IMAGES
of America

BUFFALO BLIZZARD OF 1977

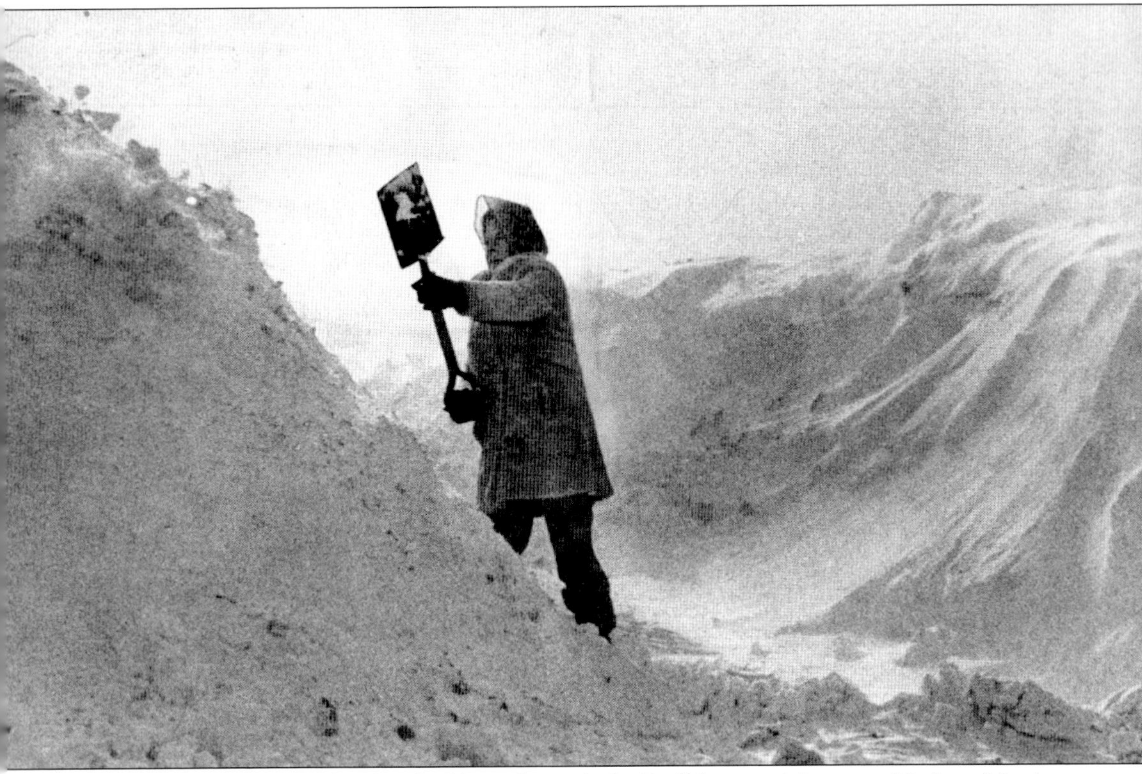

On January 28, 1977, the day the blizzard struck the Buffalo area, Marianne Hodge of Amherst, New York, fought a losing battle to clear her driveway. Her grit and determination to battle the elements speaks volumes about the character of the people of the region. (Archives & Special Collections Department, E.H. Butler Library, SUNY Buffalo State.)

On the Cover: In the aftermath of the Buffalo blizzard of 1977, which paralyzed transportation from January 28 through the first week of February, this couple found that the snowy city streets afforded a convenient and ready-made cross-country ski trail as they traveled to and from work on February 5, 1977. (Archives & Special Collections Department, E.H. Butler Library, SUNY Buffalo State.)

IMAGES
of America

BUFFALO BLIZZARD OF 1977

Timothy W. Kneeland

ARCADIA
PUBLISHING

ISBN 978-1-4671-2597-0

Published by Arcadia Publishing
Charleston, South Carolina

Printed in the United States of America

Library of Congress Control Number: 2016957951

For all general information, please contact Arcadia Publishing:
Telephone 843-853-2070
Fax 843-853-0044
E-mail sales@arcadiapublishing.com
For customer service and orders:
Toll-Free 1-888-313-2665

Visit us on the Internet at www.arcadiapublishing.com

To Laura, my partner in life, who traveled hundreds of miles with me across the Buffalo region to discover photographs to tell the story of the blizzard of 1977

CONTENTS

Acknowledgments

Several agencies and individuals shared their collections and recollections to help in the preparation of this book. At SUNY Buffalo State, Daniel DiLandro and the staff in the Archives & Special Collections Department of the E.H. Butler Library went beyond the call of duty to assist me in the initial stages of the book by providing images from the now defunct *Buffalo Courier-Express*. Ned Schimminger, of the Historical Society of the Tonawandas, provided me with pictures and some conversation about the history of the Tonawandas. Perry White, editor of the *Watertown Daily Times*, and Lisa Carr, the newspaper's archivist, were generous with their images and even allowed me to take dozens of negatives out of the archive while I worked on the book. Courtney Geerhart, the local history librarian at the Niagara Falls Public Library, provided an abundance of material from its *Niagara Gazette* collection and graciously invited me to talk and promote the book once it is published. Judy Stiles of the Genesee County History Department found nearly two dozen photographs and provided a description for each one she located. Mary Jo Monnin, sportswriter at the *Buffalo News*, found some good photographs taken in the Lancaster area. Lee Weisbeck of the *Alden Advertiser* found several good photographs from the personal collection of his father, Leonard A. Weisbeck Sr. Marissa Wilson, communications manager at Perry's Ice Cream, assisted in locating an image of its latest commemorative ice cream for the blizzard of 1977, Zero Visibility. Each caption ends with an abbreviation identifying the image source: the Archives & Special Collections at the E.H. Butler Library at SUNY Buffalo State (BLBS); the *Watertown Daily Times* (WDT); the Local History Department in the Niagara Falls Public Library (NFPL); the Historical Society of the Tonawandas (HST); the Genesee County History Department (GCHD); or Mary Jo Monnin (MM). All other photographs are cited with the owner's name.

Finally, my thanks go to the many people I contacted during my search for photographs of the blizzard. Although they may have been unable to find any original photographs of the blizzard of 1977, everyone I reached out to was unfailing in their efforts to locate images and generous in their encouragement for this project. Although too numerous to mention all of them individually, they know who they are, and I hope they will accept my gratitude and thanks for all their efforts on my behalf.

INTRODUCTION

Western New York has a long history of battling winter storms and blizzards. From lake-effect snow in Buffalo to the Tug Hill Plateau near Watertown, heavy snowfall is a regular occurrence in winter. However, the winter of 1976–1977 was the worst in the history of region, with a snowfall that year four times the normal amount. It was also the coldest winter on record, with temperatures falling below freezing in December 1976 and remaining there until February 1977. The average temperature was about 14 degrees Fahrenheit that winter, and as a result, the accumulated snow could not melt and kept piling higher and higher in the cities, towns, and suburbs. It seemed things could not get worse, but they did. On January 28, 1977, an unexpected blizzard struck the region with winds whipping up to 75 miles an hour and temperatures plummeting 30 degrees in a few hours creating wind chills of 60 or 70 degrees below zero! The powerful winds swept snow off frozen Lake Erie and aimed it at the Buffalo metropolitan region. The blowing snow created zero visibility, and traffic ground to a halt, stranding tens of thousands of people across the region, including five who froze to death in their cars. The storm raged for hundreds of miles and struck cities like Batavia and Niagara Falls. The same storm dumped five feet of new snow on Watertown, New York, 200 miles from Buffalo.

The blizzard gripped the region from January 28 until February 1, 1977. The death toll from the storm was 29. Economic losses were in the hundreds of millions of dollars due to property damage, business losses, and lost wages. During the storm, people were stranded, streets were impassible, and public services were strained beyond capacity. In response to the extreme conditions, people turned to their government leaders, like New York governor Hugh Carey, Buffalo mayor Stanley Makowski, and Erie County executive Ned Regan. Carey flew to Buffalo to inspect the scene and to promise all the assistance New York State could give. Knowing that would not be sufficient in light of the magnitude of the storm, Governor Carey called on Pres. Jimmy Carter to assist the stricken region. People also turned to one another. Incredible acts of self-sacrifice and bravery occurred during the blizzard as neighbors helped neighbors, and fire and police did all they could to help stranded motorists find shelter from the subzero weather. Thirteen thousand people were stranded in the city of Buffalo alone and thousands more in the counties bordering Buffalo. Total strangers found themselves huddled in firehouses, farmhouses, and community centers. Snowmobilers, guided by citizens-band radio operators, were dispatched to help storm victims, rescuing those stuck in cars, delivering needed medicine, or bringing food to people trapped by the storm. Together, the people of Western and Northern New York pitched in and dug out of the blizzard, and entire neighborhoods created shovel brigades to open up their streets. These individual and collective efforts turned the tragedy into a time for togetherness and an enhanced sense of community.

After February 1, the weather improved, and so did the spirit of the people. With mountains of snow to move off roads and away from buildings, many communities imposed or continued driving bans through the first week of February, and schools in many places were closed until

February 7 or later. Citizens unable to use their cars traveled by bus or snowmobile, walked, skied, biked, tubed, sledded, and even rode horses to get around and run errands. Despite people's best efforts, the region was still in need of help, and President Carter responded to Buffalo's plight by sending his son James Earl "Chip" Carter III to Buffalo on February 4, 1977, to survey the scene and report back to the White House. Chip Carter, accompanied by the local congressional delegation and US senators from New York Jacob Javits and Daniel Patrick Moynihan, was moved by the friendliness of the people and awed by the tons of snow that still lay on the ground. The day after the visit, President Carter issued the first major disaster declaration for a snowstorm in US history. By granting disaster status to nine counties in New York—Cattaraugus, Chautauqua, Erie, Genesee, Jefferson, Lewis, Niagara, Orleans, and Wyoming—President Carter provided aid and financial support to the people of Western New York. The government provided unemployment compensation for those thrown out of work by the storm and food stamps to assist people. The financial rewards greatly benefited the region.

In the aftermath of the blizzard of 1977, Buffalo became the punch line of many a joke on late-night television and the putative snow capital of America. Happy to have survived the ordeal, the people of Buffalo and Western New York remembered the blizzard and celebrated their survival and resilience through balls, board games, and a new variety of ice cream.

This book focuses on the regional response to the extreme weather conditions from Buffalo to Batavia and from Niagara Falls to Watertown. It discusses the storm, how officials worked to protect the people of Western New York, how people responded to the travel restriction by adapting old and new styles of transportation, how they helped one another, and once the emergency was over, how they had fun and remembered the blizzard.

The following explains terms used throughout this book: Western New York is the westernmost part of New York State and includes cities such as Buffalo, Niagara Falls, and Batavia. Northern New York is the region of Jefferson County and Watertown. A blizzard is a weather system lasting over three hours with sustained winds or frequent gusts of 35 miles an hour or higher and considerable falling or blowing snow that reduces visibility to less than a quarter of a mile. Wind chill is a weather condition in which increased wind speeds accelerate heat loss from exposed skin. The National Weather Service suggests that a potentially dangerous wind chill is about 20 degrees below zero.

One

The Blizzard of 1977

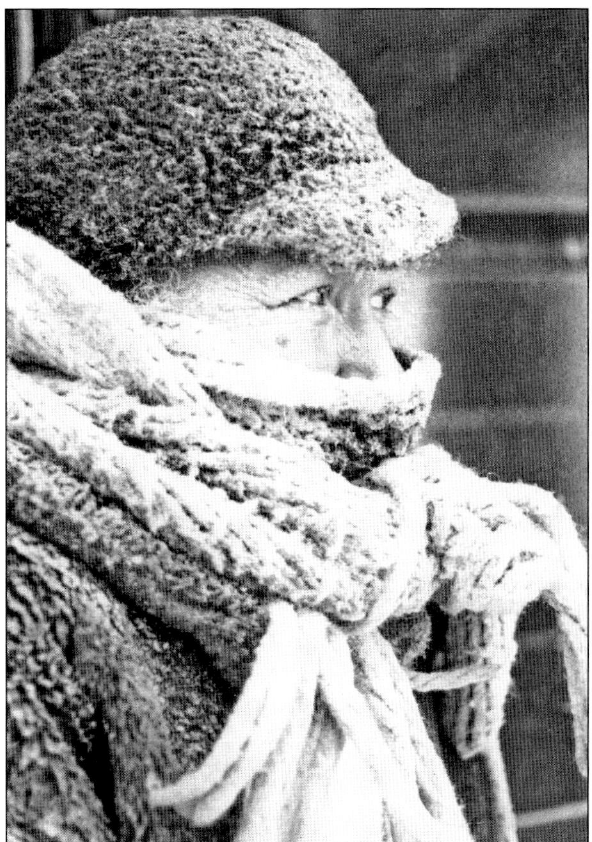

During the winter of 1976–1977, the eastern half of the United States experienced one of its coldest winters on record. In Western New York, the temperature dropped below freezing before Christmas and remained that way until February 1977. The people of Western New York responded by bundling up. (BLBS.)

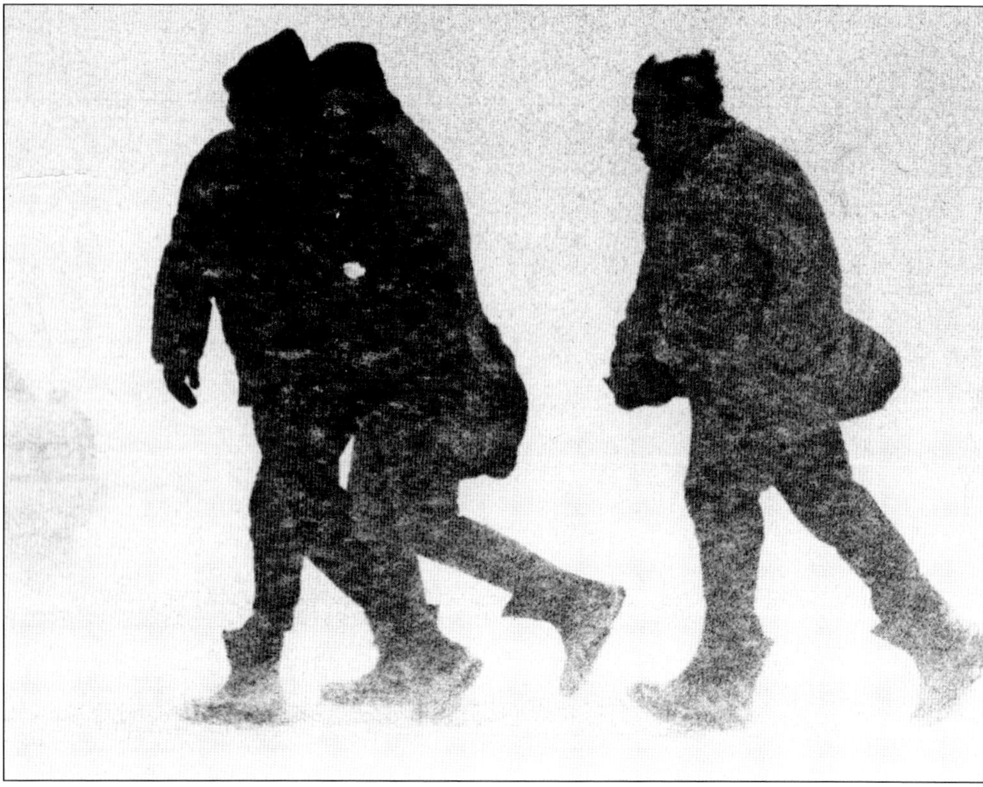

Snowstorm after snowstorm lashed Buffalo during the winter of 1976–1977. Here, residents of Buffalo try to cross Main Street during a December 1976 storm. (BLBS.)

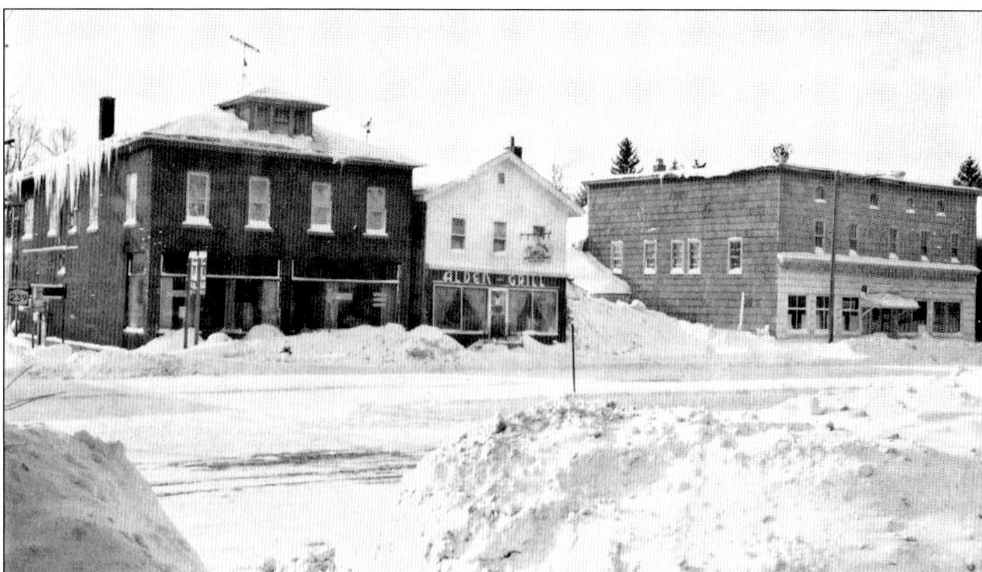

By January 1977, nearly 150 inches of snow had fallen in Western New York. In combination with the extreme cold, cities, towns, and villages, like Alden, were left with piles of unmelted snow and very few ideas of where to put it. (Leonard A. Weisbeck Sr.)

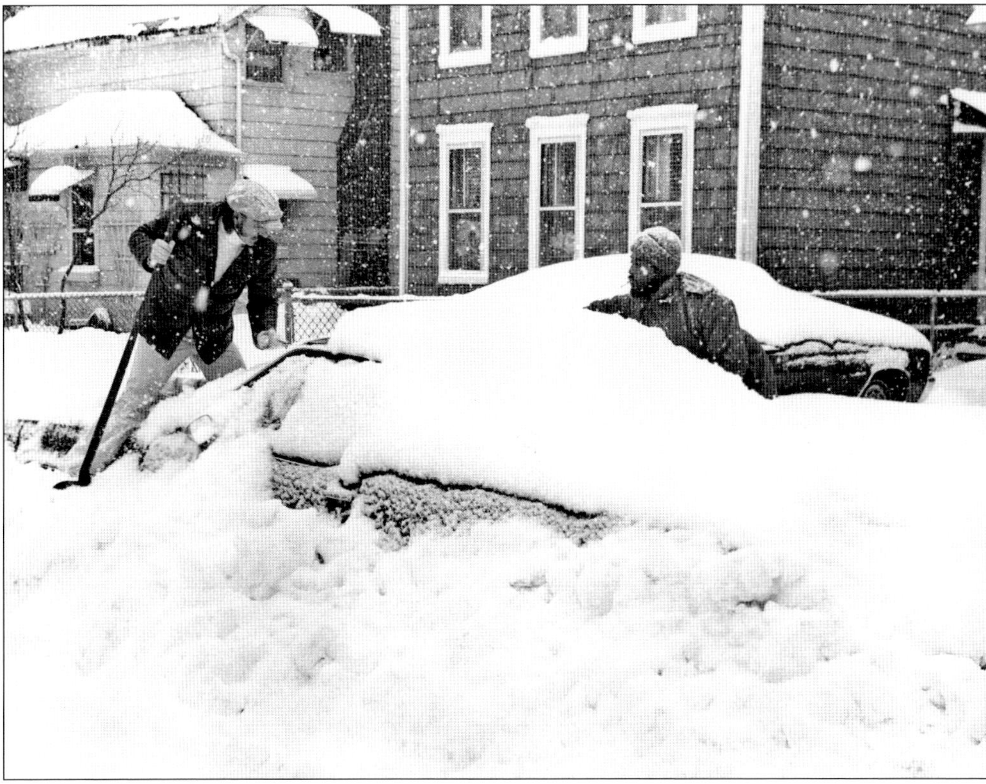

Throughout the winter of 1976–1977, residents struggled to keep their cars from being buried by snow, while plow drivers tried to keep the streets open. Merton Kreps (left) and Albert Colbert work to dig out their cars on Willow Avenue near Main Street in Niagara Falls on December 6, 1977. (NFPL.)

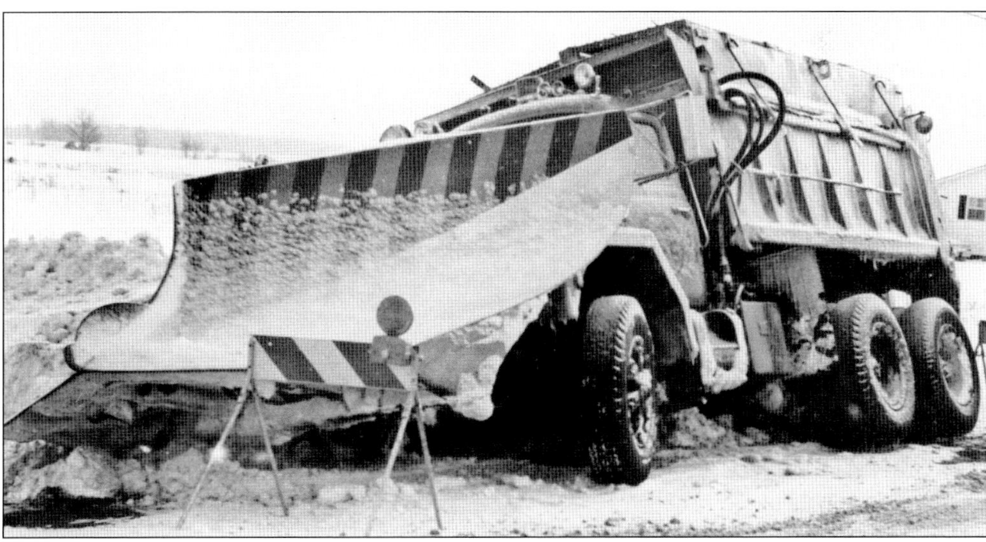

The relentless winter of 1976–1977 made it impossible for snowplows to keep roads and streets clear, and many plows across the region broke down. The problem was most severe in the city of Buffalo, which due to financial distress had deferred maintenance on its fleet of plows. (GCHD.)

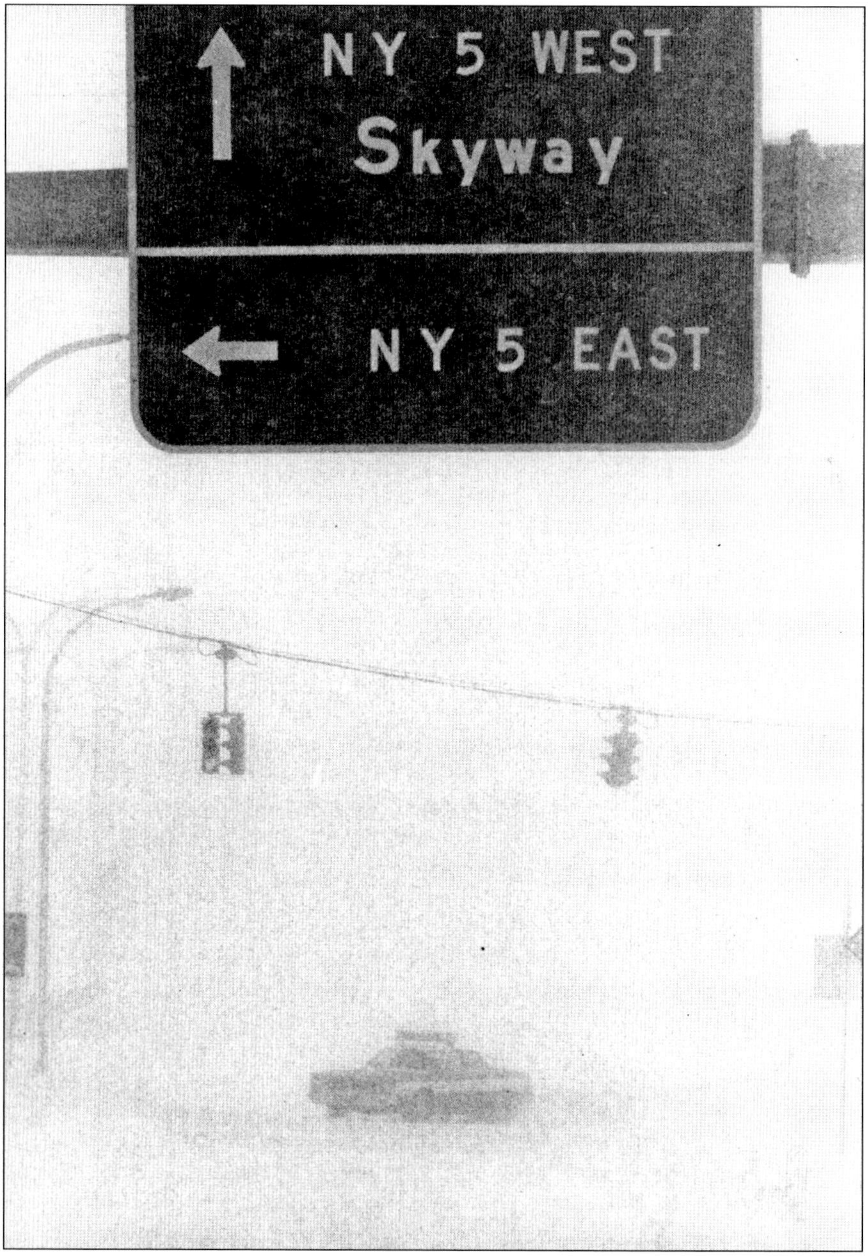

Just after 11:00 a.m. on Friday, January 28, 1977, an unexpected blizzard struck Buffalo and Western New York. Within a matter of minutes, the sky darkened and visibility dropped to zero. Within hours, the temperature dropped below zero, with wind chills as low as 60 below zero. Winds were recorded as high as 70 miles per hour. The storm lasted four days and paralyzed the region until Tuesday, February 1, 1977. The storm blew out of Ohio, where it also caused blizzard conditions, and spread south to Pennsylvania and north to the province of Ontario in Canada. There were 29 deaths and economic losses of nearly $300 million for the city of Buffalo. What made the storm so long-lasting and devastating was that it picked up the 30 inches of snow that lay atop frozen Lake Erie and aimed this at the city of Buffalo, acting more like a sandstorm than a blizzard. (BLBS.)

Tens of thousands of people tried to leave work at the same time, but blowing snow quickly brought travel to a standstill. An estimated 13,000 were stranded in the city of Buffalo. (BLBS.)

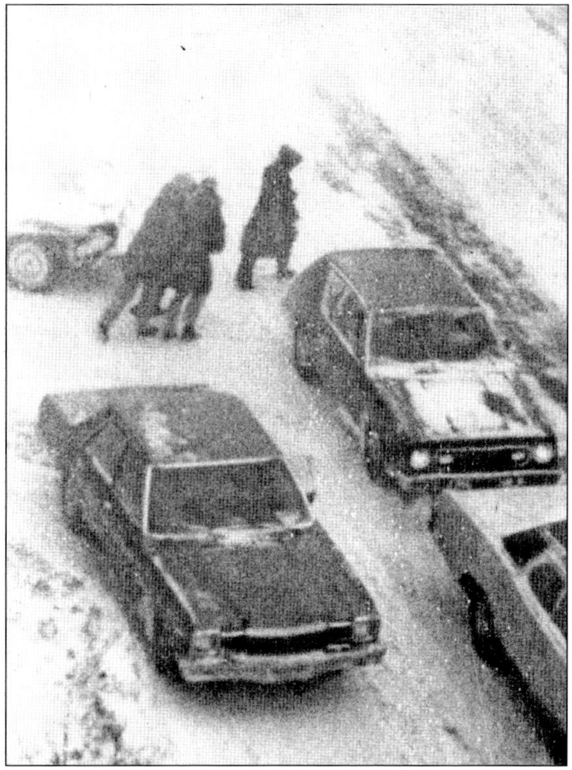

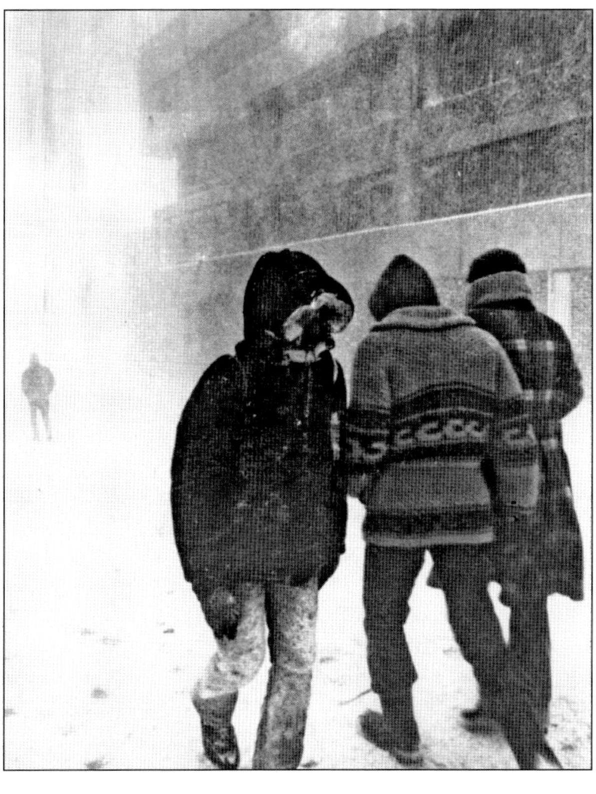

The winds blew and the snow came roaring in off the frozen surface of Lake Erie. This snow hit the region so quickly that people in Buffalo were caught unawares. These Buffalo State College students are surprised by the sudden snow and darkness that descended at noon. (BLBS.)

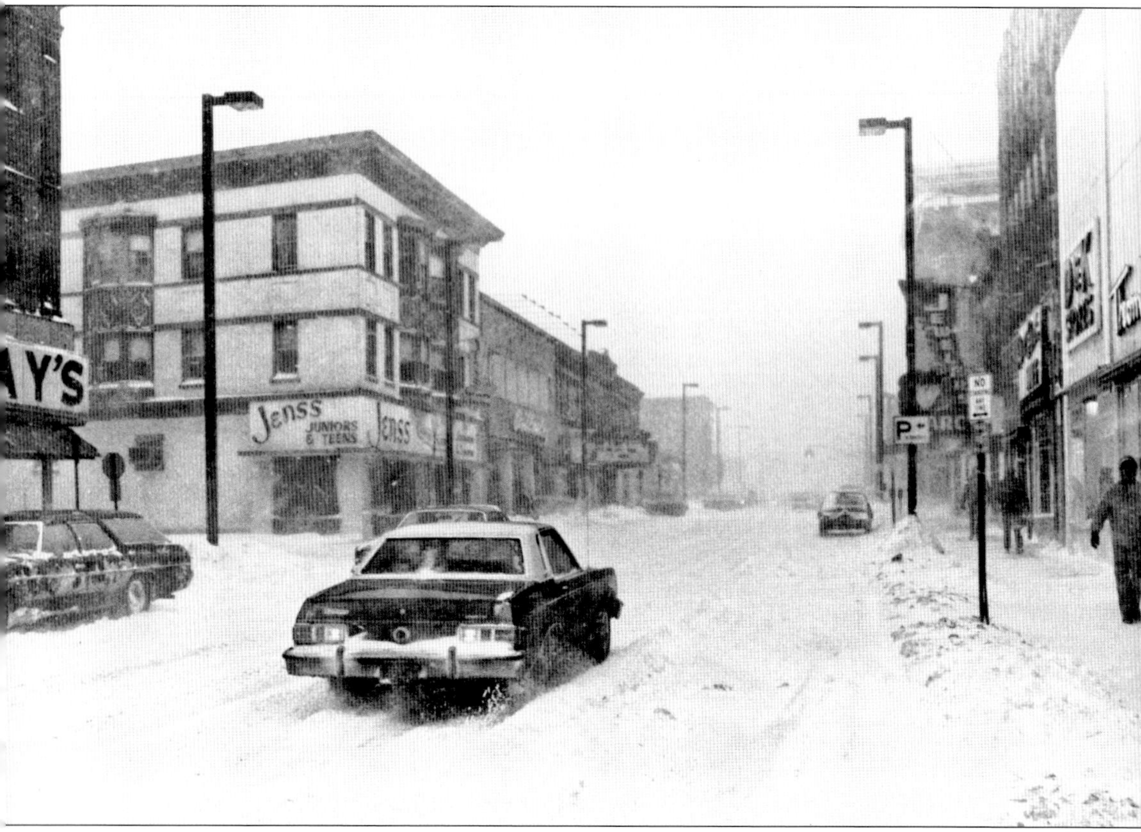

Twenty-five miles north of Buffalo, the city of Niagara Falls was similarly surprised on the morning of January 28, 1977. Drivers at Main Street and Lincoln Avenue were stunned to see darkness falling on the city. (NFPL.)

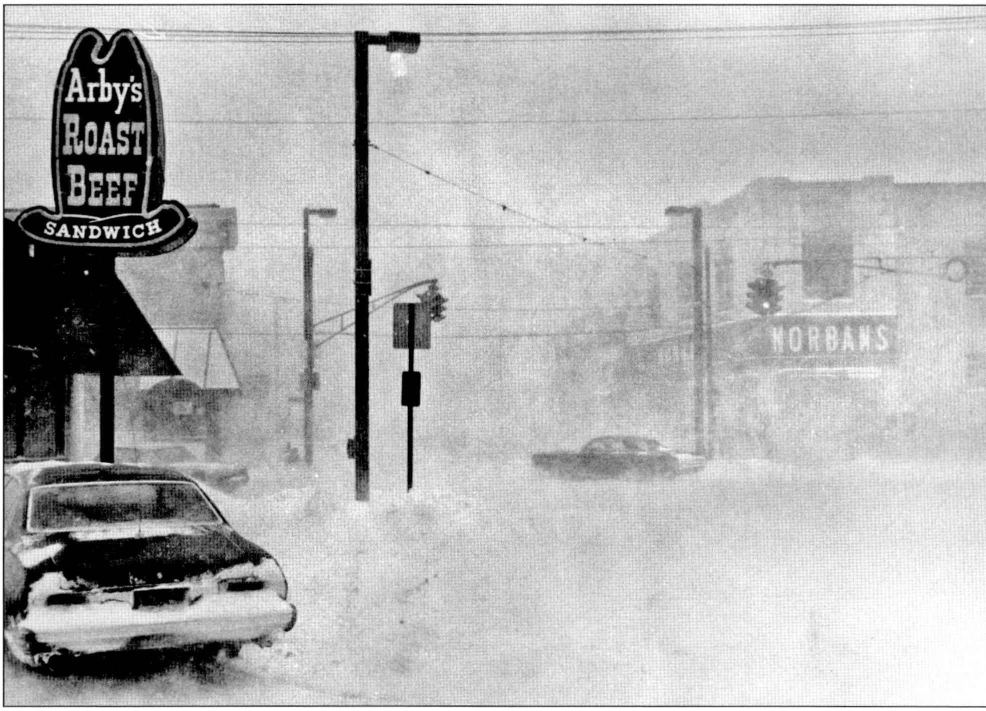

Minutes after the blizzard of 1977 descended upon Main and Cleveland Streets in Niagara Falls, visibility dropped from three-quarters of a mile to zero. In the 1970s, the city was still home to over 80,000 residents, all of whom struggled against the snow during and after the blizzard. (NFPL.)

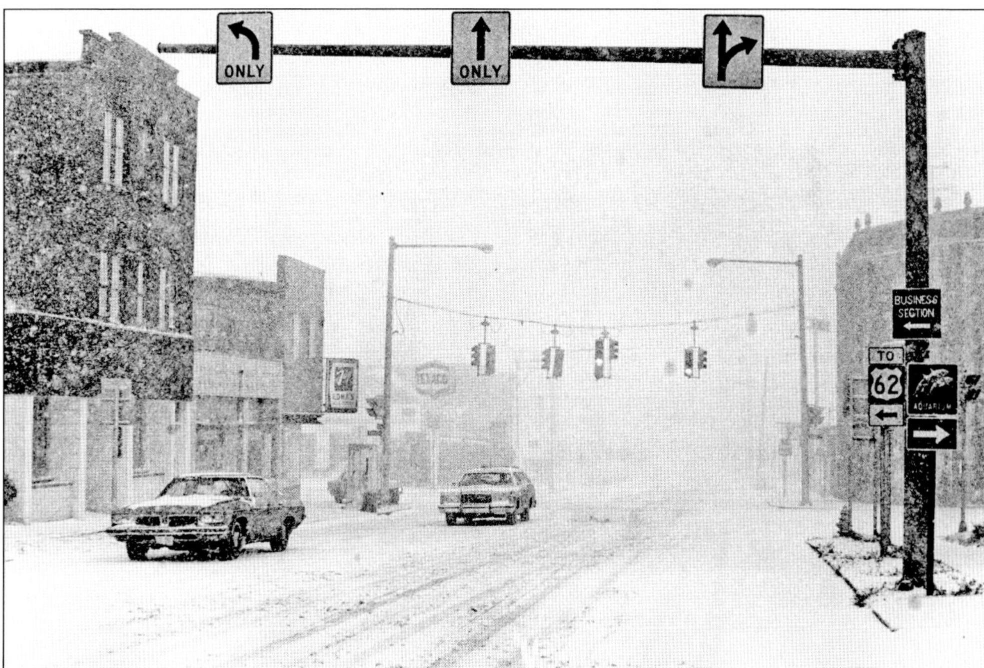

Although still morning on January 28, 1977, it began to look like early evening along the major thoroughfares of Niagara Falls. (NFPL.)

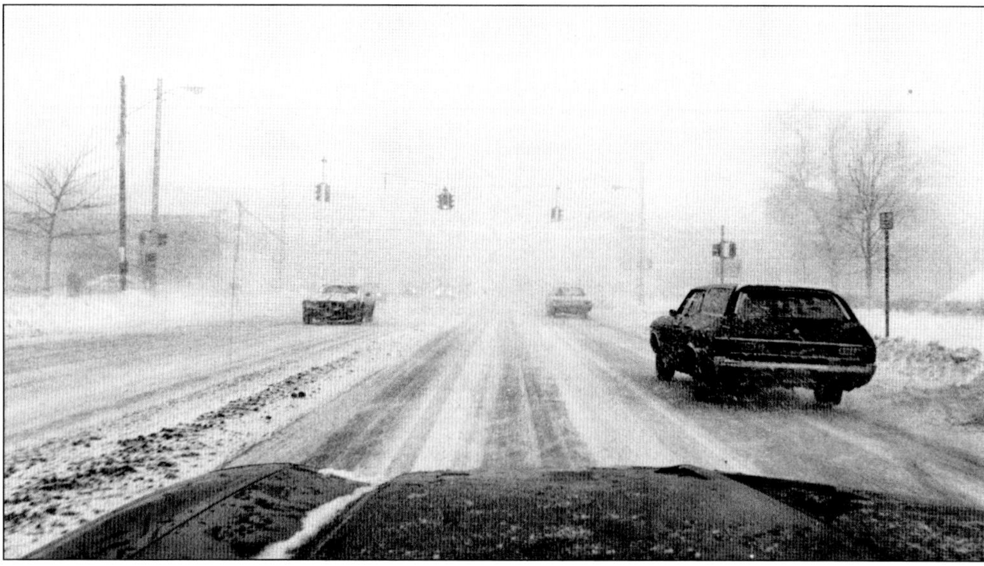

The blizzard of 1977 was so massive that it was felt 45 miles east of Buffalo in the city of Batavia in Genesee County. Cars along Main Street near Court Street drove right into whiteout conditions. (GCHD.)

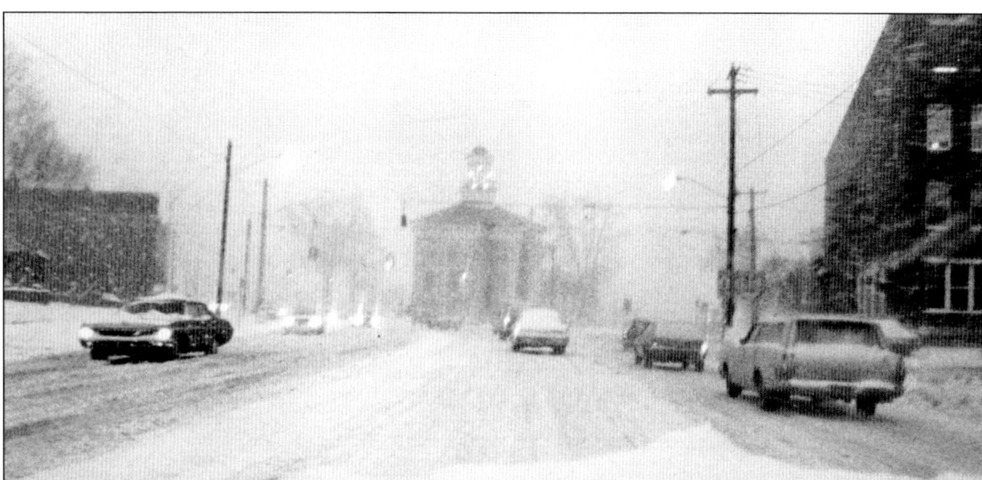

Darkness fell early on January 28, 1977. In Batavia, drivers on Main and Ellicott Streets found themselves unable to distinguish the horizon from the road. (GCHD.)

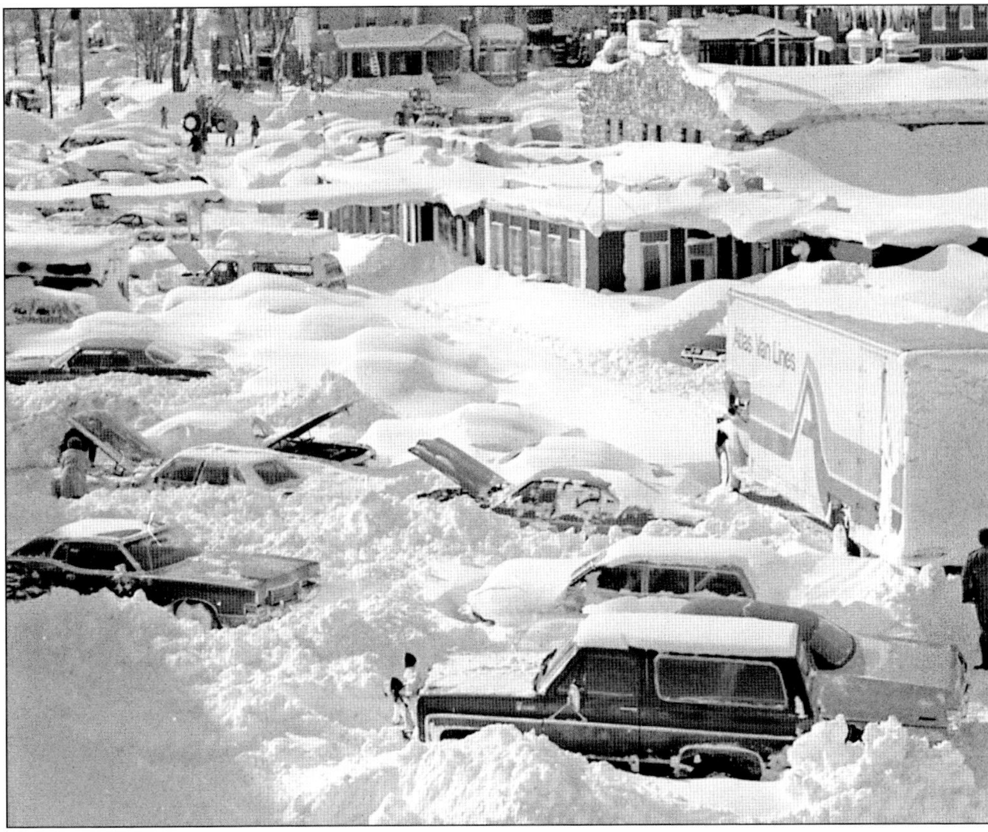

The blizzard was so ferocious and widespread that it was felt 215 miles away from Buffalo in the city of Watertown, which sits east of Lake Ontario in Northern New York. Unlike Buffalo, which received a good deal of snow from atop frozen Lake Erie, here the winds brought snow from the unfrozen Lake Ontario. Watertown received 66 inches of snow between January 28 and February 1, 1977. At least five deaths were attributed to the snowstorm, which trapped thousands of people in that area and caused hundreds of thousands of dollars in damage. This photograph shows the parking lot of the Carriage House in Watertown. (WDT.)

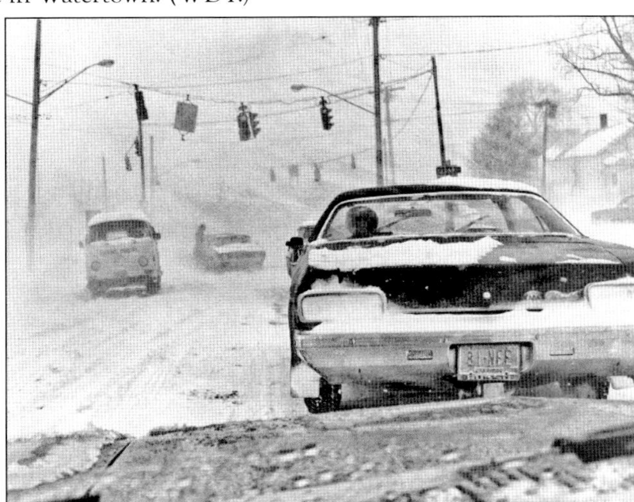

For hundreds of miles, the blizzard cut visibility to zero and whipped snow into drifts that stranded cars and drivers. Traffic ground to a halt at the intersection of Whirlpool and Cedar Streets in Niagara Falls. (NFPL.)

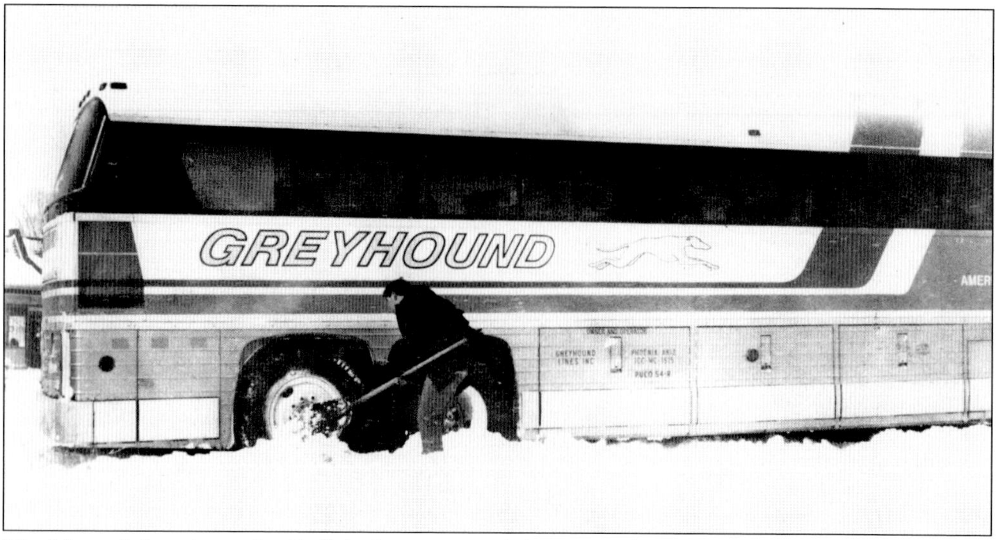

The blizzard shut down the Buffalo International Airport, other regional airports, Amtrak, and bus lines, making travel into and out of the region impossible for several days after it struck on January 28, 1977. (GCHD.)

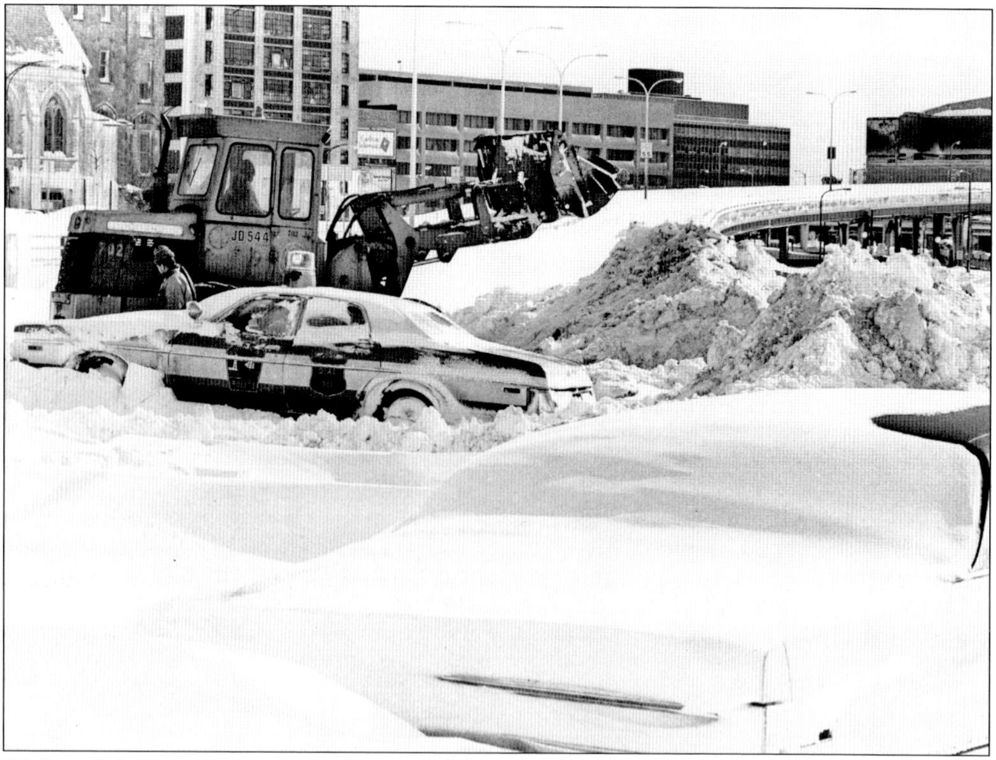

With visibility at zero, every major road and thoroughfare was shut down. The Skyway, a Buffalo lifeline, and one of the first roads to close during a snowstorm, remained closed due to snow and abandoned cars until February 1, 1977. (BLBS.)

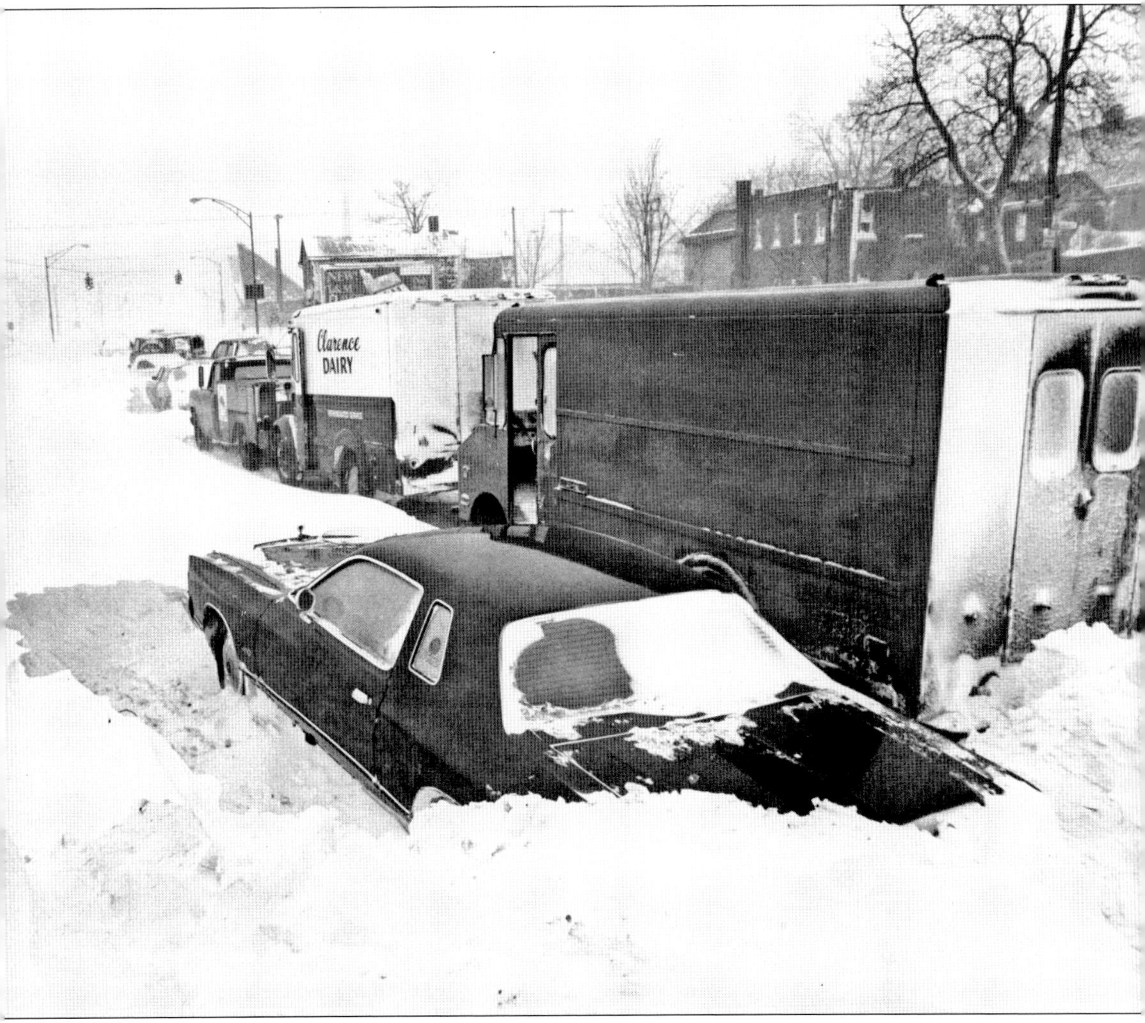

The storm dropped less than a foot of snow on Buffalo, but adding to this total was loose snow from frozen Lake Erie that created snowdrifts that buried cars in a matter of minutes along the Kensington Expressway in Buffalo. Many people who lived through the storm have harrowing tales of finding themselves on roads in whiteout conditions. They were unable to drive ahead for fear they would run into someone else and fearful that someone might drive into them, which all too often happened. Once they stopped, they had a choice: stay with the vehicle and hope that help would come or try to find shelter in conditions that made even finding a visible landmark a challenge. One of these people was Cynthia Toy of East Aurora, who went into labor. She and her husband, Don, were on their way to Sisters Hospital in Buffalo during the blizzard but got stuck in the snow on Route 400. Holding hands so they would not be separated in the whiteout, they were rescued by fire crews who got them home, where they delivered their son Brennan. (BLBS.)

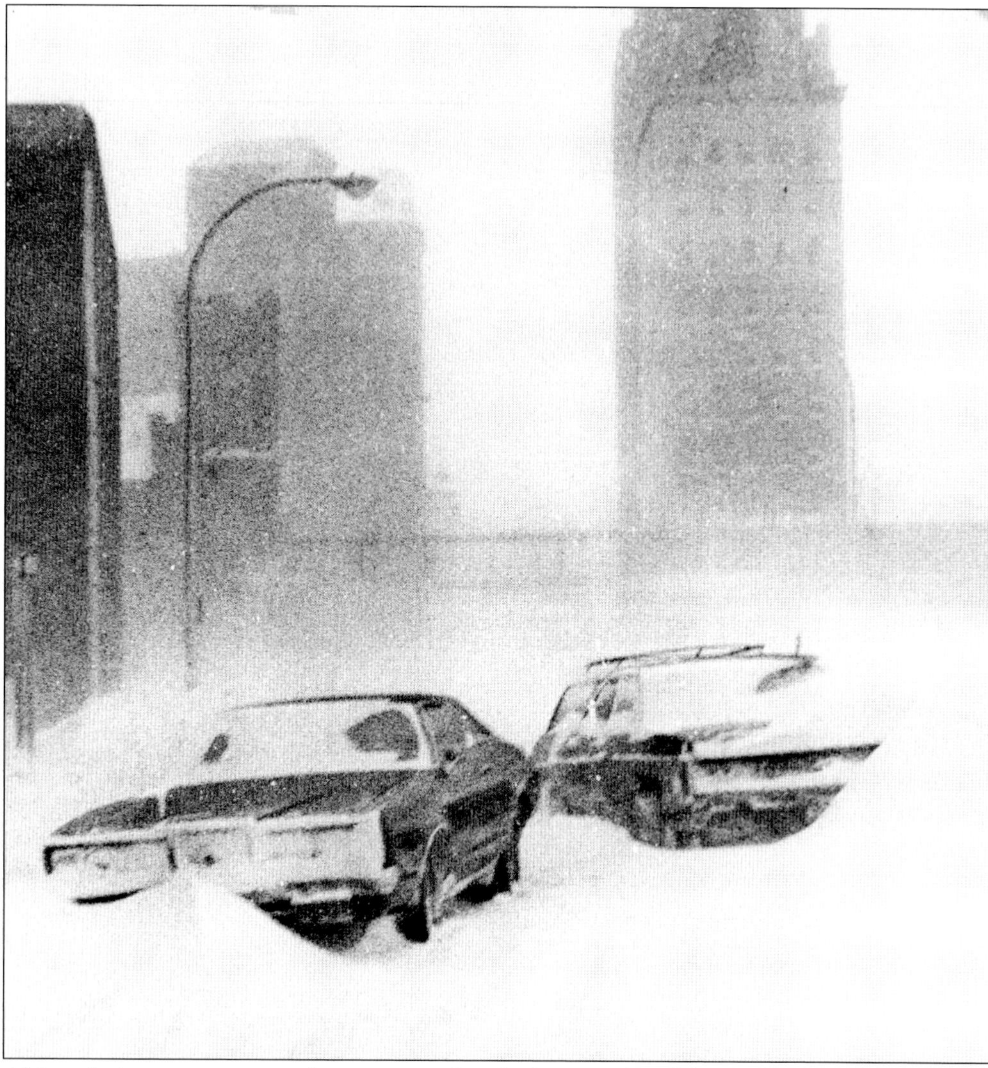

Although the storm is most often associated with the city of Buffalo, residents of other villages, towns, and cities were subject to the dangerous conditions. Niagara Falls is only 25 miles north of Buffalo, and it too was in the throes of the storm that fell on that city with savage force on January 28, 1977. The city of Niagara Falls incorporated in 1892, and in the 20th century, it was known as the "Honeymoon Capital of the World," but it was also the site of several chemical industrial plants and hydroelectric power plants. When the blizzard struck, Niagara Falls was already losing its place as the top spot for honeymooners and was suffering economic decline as chemical plants were relocating elsewhere. Economic losses from the blizzard were in the tens of millions. (NFPL.)

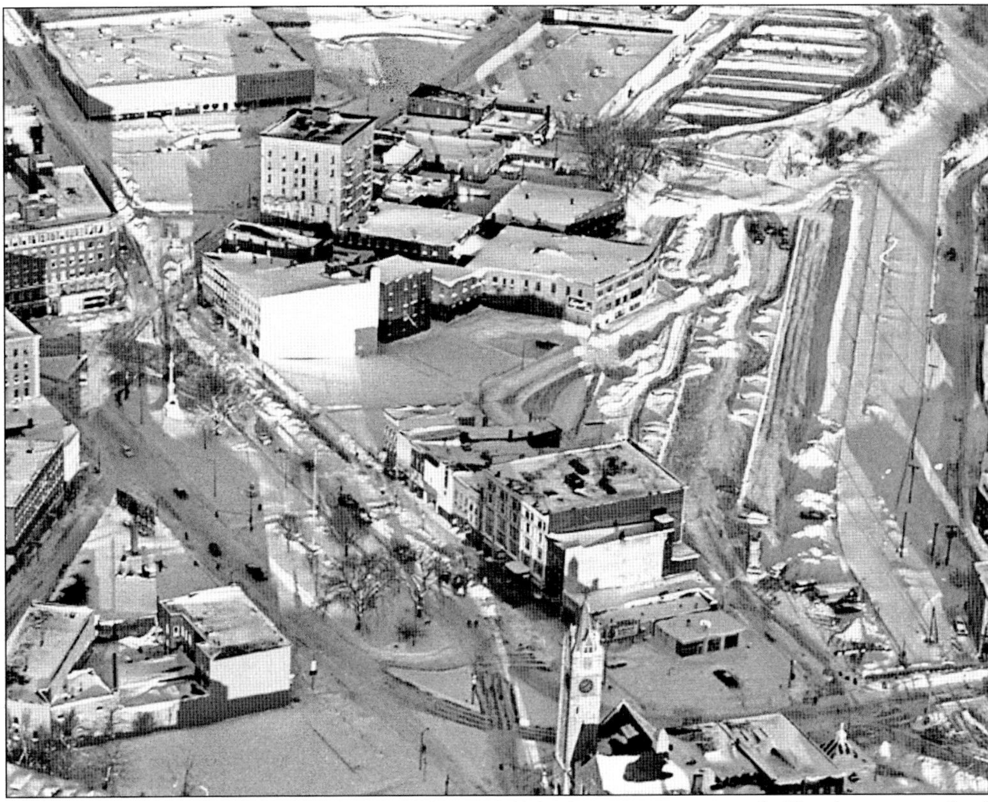

The city of Watertown is 200 miles away from Buffalo, but it too was crippled by the storm, which left thousands of people stranded. Many of those stuck in Watertown were Canadians passing through on their way to Florida. Watertown, just 20 miles south of the Thousand Island recreation area, gets its name from the many falls along the Black River, which led to a large number of industrial mills in the 19th century. (WDT.)

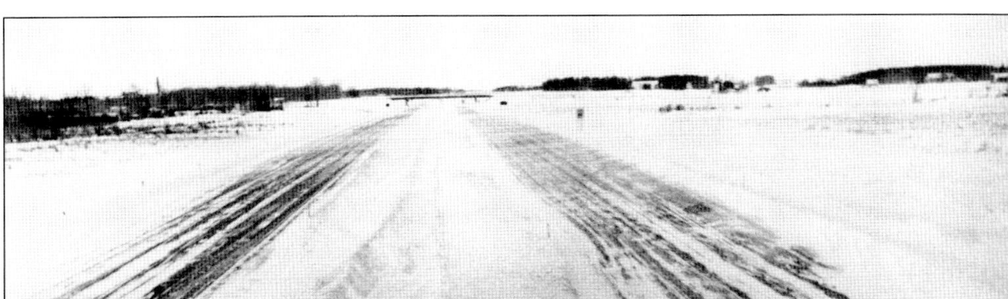

The New York State Thruway was shut down from Batavia through Fredonia. Jackknifed trucks and abandoned cars made travel impossible, and once stopped, cars were buried in the snow. An empty New York State Thruway is seen here just outside of Batavia. (GCHD.)

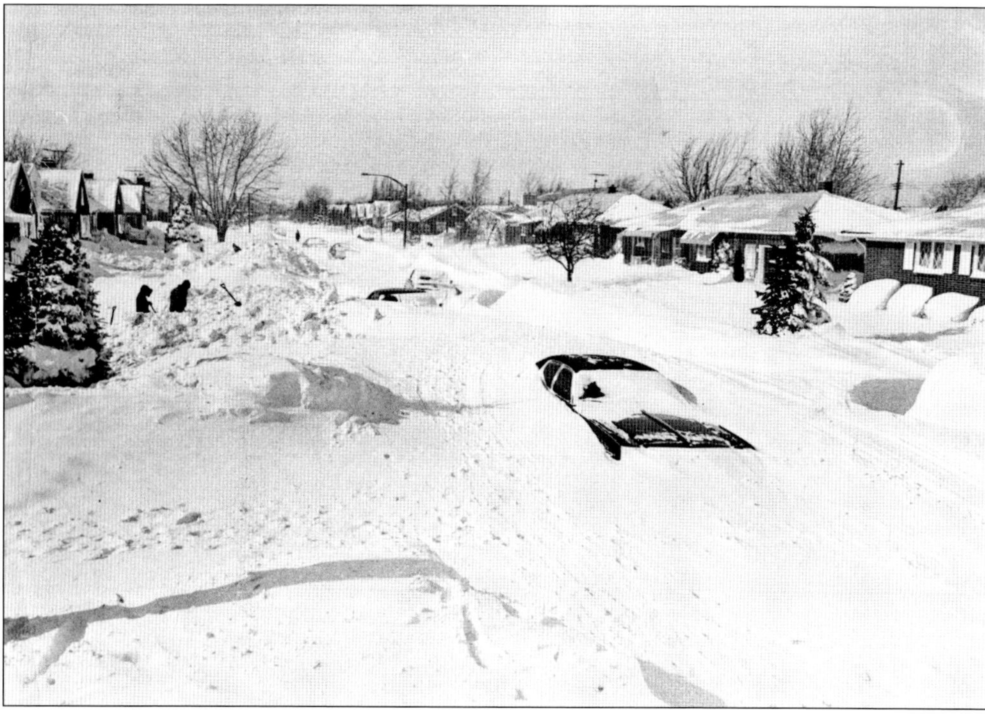

Cheektowaga, which is 10 miles east of Buffalo, was also prostrated by the storm, which buried its streets and cars. Tudor Road in Cheektowaga remained buried by snow for over a week. (BLBS.)

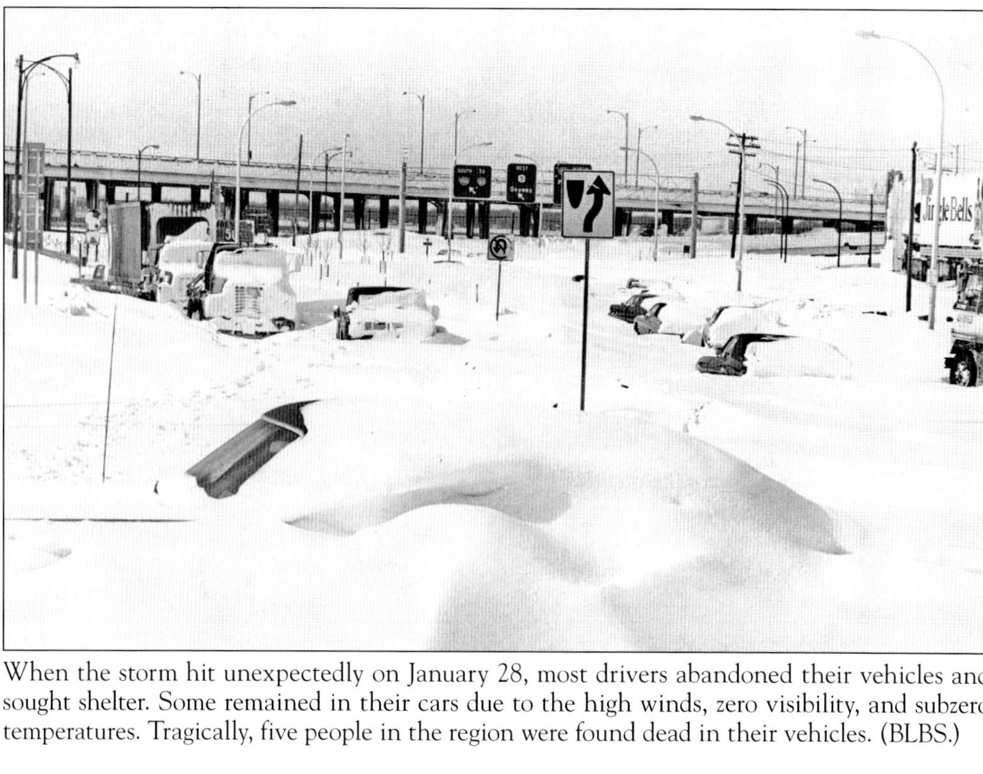

When the storm hit unexpectedly on January 28, most drivers abandoned their vehicles and sought shelter. Some remained in their cars due to the high winds, zero visibility, and subzero temperatures. Tragically, five people in the region were found dead in their vehicles. (BLBS.)

Surprised by the blizzard of 1977, pedestrians strained to find shelter against the cold and winds that gusted as high as 70 miles per hour. Some people were knocked off their feet. Others clung to light poles to resist the winds. Some formed a human chain to get individuals blinded by the snow and blown over by the wind to safety. (BLBS.)

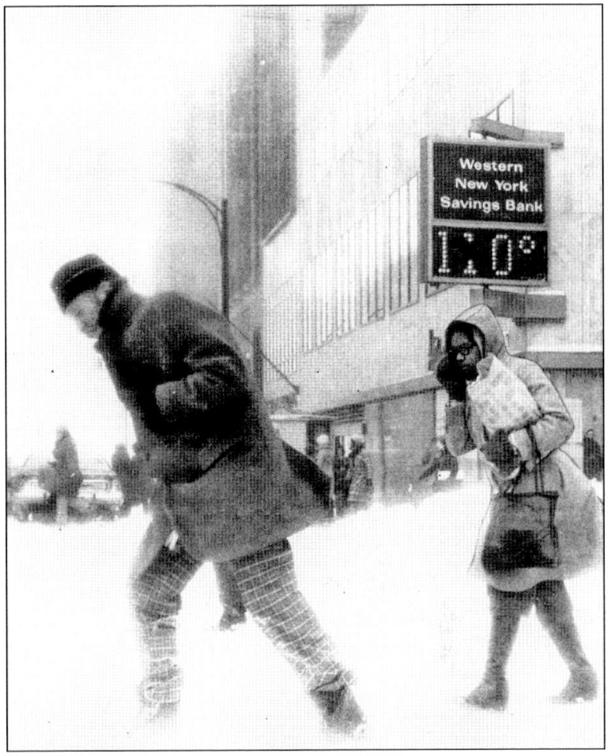

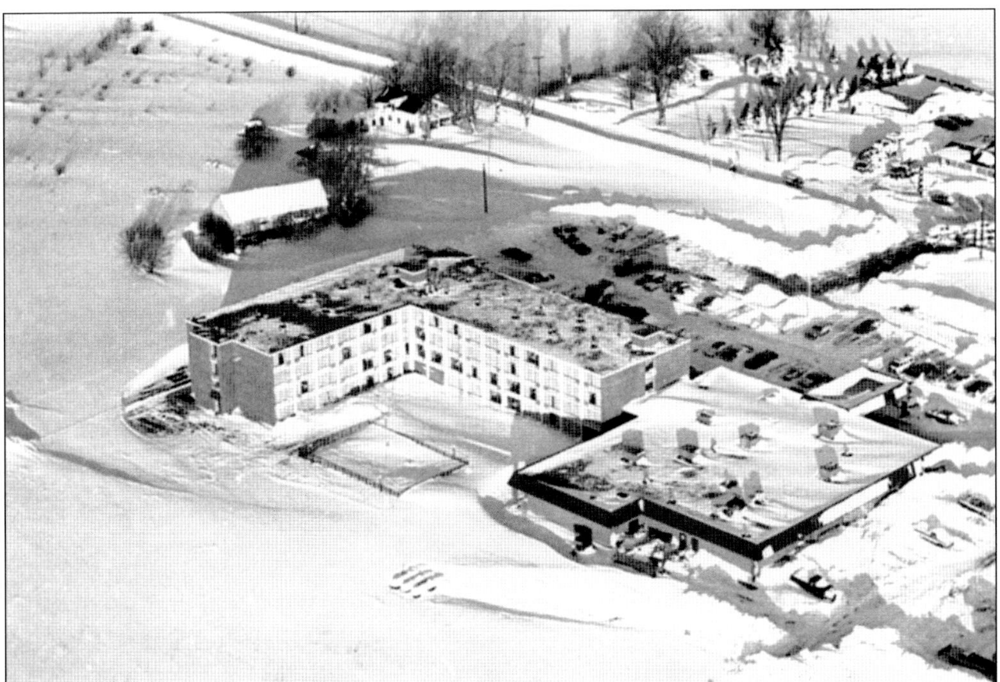

For hundreds of miles around Buffalo, motorists became stranded and sought shelter. The Ramada Inn on Outer Arsenal Road in Watertown was full of people seeking escape from the storm and cold. (WDT.)

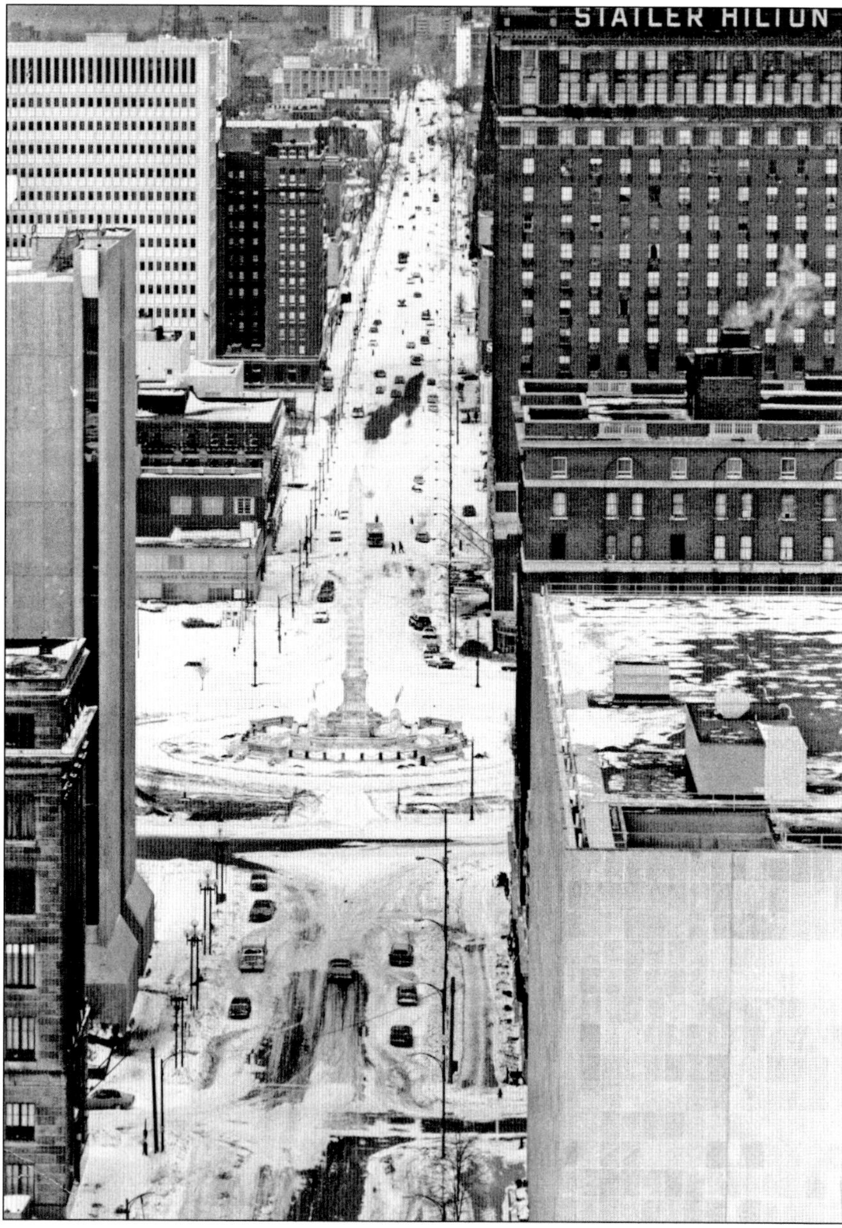

Caught unawares by the blizzard, 13,000 people were stranded in the city of Buffalo. Some were fortunate to find a bed at the Hotel Statler, which overlooks Niagara Square in Buffalo. In 1977, the building was a mix of offices and hotel rooms. All 400 rooms were booked on January 28, and another 400 beds were set up in hallways, in meeting rooms, and in the lobby to accommodate those trapped by the storm. It was a significant meeting place for people and politicians working to clean up from the storm. An iconic structure, the building was opened in 1923 and was the second Statler Hotel in the city. The Buffalo landmark was a thriving hotel through the mid-20th century. In the late 1940s, it began to include office space. The history of the building reflects the ups and downs of Buffalo. Once part of a chain of hotels, the building has been sold and resold many times as developers have sought a means to increase tenancy in the office spaces, reinvigorate the hotel rooms, or use the grand ballrooms for public events. (BLBS.)

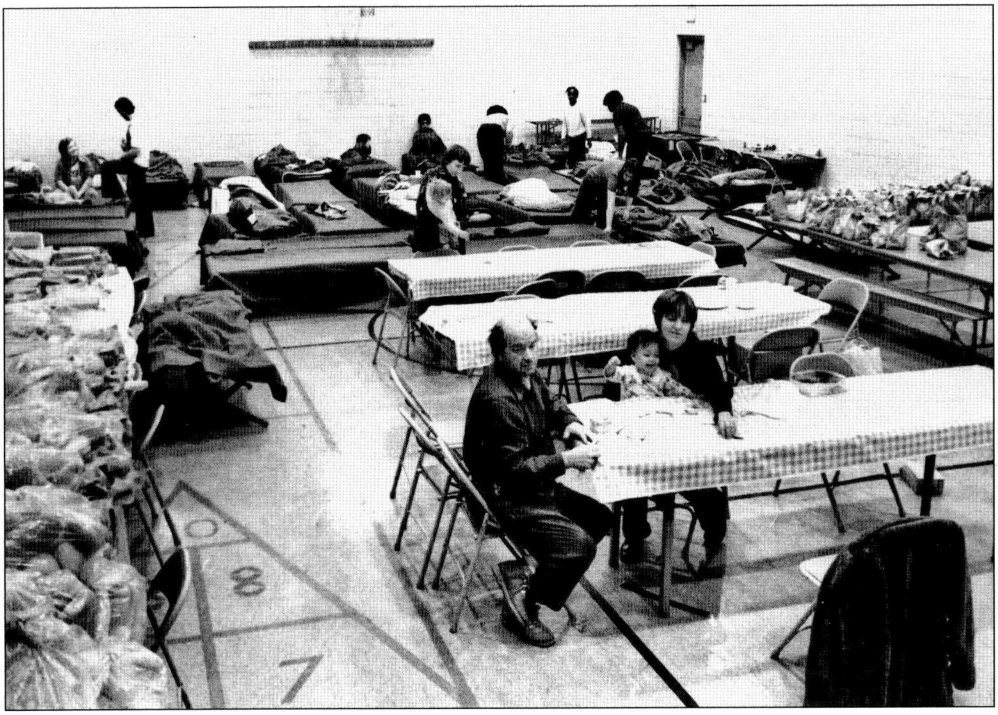

Stranded motorists found refuge in the airport, fire stations, office buildings, and recreation centers, like this one in Niagara Falls. Four hundred people found refuge in the Buffalo Auditorium, home of the Sabres hockey team. Bell Aerospace in Niagara County hosted 1,600 people. The Ford Woodlawn plant near Hamburg housed 1,800 employees. One department store in Buffalo, Hens & Kelly, provided food and linens to those trapped by the storm. After the blizzard, the store donated the linens to the Salvation Army. (NFPL.)

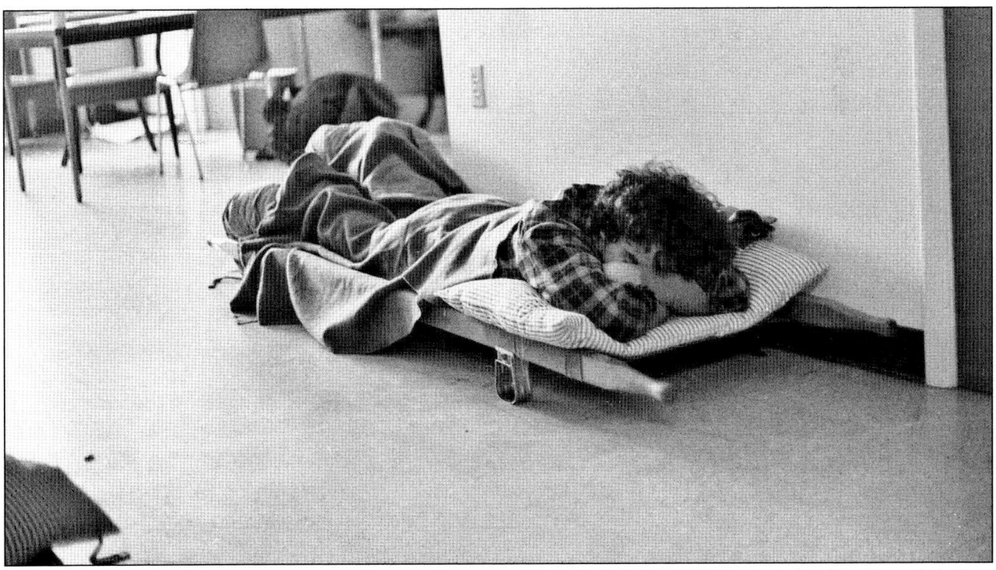

After the blizzard trapped people in the cities of Western and Northern New York, they found shelter wherever they could—in offices, factories, firehouses, taverns, and restaurants—to wait out the storm. This young man found a cot in his office where he spent 72 hours after the storm. (WDT.)

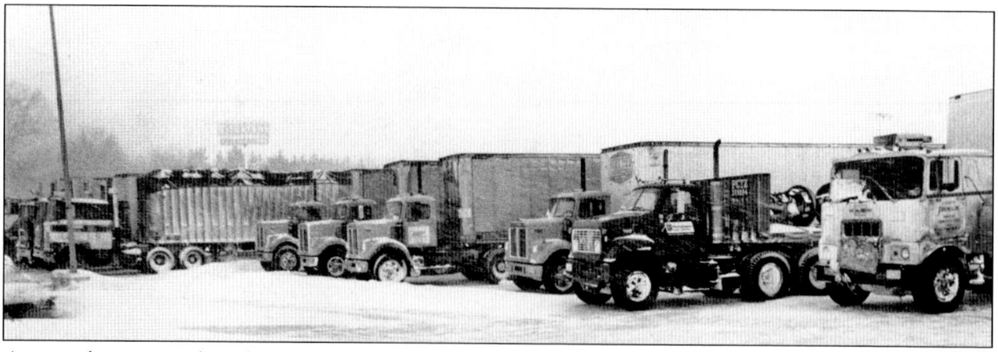

Across the region, hundreds of truckers had to get off roads and hunker down until snow could be cleared and roads reopened. (GCHD.)

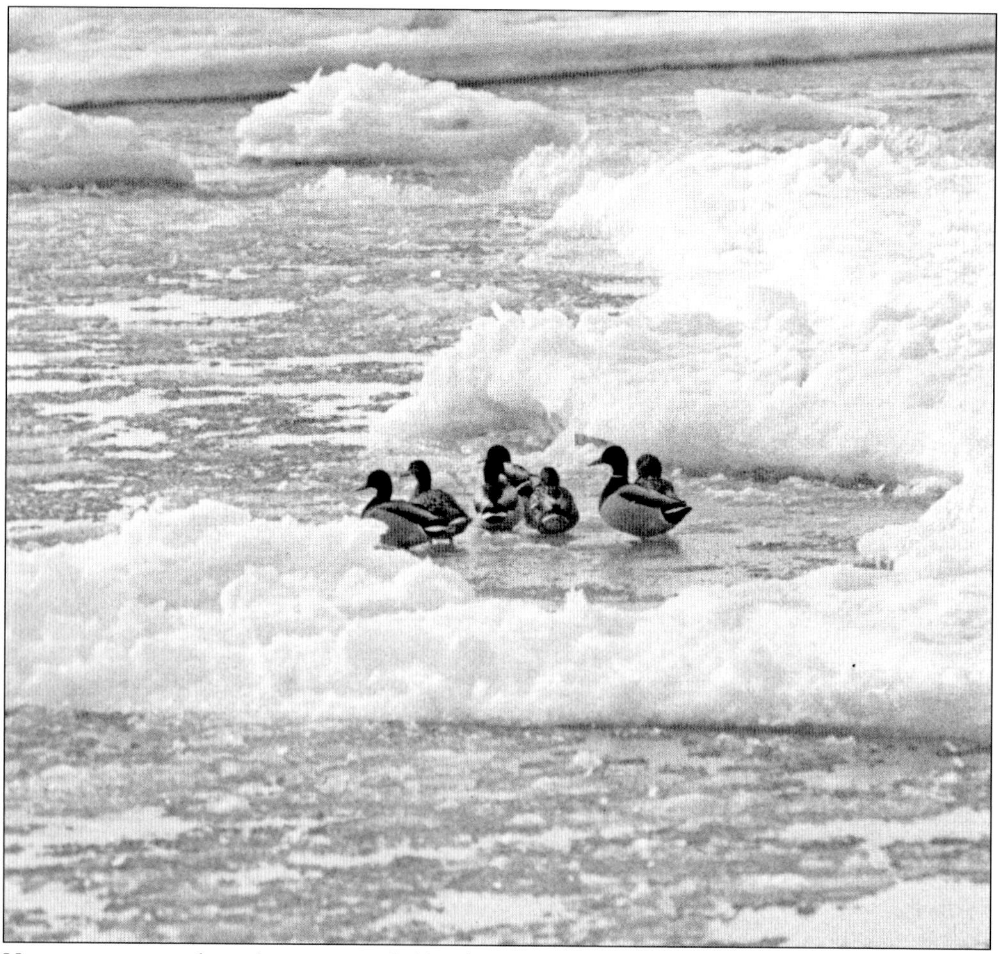

Humans were not the only ones stranded by the storm. Ducks were among the many species that waited for the storm to clear. At the Buffalo Zoo, three reindeer used snowdrifts created by the storm to escape, and they ran loose for hours during the blizzard. Sadly, 20 animals at the zoo perished due to the cold and extreme weather conditions. (NFPL.)

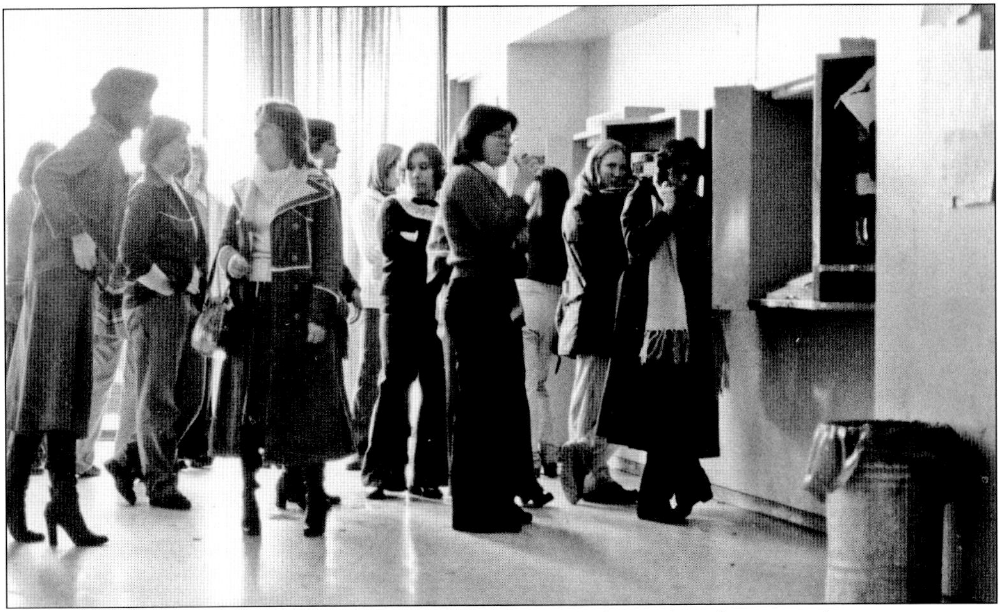

Tens of thousands of people who found themselves stranded away from home tried to communicate with the only technology then available, the telephone. These Buffalo State College students are waiting for their turns to call home. Across the region, the telephone system was overwhelmed by people trying to call friends and family. (BLBS.)

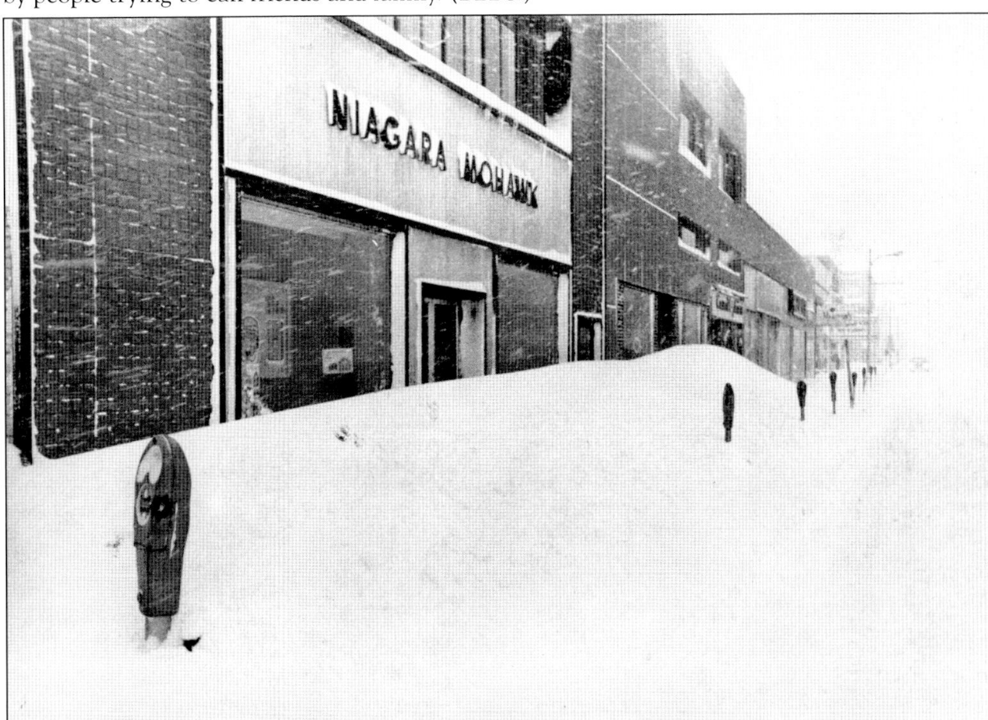

During the storm, most people were able to stay warm. However, 7,500 Niagara Mohawk customers in Erie, Genesee, and Niagara Counties lost power, which only compounded their misery. (GCHD.)

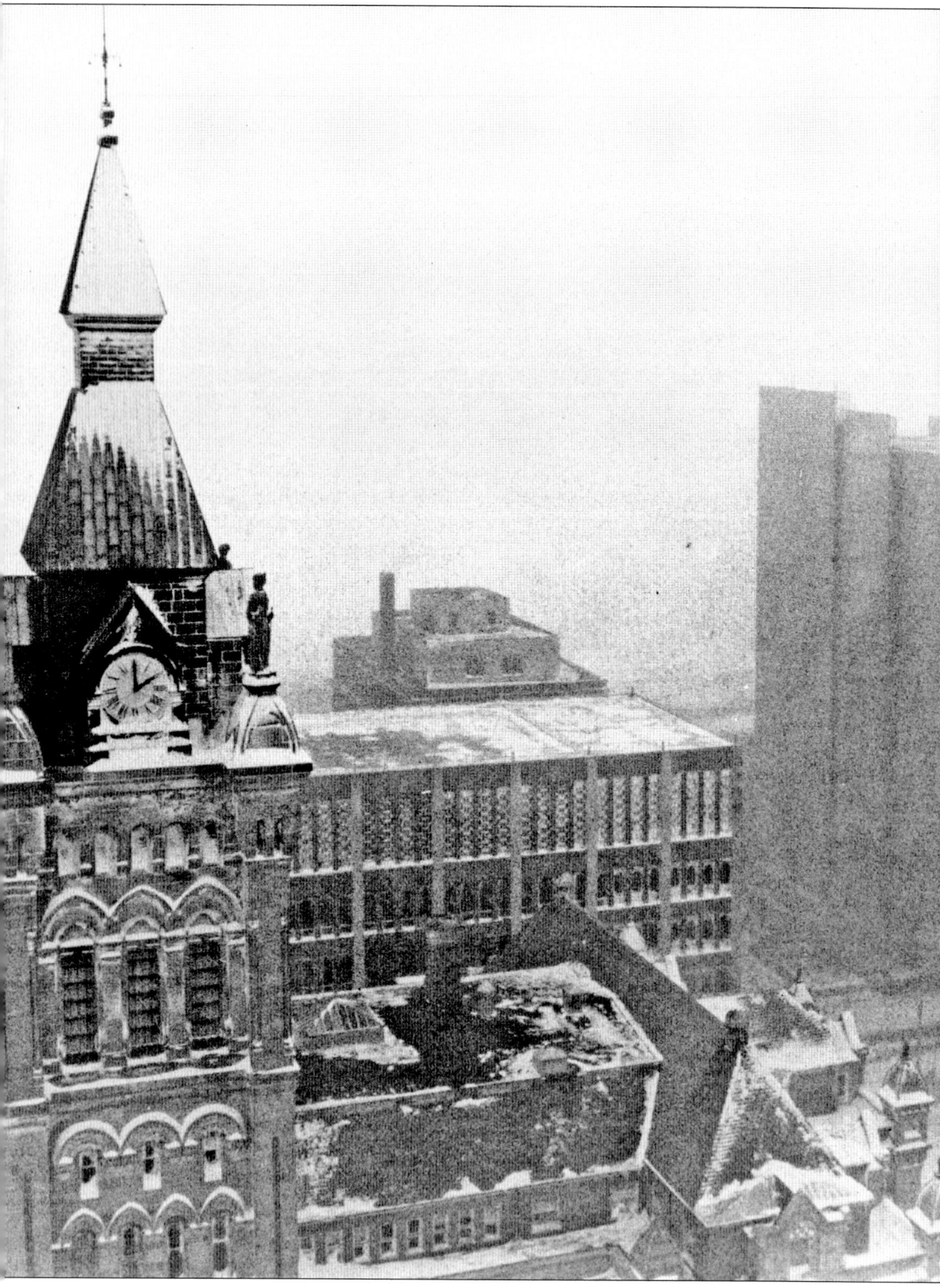

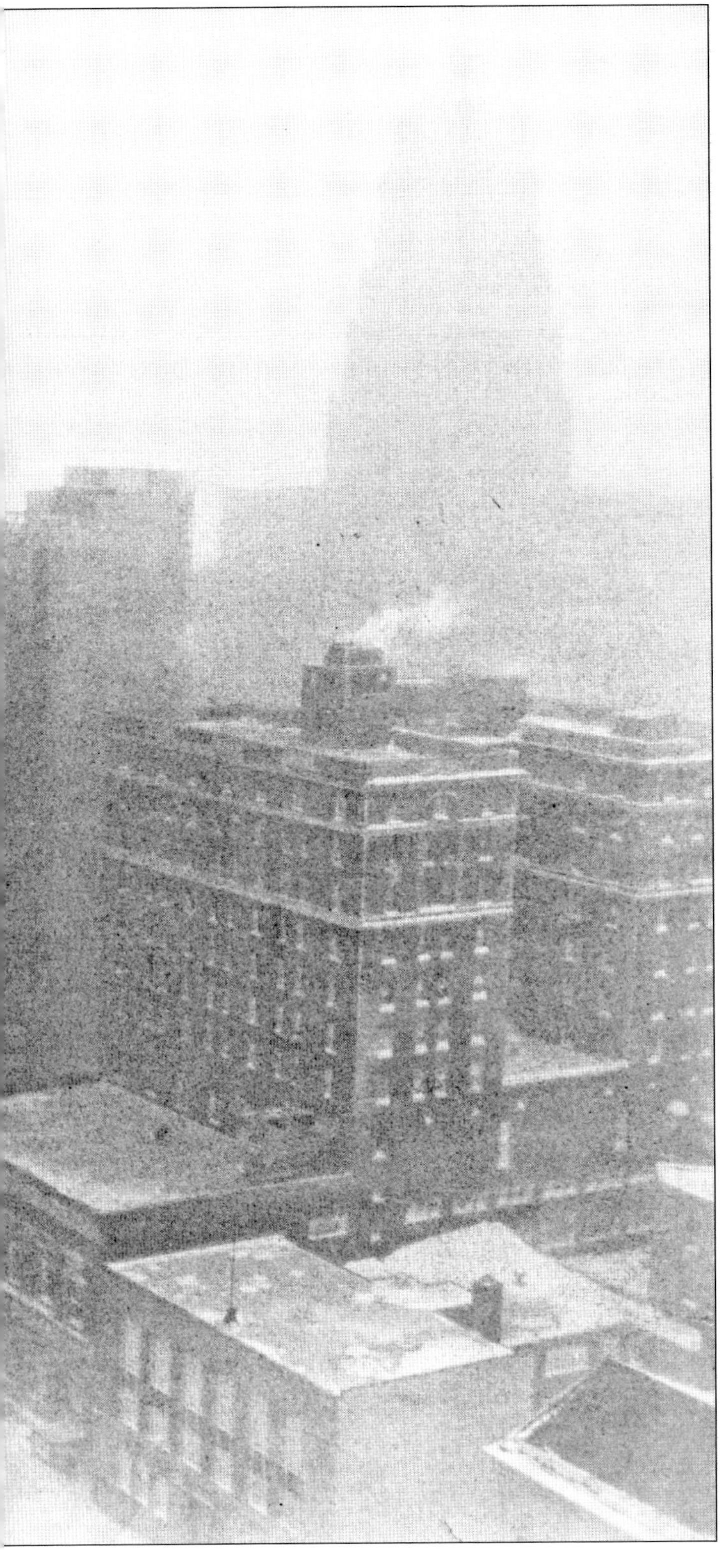

Buffalo City Hall is pictured on the right. On the night the blizzard struck, January 28, city hall was refuge for over 600 people. Politicians slept in their offices, and people stranded by the storm gathered in meeting rooms and the lobby. Many tuned in to watch *Roots*, which was broadcast over eight nights from January 23 to January 30, 1977. An estimated 33 million people were tuned in on January 28. Buffalo City Hall is an architectural icon of the city. Completed in 1931, it features Art Deco style, much like the Empire State Building. It was built by the same firm that built the Hotel Statler and was, until 1970, the tallest building in the city of Buffalo. From city hall, one can see Canada, Lake Erie, and the entire downtown area. (BLBS.)

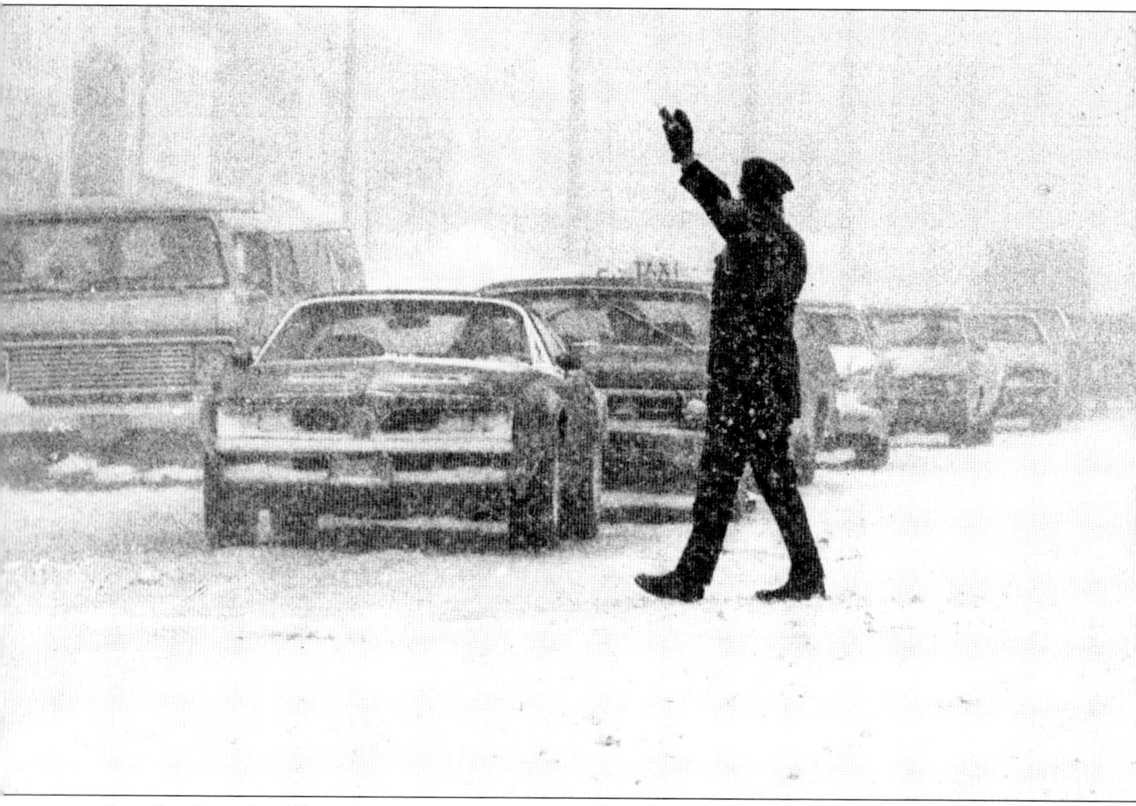

Local police, sheriffs, and state troopers remained on the job throughout the emergency, and many suffered frostbite in the harsh conditions. One police officer, Carl Reese of Buffalo, represents many of the finest and bravest who worked to serve and protect the public during the blizzard. Reese, badge no. 1317, worked 25 hours during the crisis, pushing cars stuck in the snow, helping stranded motorists, and walking miles in the blizzard to bring needed medication to people unable to get out in the storm. He tended to the needs of nearly 220 people trapped in Chef's restaurant on Seneca Street in Buffalo. Patrolman Reese suffered a heart attack and died on February 1, 1977, as a direct result of his strenuous efforts during the blizzard. In this picture, an unidentified Buffalo policeman tries to move traffic along despite whiteout conditions. (BLBS.)

"Neither snow nor rain nor heat nor gloom of night stays these couriers from the swift completion of their appointed rounds," but in fact the blizzard stopped mail for days. Once conditions were back to normal, mail carriers like Mathew Drylewski of Niagara Falls hefted their loads and walked through the snowdrifts to deliver the mail. (NFPL.)

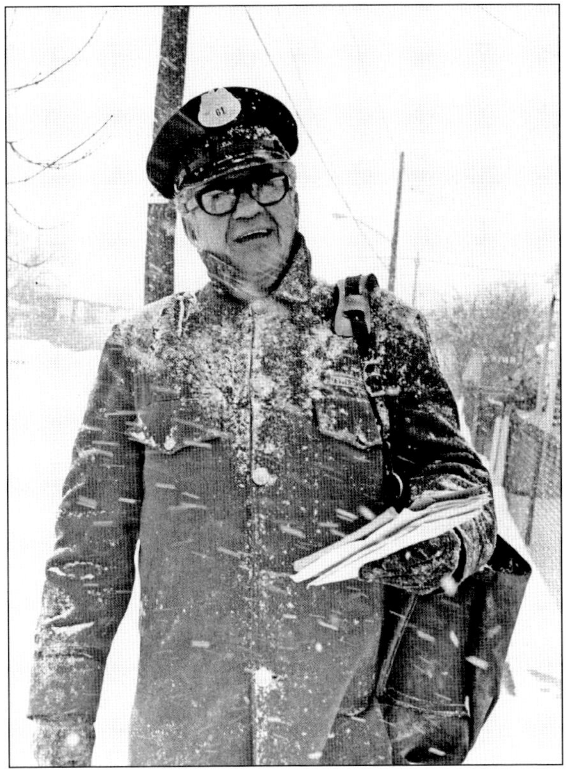

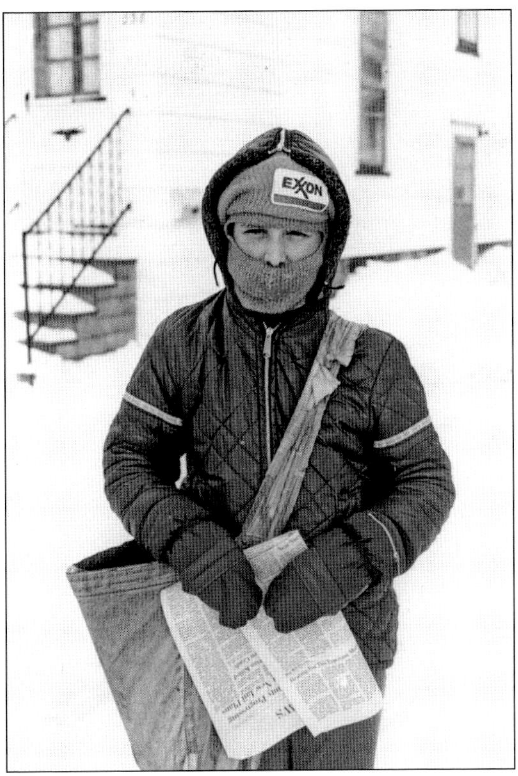

The snowstorm forced many local newspapers to suspend or delay publication, but once they were back in business, so was the army of news carriers. This carrier is from Batavia. (GCHD.)

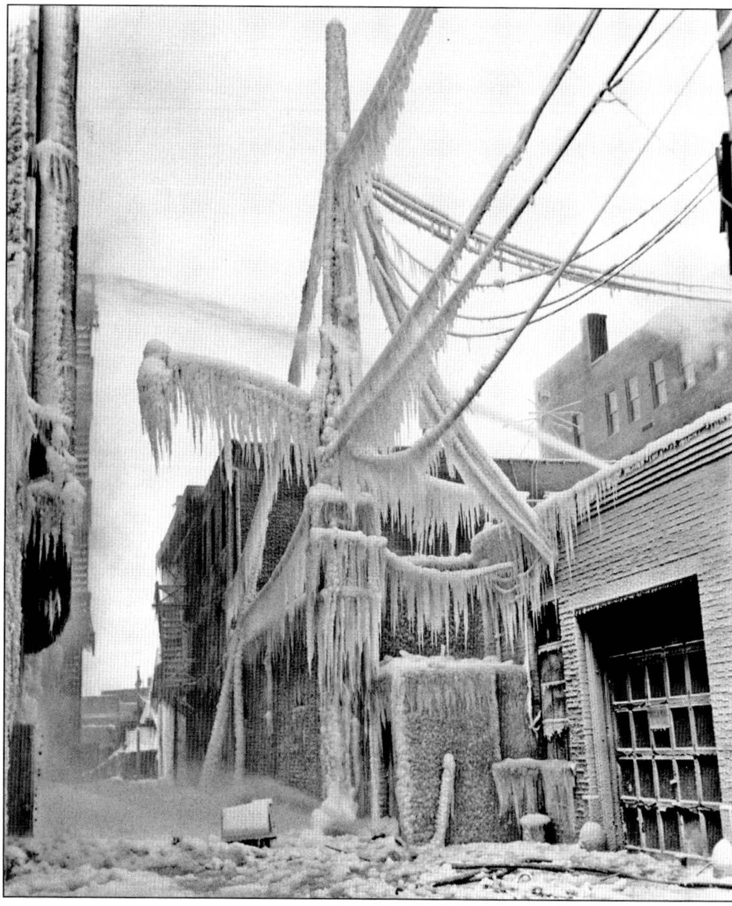

The extreme cold made fighting fires a challenge. Hoses and equipment froze, as did anything the hoses touched. (NFPL.)

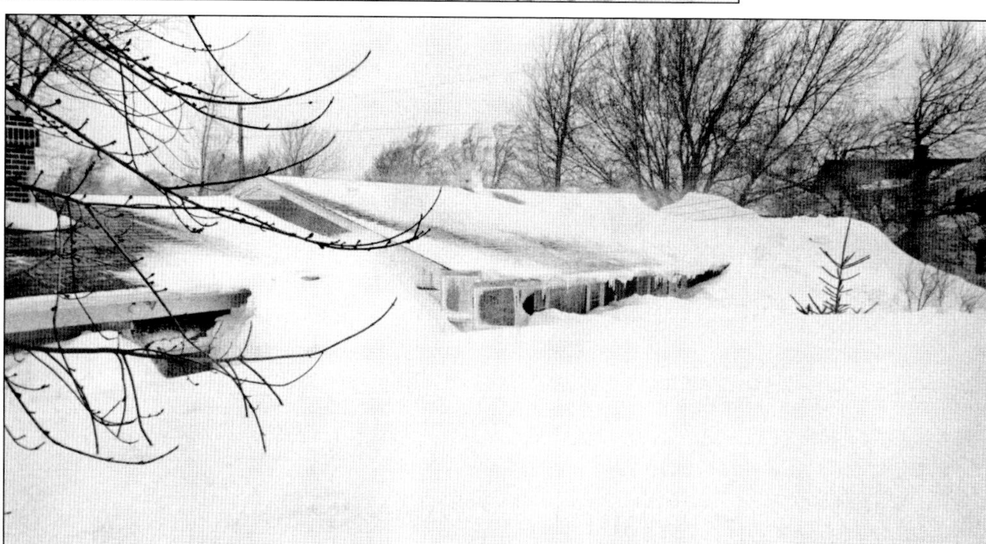

The total amount of snow that fell during the blizzard in the Buffalo area was less than a foot, but blowing and drifting snow buried houses up to the second floor. This house on Keck Road in Lockport is nearly totally covered in snow. (NFPL.)

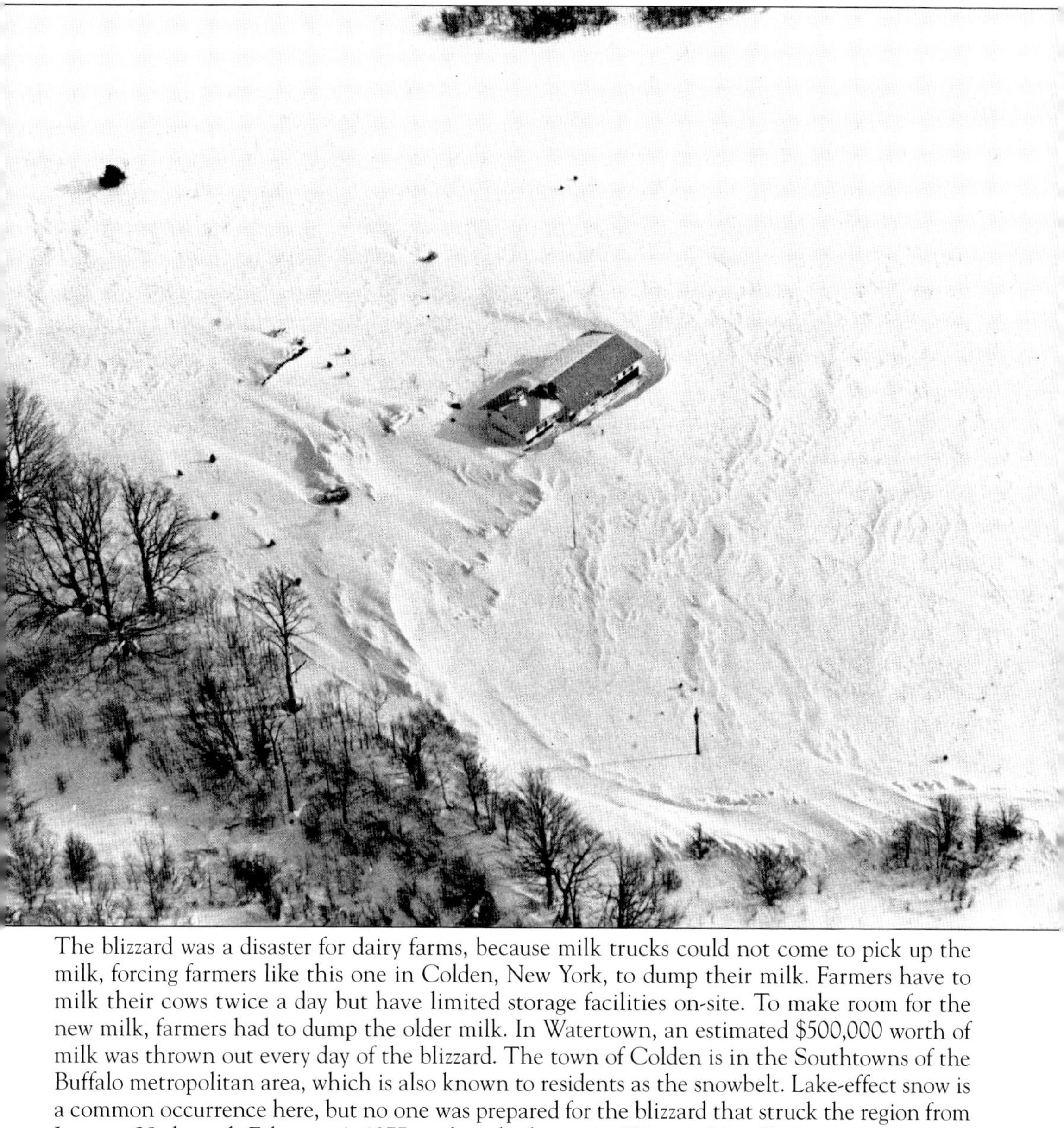

The blizzard was a disaster for dairy farms, because milk trucks could not come to pick up the milk, forcing farmers like this one in Colden, New York, to dump their milk. Farmers have to milk their cows twice a day but have limited storage facilities on-site. To make room for the new milk, farmers had to dump the older milk. In Watertown, an estimated $500,000 worth of milk was thrown out every day of the blizzard. The town of Colden is in the Southtowns of the Buffalo metropolitan area, which is also known to residents as the snowbelt. Lake-effect snow is a common occurrence here, but no one was prepared for the blizzard that struck the region from January 28 through February 1, 1977, and made the entire Western New York region one giant snowbelt. (BLBS.)

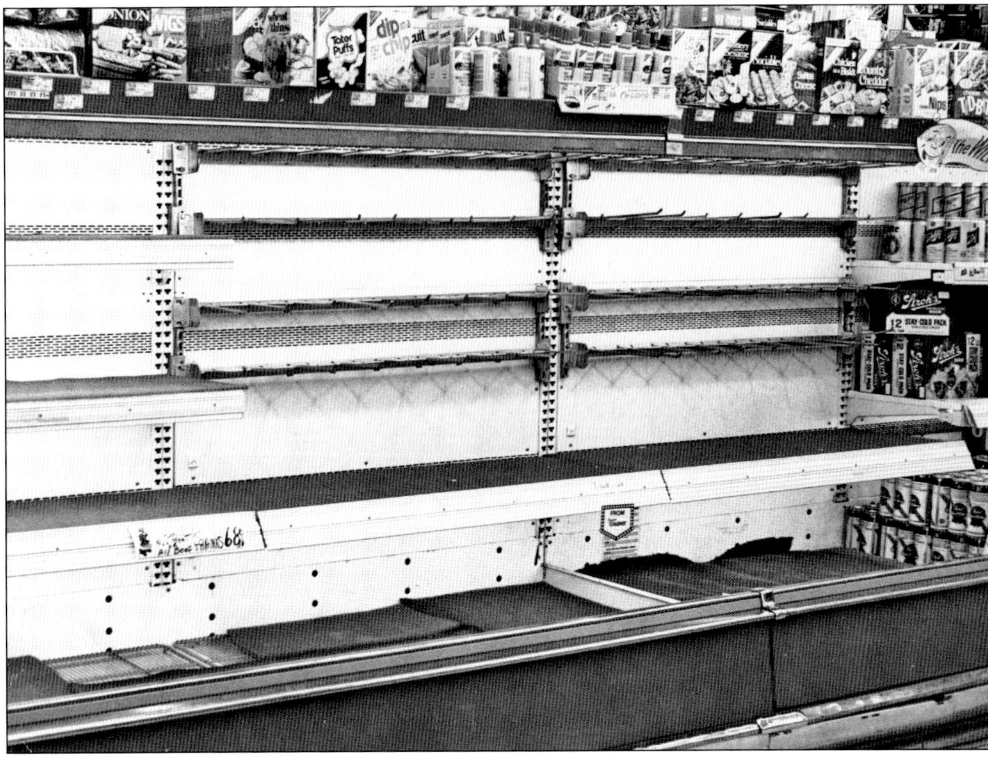

Milk was one of the common staples in short supply during the blizzard. Because of their short shelf life, items like bread and milk must be delivered more frequently than other goods. Grocery stores across the area saw stocks of these items dwindle to nothing, leaving shelves bare. (NFPL.)

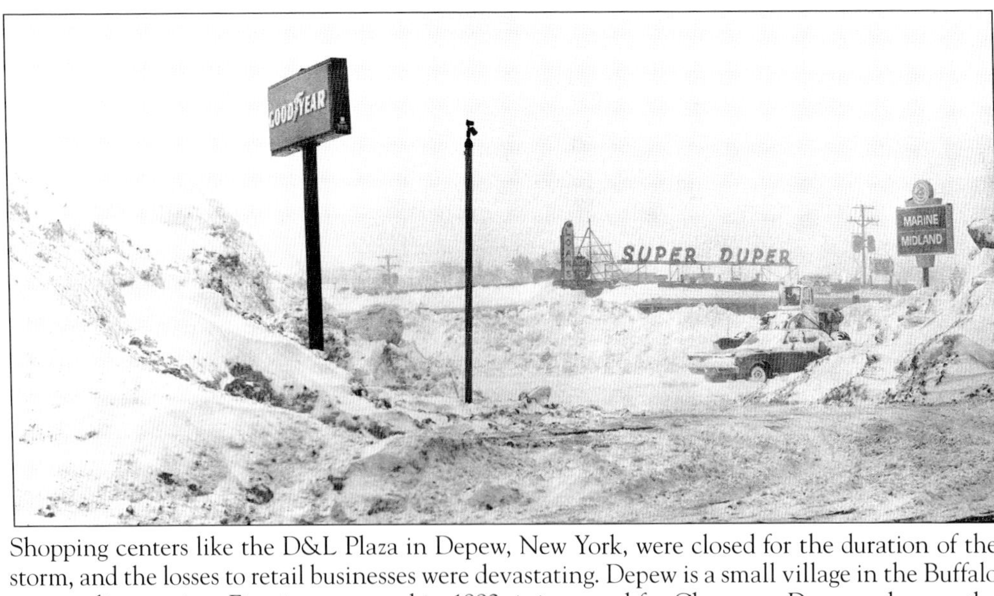

Shopping centers like the D&L Plaza in Depew, New York, were closed for the duration of the storm, and the losses to retail businesses were devastating. Depew is a small village in the Buffalo metropolitan region. First incorporated in 1892, it is named for Chauncey Depew, who ran the New York Central Railroad, which had its headquarters in Depew. Chauncey Depew served in the US Senate from 1899 until 1911. (MM.)

Malls throughout Western New York were closed by the storm. The Summit Park Mall was one of the newer malls in the Buffalo area, having only been opened in 1972. Located in Wheatfield, between Niagara Falls Boulevard and River Road, it made it through the blizzard of 1977, but like many shopping malls in the Buffalo region, it is today struggling to survive. (NFPL.)

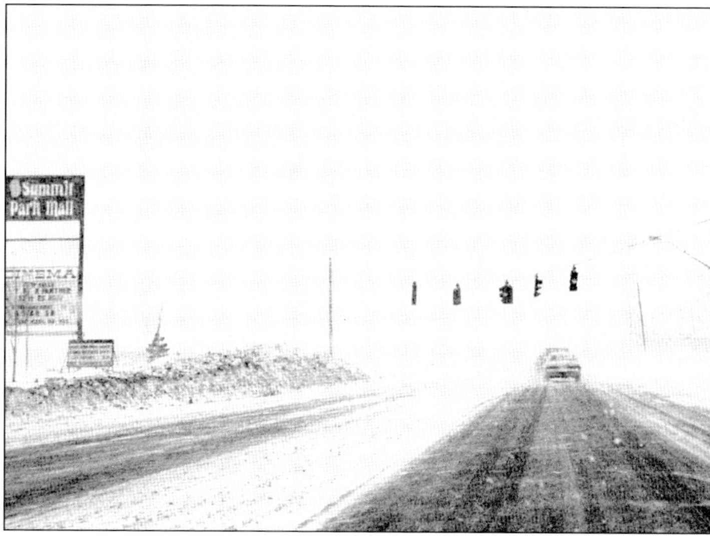

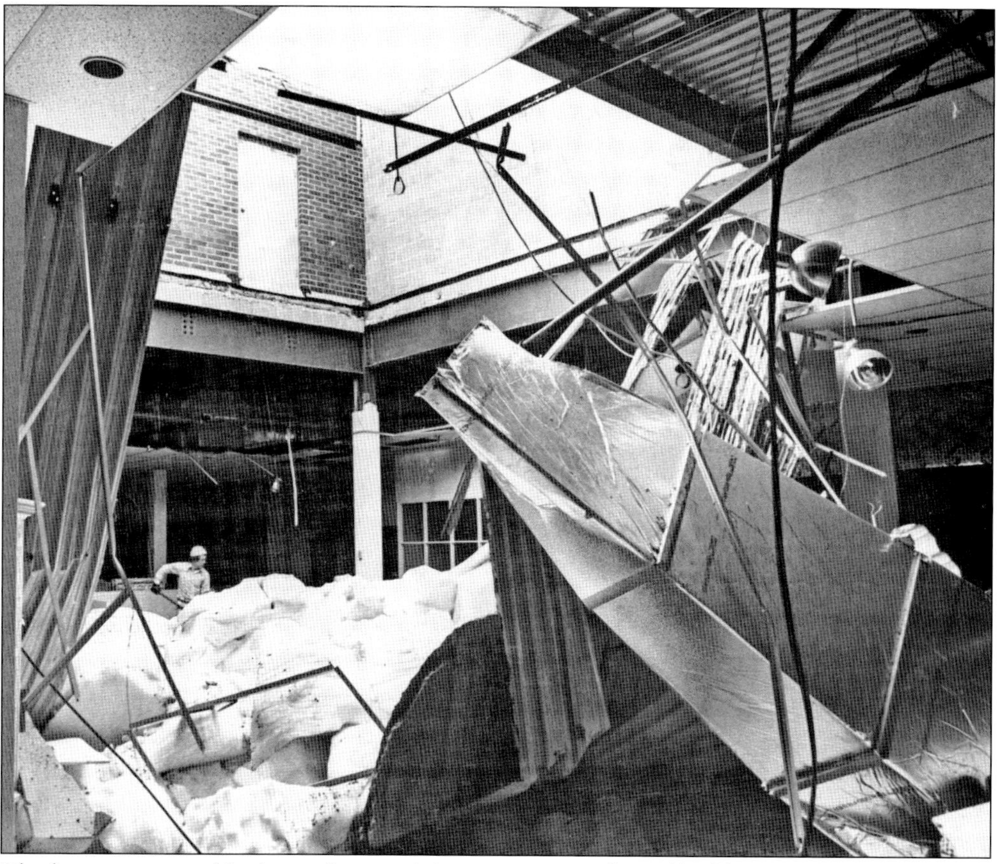

The heavy snow and high winds caused damage to a number of buildings in the area. In some cases, hurricane-force winds blew out windows and blew off roofs. The roof on the Hens & Kelly department store at the Como Mall in Cheektowaga collapsed, causing damage to the store and its merchandise. Hens & Kelly had a chain of department stores in the region, but the company went out of business in 1982. The Como Mall is no longer a mall but is now a business park. (BLBS.)

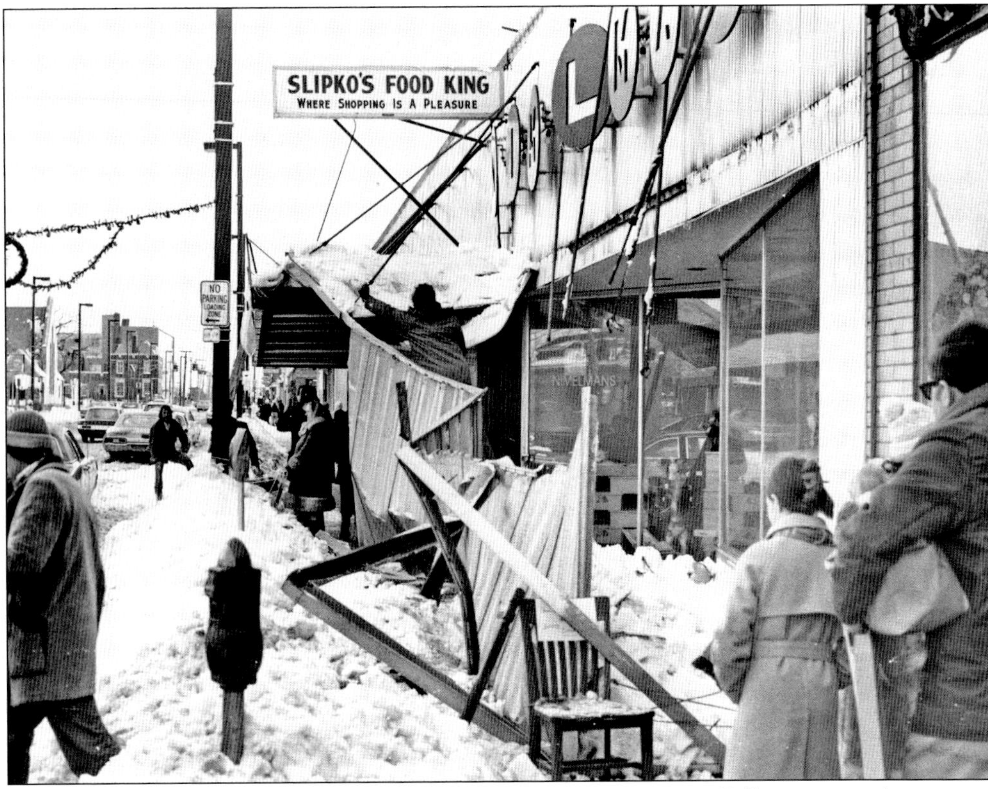

Slipkos grocery store on Main Street and Linwood Avenue in Niagara Falls was a popular grocery. Its motto was "Where Food Shopping Is King." Heavily damaged by the blizzard, the store was renovated and reopened. Like many Niagara Falls landmarks, Slipkos is now gone. (NFPL.)

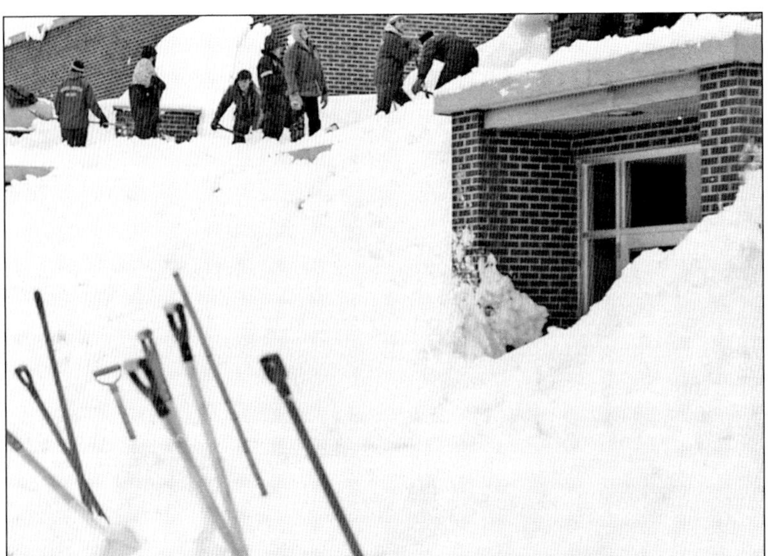
Heavy snow collapsed the roof of this school in Adams Center, New York. When the storm abated, dozens of volunteers turned out to clear the snow so the roof could be repaired. (WDT.)

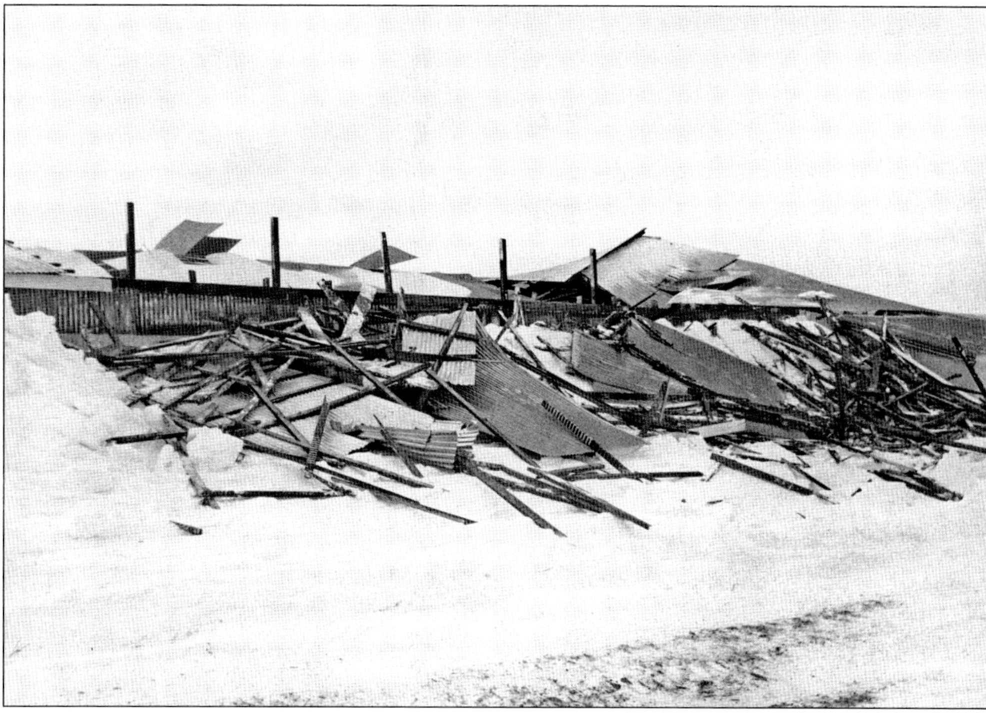

Wind and snow brought down a barn belonging to John W. Barber of Warsaw Road in Perry, New York. Sadly, the collapse led to the death of 10 of his cows. (BLBS.)

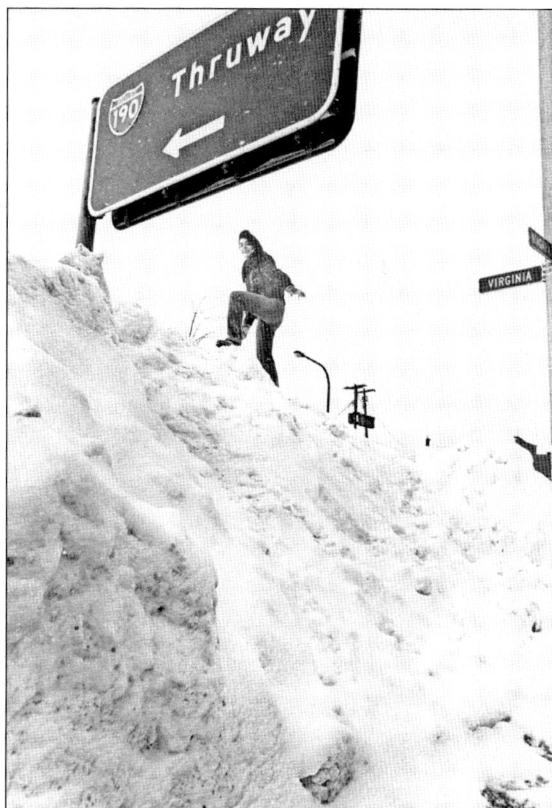

Throughout the Buffalo metropolitan area, the storm left mountains of snow and drifts of 30 or more feet in some places. This young woman uses the snow to get a new perspective on Buffalo near Virginia and Niagara Streets. (BLBS.)

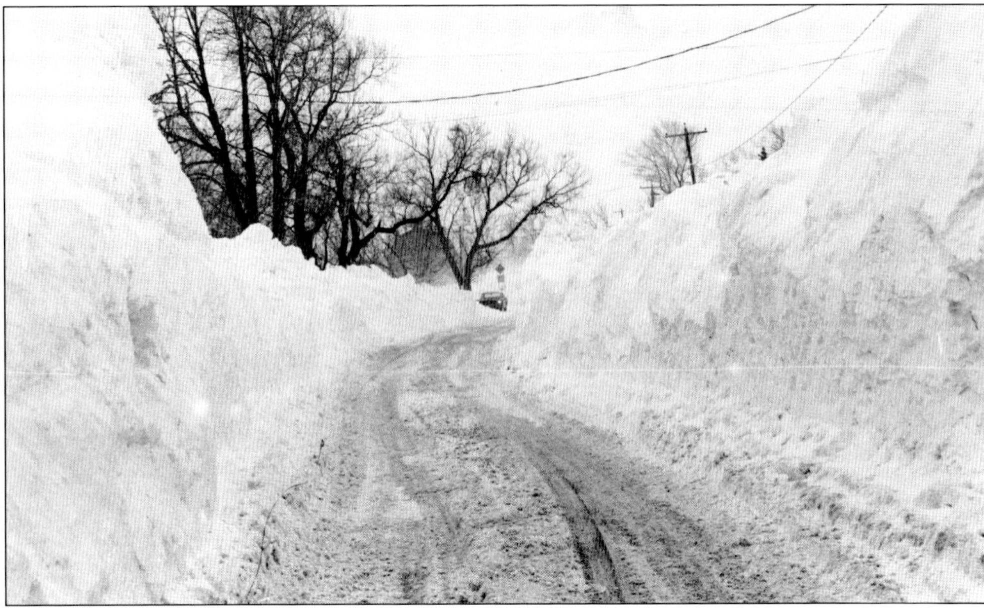

The snowdrifts created by the blizzard were impressive. When plows did open up roads, they often looked more like canyons, like this street within the city of Batavia. (GCHD.)

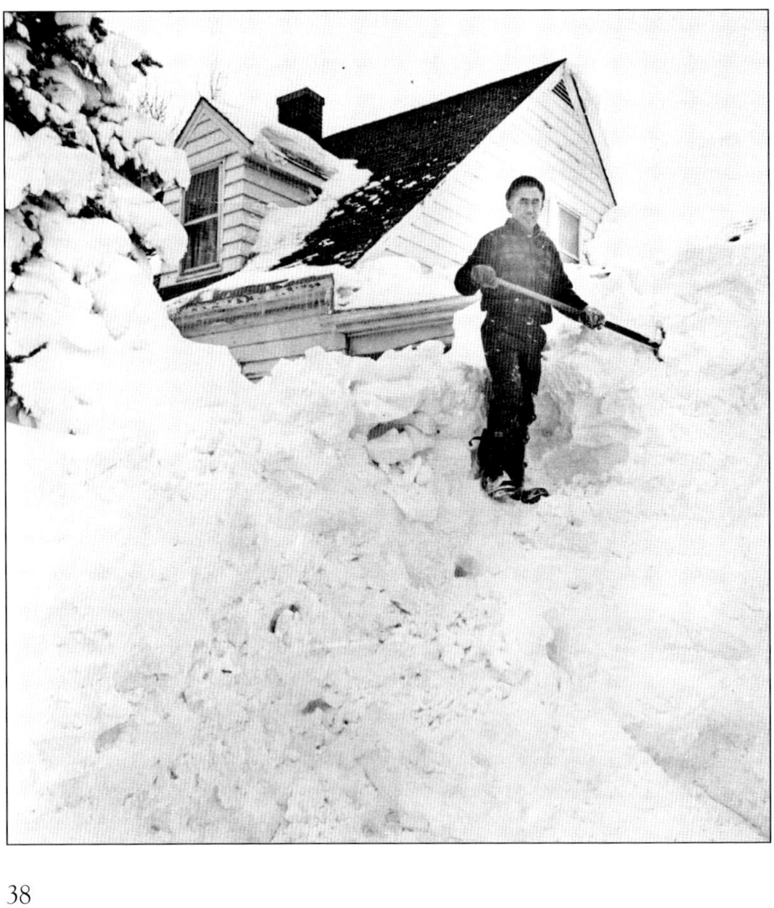

During a lull in the storm, many people tried to get out of their houses. Due to the enormous snowdrifts, some people had to climb down from the second floor. (BLBS.)

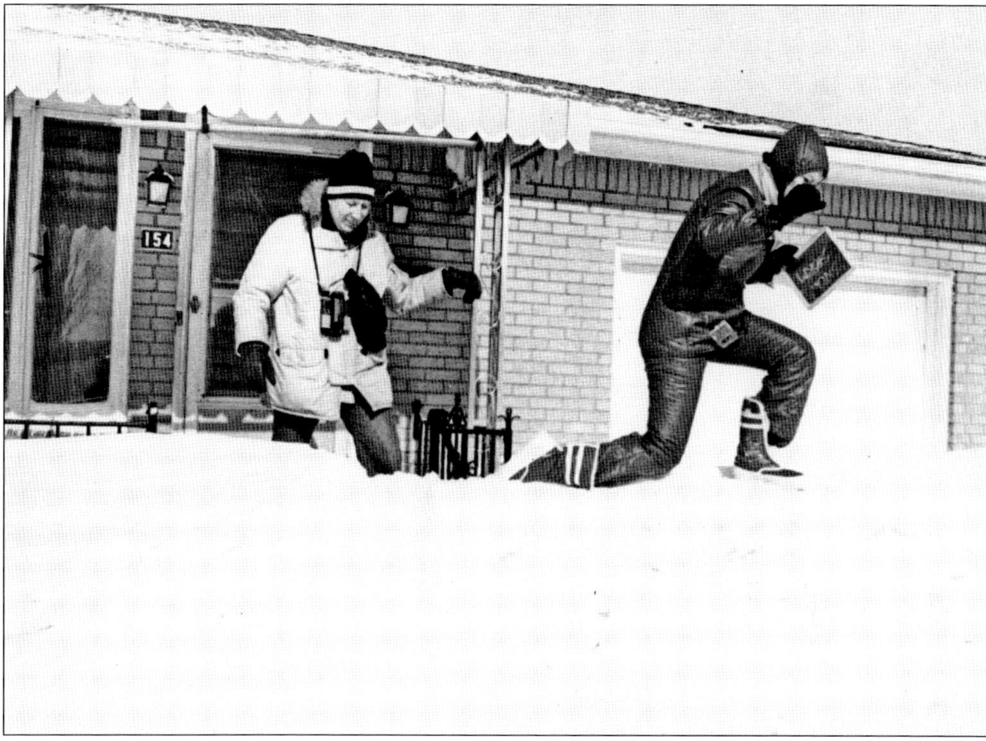

This family had to climb up a snowbank to get out of their house. (BLBS.)

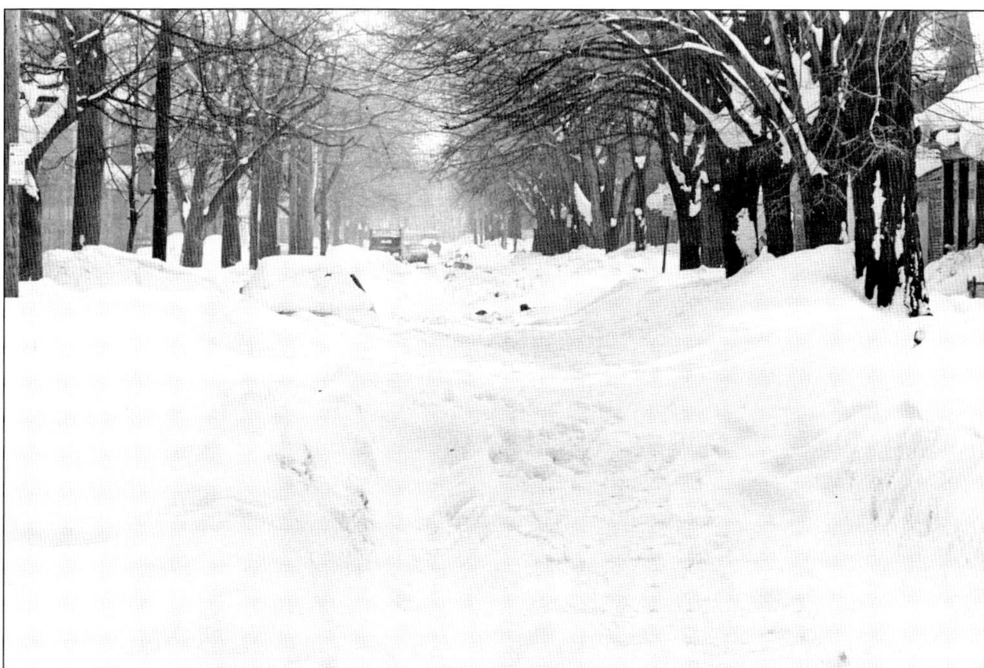

Getting out of the house after the blizzard was only the beginning. Getting to the road was quite another issue, and some would wait more than a week for their streets to get plowed, like the residents who lived on Hickory Street in downtown Buffalo. (BLBS.)

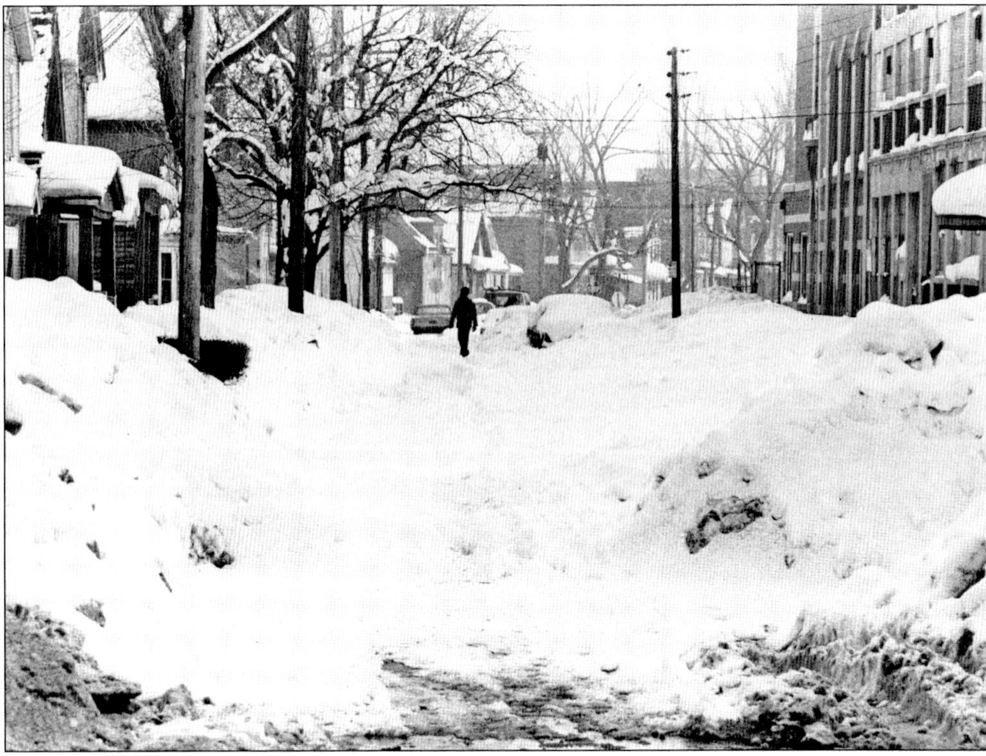

Pratt Street in Buffalo was also choked with snow. For many residents of Buffalo, it was weeks before things returned to normal. (BLBS.)

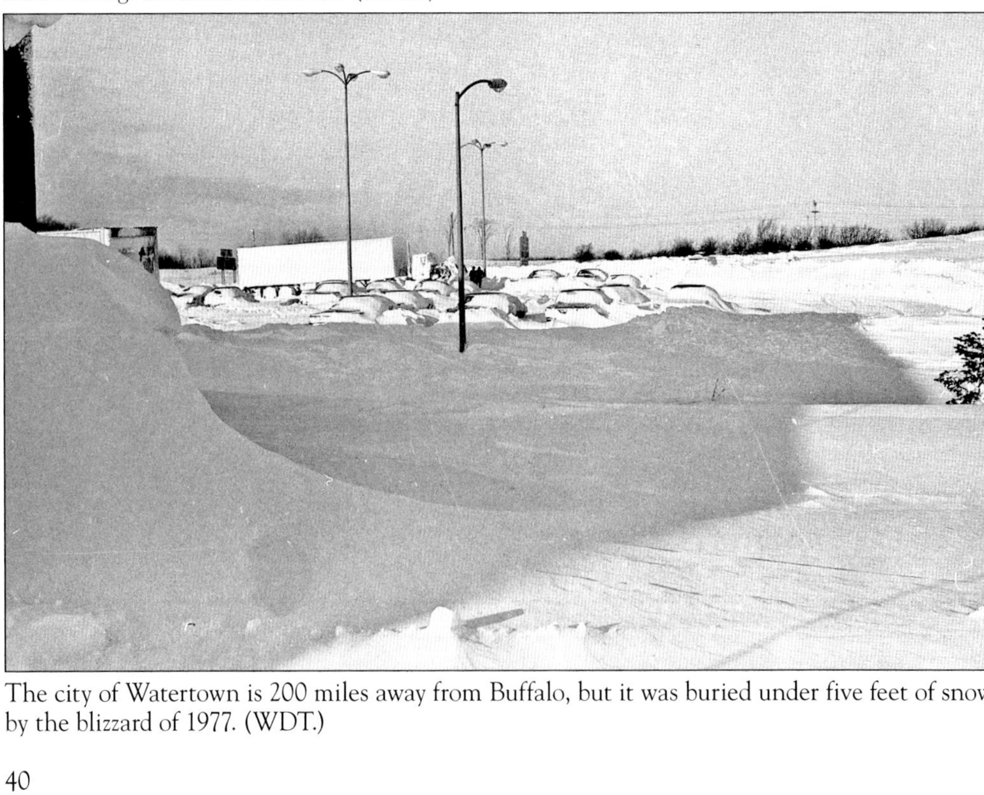

The city of Watertown is 200 miles away from Buffalo, but it was buried under five feet of snow by the blizzard of 1977. (WDT.)

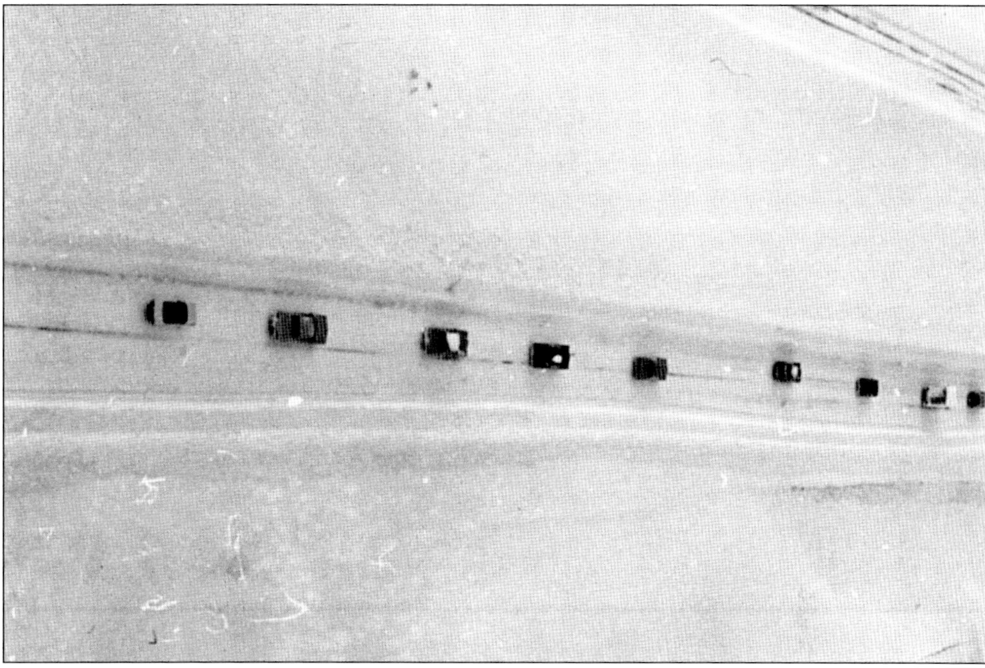

Once authorities opened Interstate 81 on Wednesday, February 2, some 1,800 people trapped by the storm made their way south out of Watertown. The decision to open the road was prompted by a concern that the city would run out of food. (WDT.)

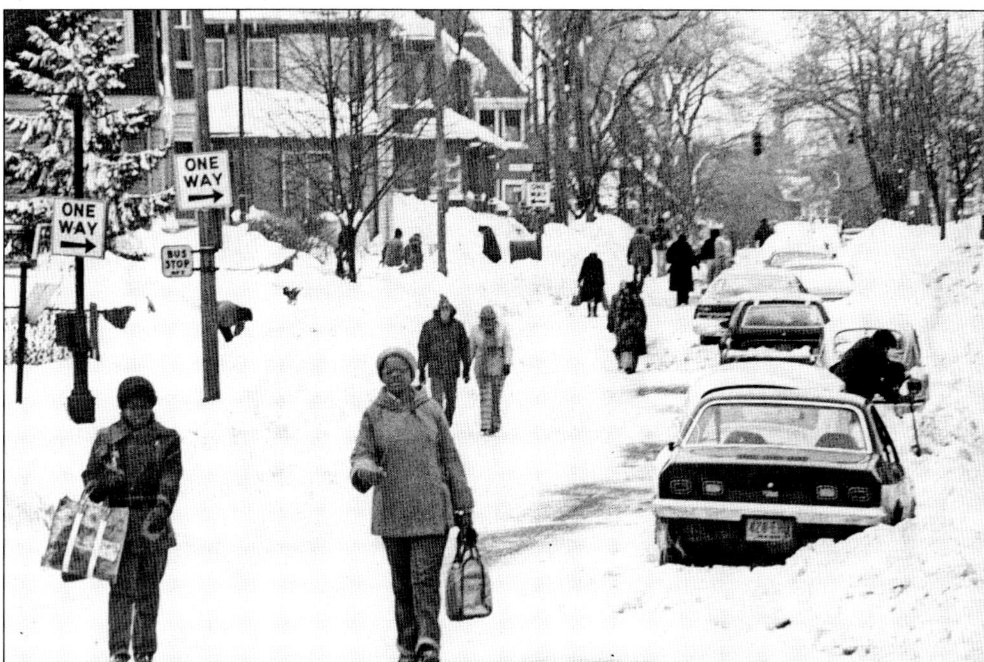

Even if roads were open, not everyone was able to get his or her car started in the extreme wind chills of 30 to 60 below zero. Residents at Richmond and West Utica Streets chose to walk rather than drive after the blizzard. (BLBS.)

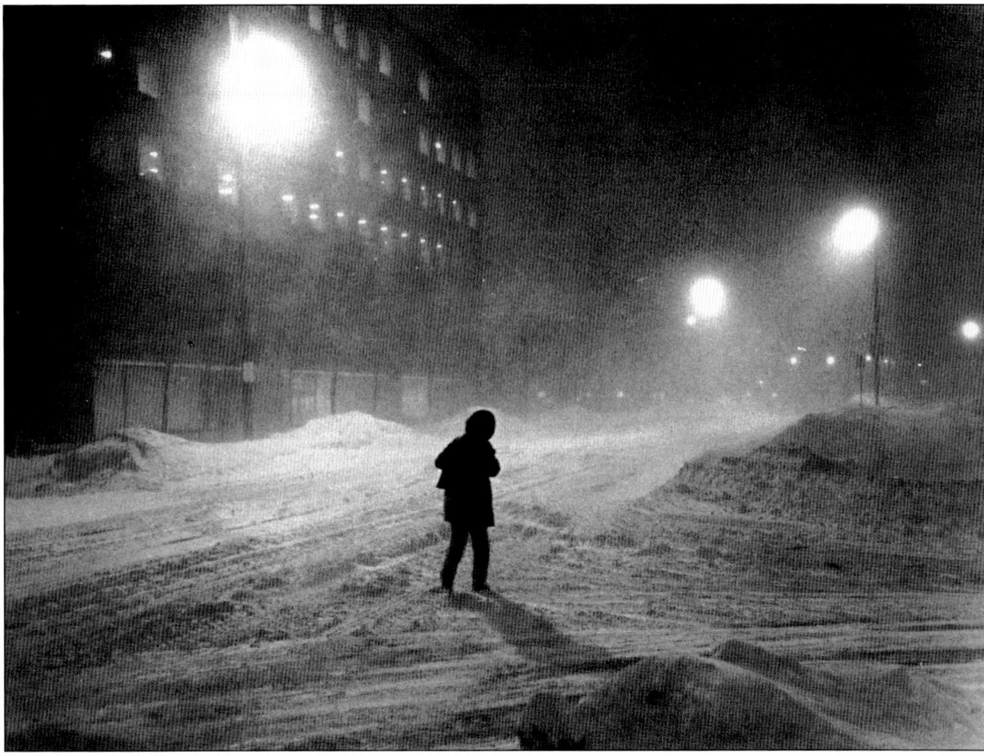

The traffic-free, snow-clogged, and therefore quiet streets provided some with a peaceful feeling and a sense of calm after the storm. (NFPL.)

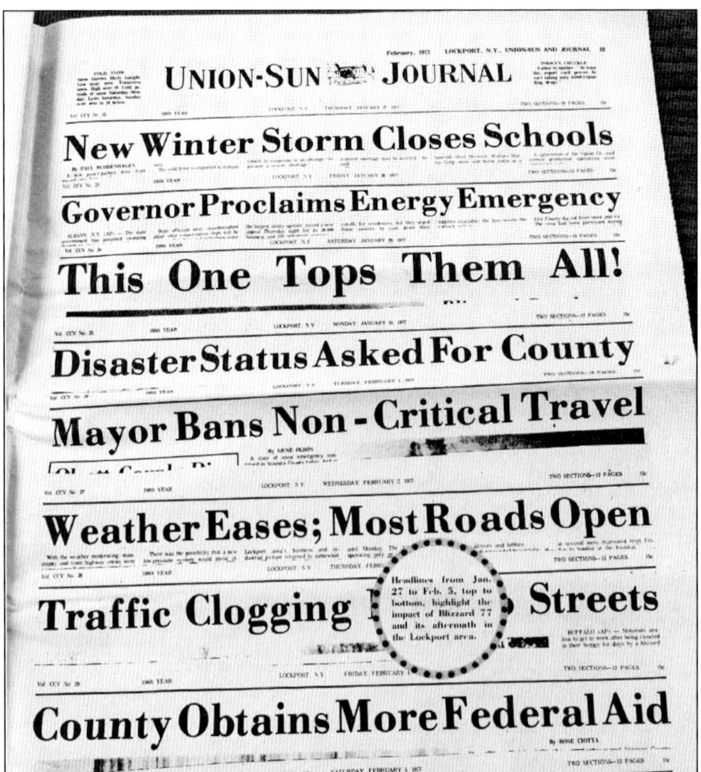

UNION-SUN JOURNAL

New Winter Storm Closes Schools

Governor Proclaims Energy Emergency

This One Tops Them All!

Disaster Status Asked For County

Mayor Bans Non-Critical Travel

Weather Eases; Most Roads Open

Traffic Clogging … Streets

County Obtains More Federal Aid

Headlines from Jan. 27 to Feb. 5, top to bottom, highlight the impact of Blizzard 77 and its aftermath in the Lockport area.

The blizzard of 1977 provoked a series of headlines, all collected here from the *Lockport Sun Journal*. (Author's collection.)

Two

The Government Responds

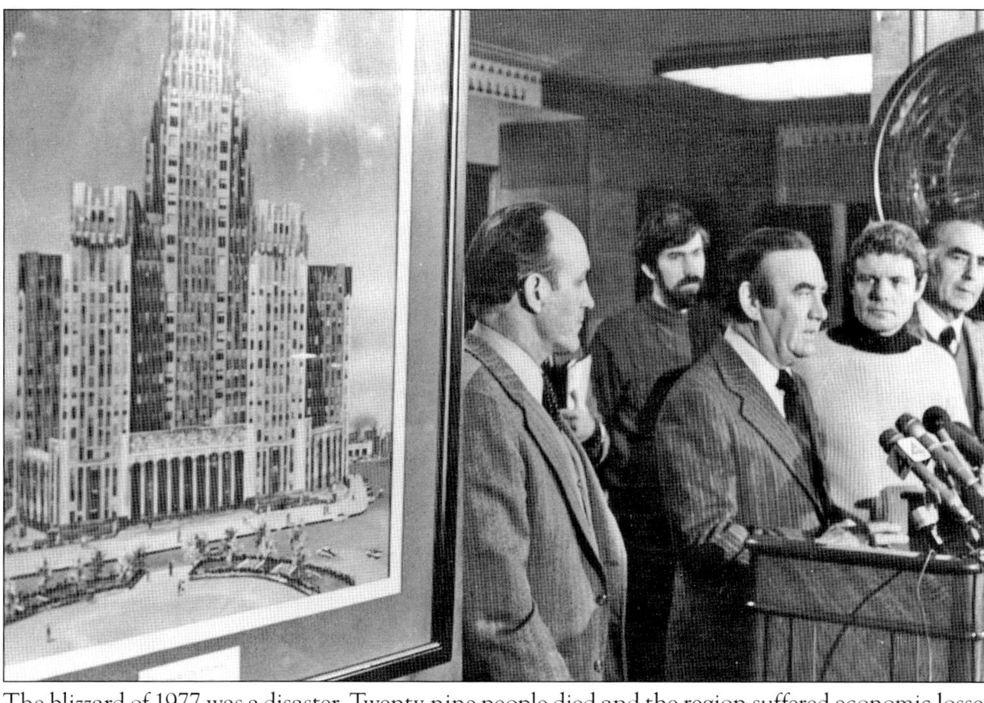

The blizzard of 1977 was a disaster. Twenty-nine people died and the region suffered economic losses in the hundreds of millions of dollars. The event led to a coordinated response by state and local officials, such as, from left to right, Buffalo mayor Stanley Makowski, New York governor Hugh Carey, Erie County executive Edward "Ned" Regan, and Tom Casey of the Federal Disaster Assistance Administration. The man in the background is unidentified. (BLBS.)

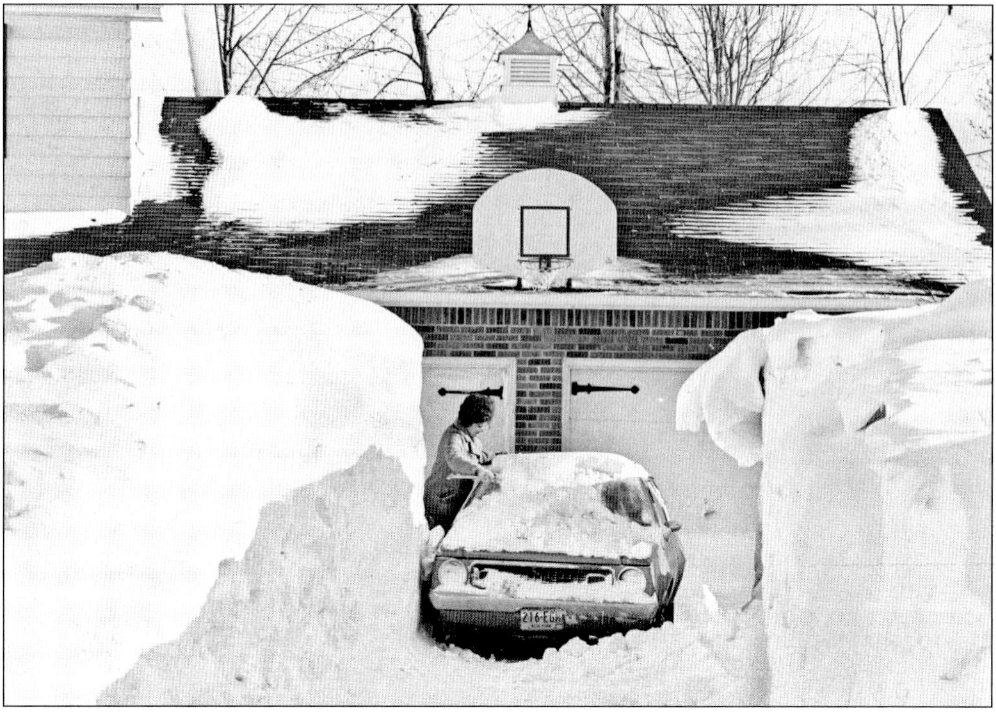

Before the blizzard of 1977 buried houses, like this one on Willowgrove Street in the town of Tonawanda, the winter had been cold and snowy and had left local and city governments throughout the region in financial crises as they tried to keep roads and streets open while exceeding their annual snow removal budgets. (BLBS.)

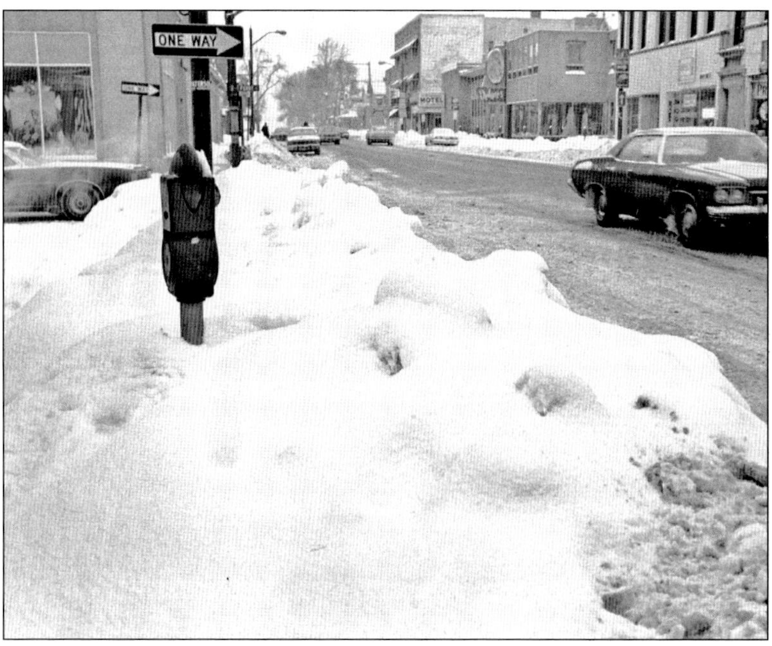

With 150 inches of snow on the ground by the end of January, local governments had spent their entire snow removal budgets and were running financial deficits. Main Street near Ferry Avenue in Niagara Falls already looked snowed under on January 11, but there was more to come before spring. (NFPL.)

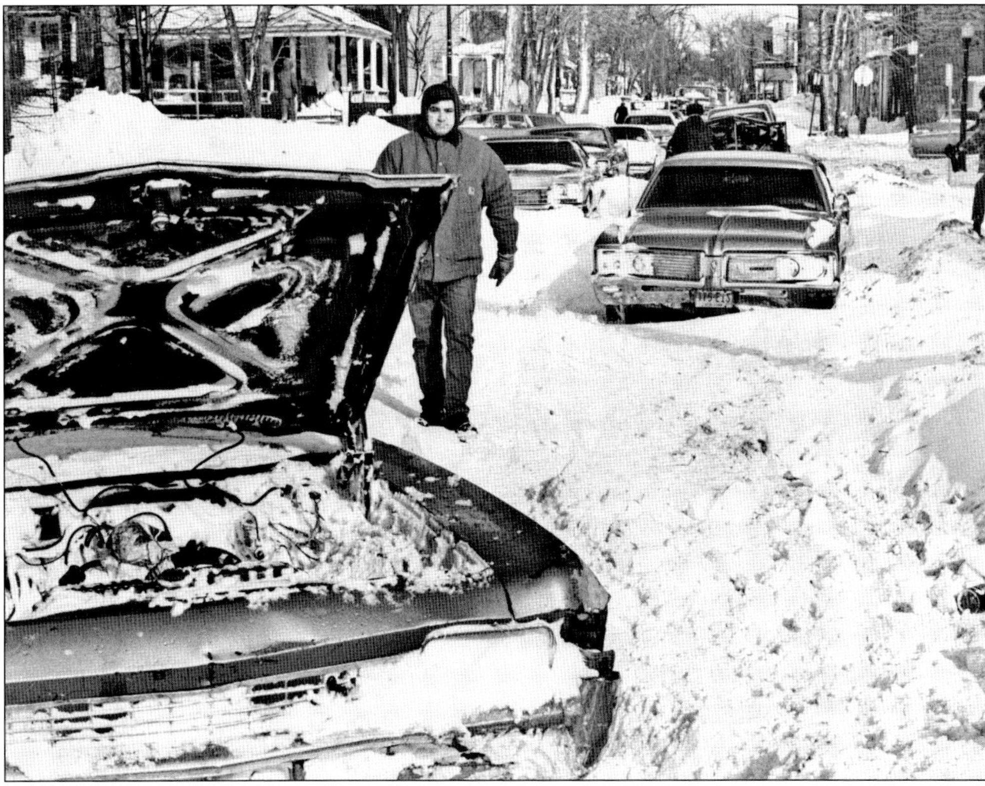

Buffalo, the second-largest city in New York State, was especially hard-hit by the winter of 1976–1977. From December through January, side streets were clogged with snow and illegally parked cars, which made it difficult if not impossible for snowplows to drive down these streets. (BLBS.)

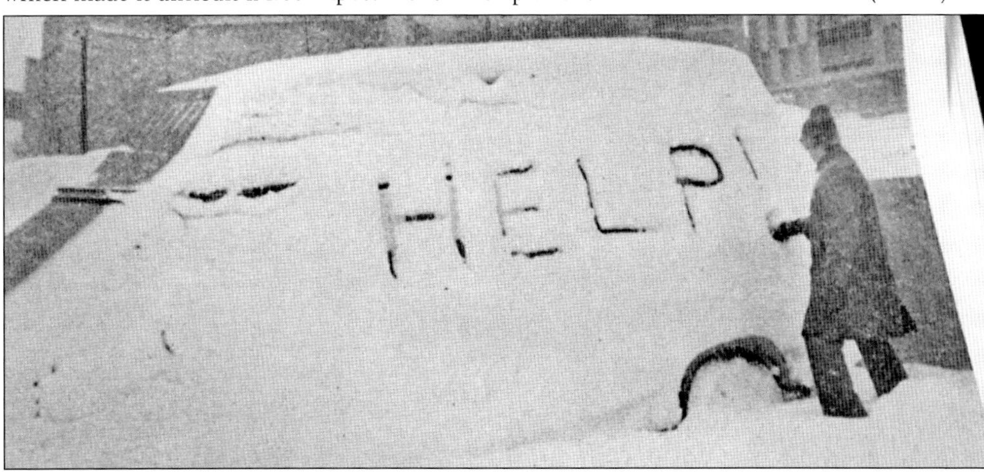

The situation in Buffalo was exacerbated by the financial crisis that beset the region in the 1970s. Thousands of manufacturing jobs had left the region, and the unemployment rate was one of the highest in the nation at 13 percent. Nearly half of Buffalo's snow-fighting equipment was broken down by January 1977, and the city had no money to fix or replace it. Just days before the blizzard, Mayor Stanley Makowski had requested Gov. Hugh Carey to provide assistance to Buffalo in snow removal operations. Newspapers such as the *Lockport Sun Journal* carried images conveying the plight of the people. (Niagara County Historical Society.)

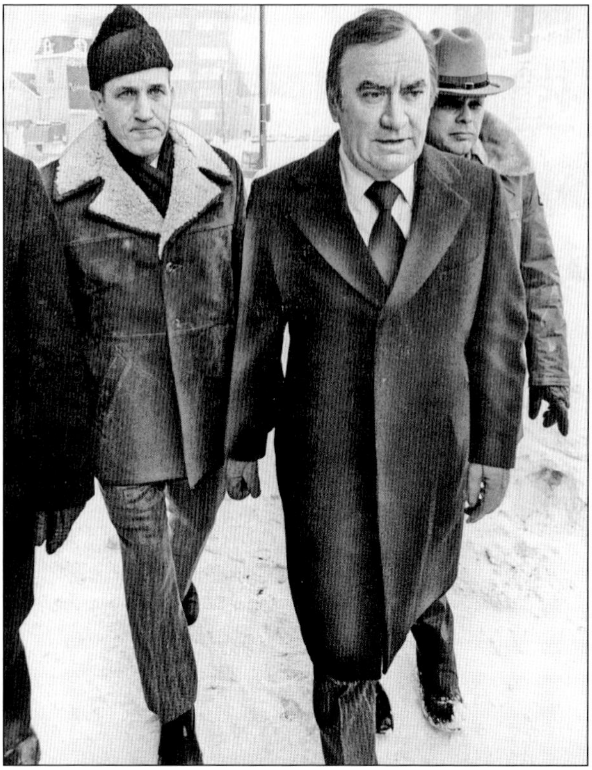

On January 27, 1977, one day before the blizzard struck, Mayor Makowski (left) accompanied Gov. Hugh Carey (center) and state troopers on an inspection tour of the area. Carey agreed to send snow-fighting equipment and National Guard troops to Buffalo. (BLBS.)

Equipment and personnel to assist in snow removal were delayed by the blizzard and unable to get to the city until January 30, 1977. Much of the equipment was delivered on Air Force planes, including the C-5 Galaxy, one of the largest planes in the world. Because the runways at the Buffalo International Airport were unable to accommodate such large aircraft, these planes landed at the Niagara Falls International Airport. (NFPL.)

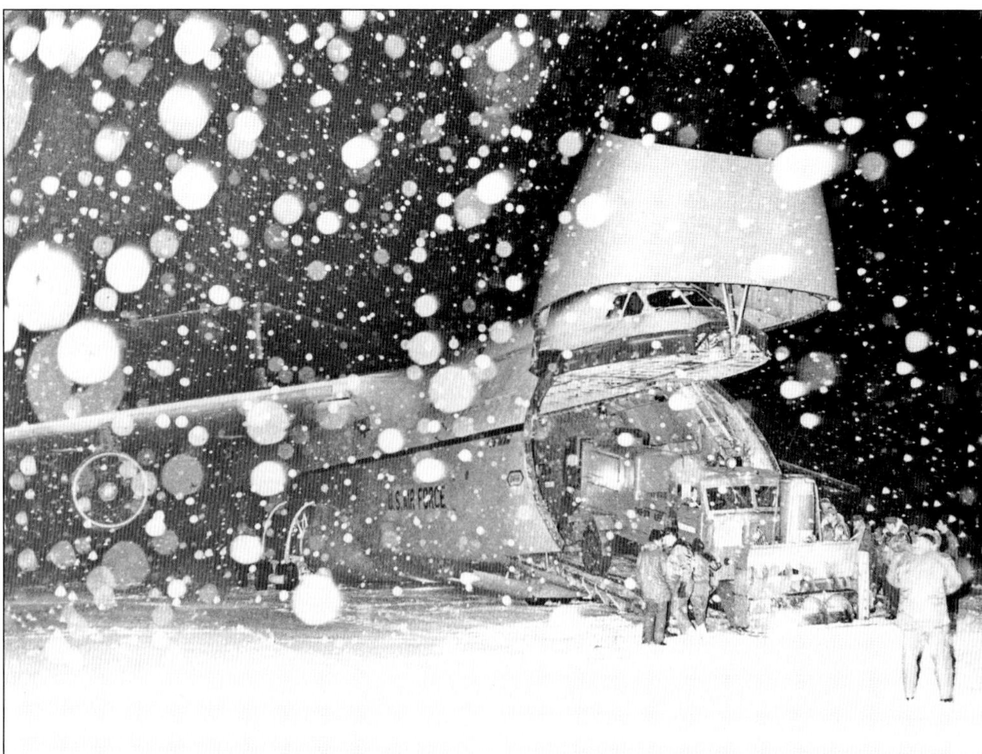

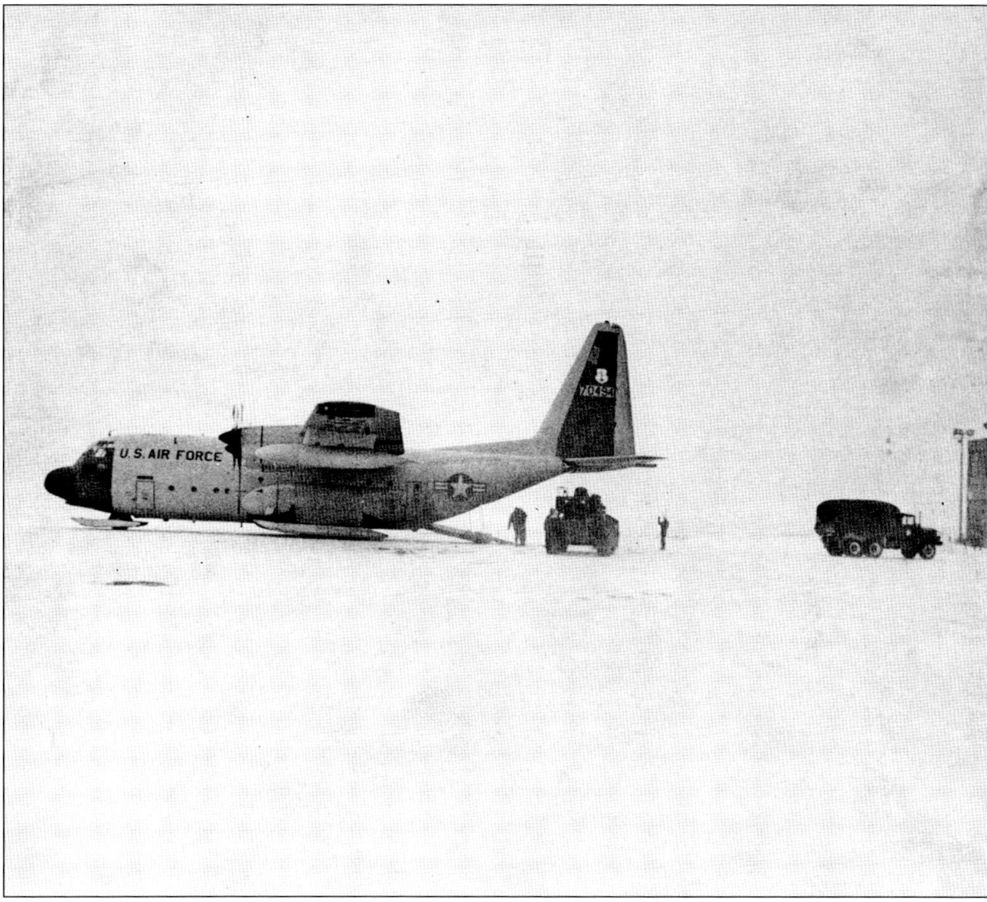

On January 30, 1977, during a lull in the storm, Gov. Hugh Carey flew into Buffalo on a C-130 cargo plane. Accompanying Governor Carey were federal disaster officials sent to inspect the area. Governor Carey led an inspection tour of Buffalo and praised "the spirit and morale of the people" afflicted by the blizzard. After touring the area with Erie County executive Ned Regan and Buffalo mayor Stanley Makowski, Governor Carey requested that Pres. Jimmy Carter declare the city of Buffalo and Cattaraugus, Chautauqua, Erie, Genesee, Jefferson, Lewis, Niagara, Orleans, and Wyoming Counties major disaster areas. The president had declared an emergency for these counties on January 28, 1977, but stopped short of declaring a disaster. Under the guidelines of the emergency declaration, the federal government was willing to provide $200,000 in assistance to the City of Buffalo. (BLBS.)

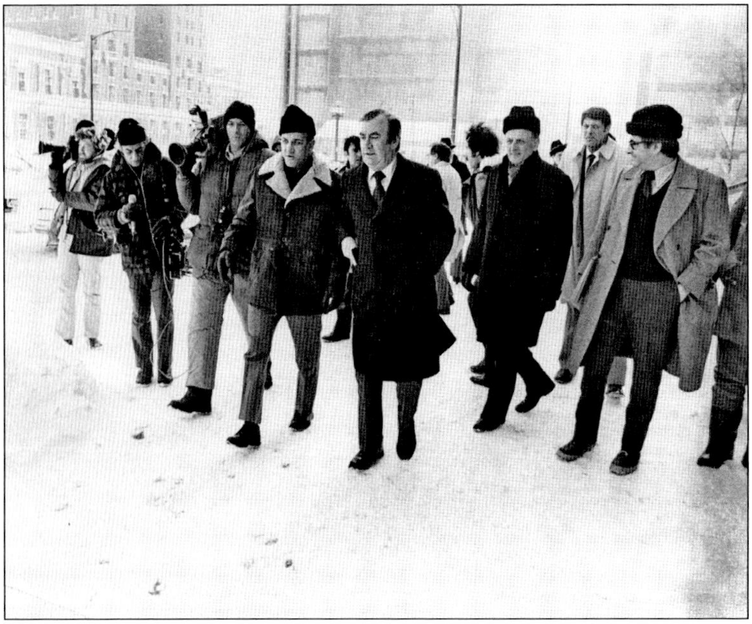

Governor Carey, pictured here on his tour of Buffalo on January 30, 1977, returned to Albany but left a team of officials to liaise with local government. These officials included his assistant, Ray Harding, William Hennesey from the State Department of Transportation, and Vito Catellano from the New York Office of Military and Naval Affairs. (BLBS.)

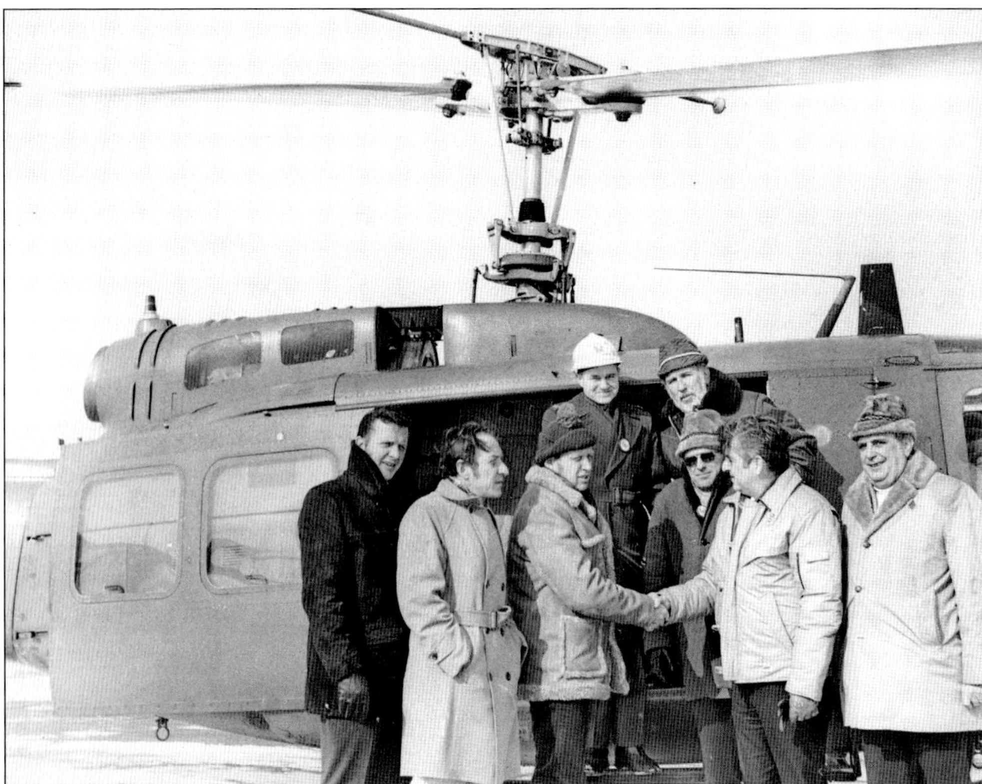

President Carter sent members of the Federal Disaster Assistance Administration (FDAA), the forerunner to the Federal Emergency Management Agency (FEMA), to inspect Western New York and to assess whether the federal government should declare a disaster. (BLBS.)

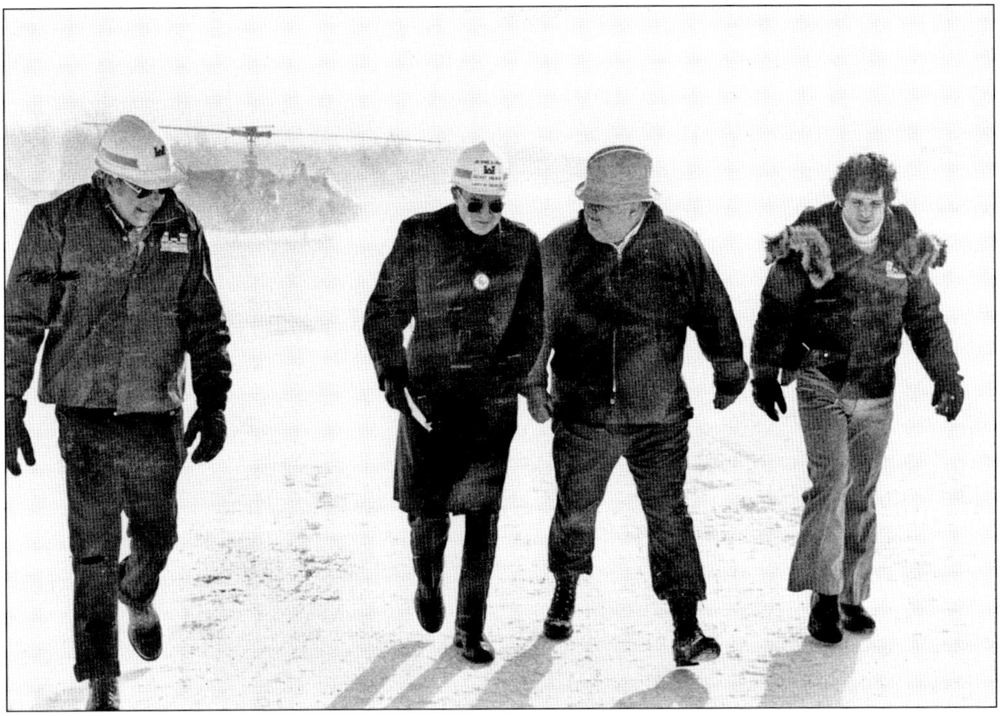

Tom Casey (second from left) was in charge of FDAA operations in New York. The FDAA was housed in the Department of Housing and Urban Development and coordinated the work of all federal branches of government, such as the Army Corps of Engineers, who assisted in snow removal operations. (BLBS.)

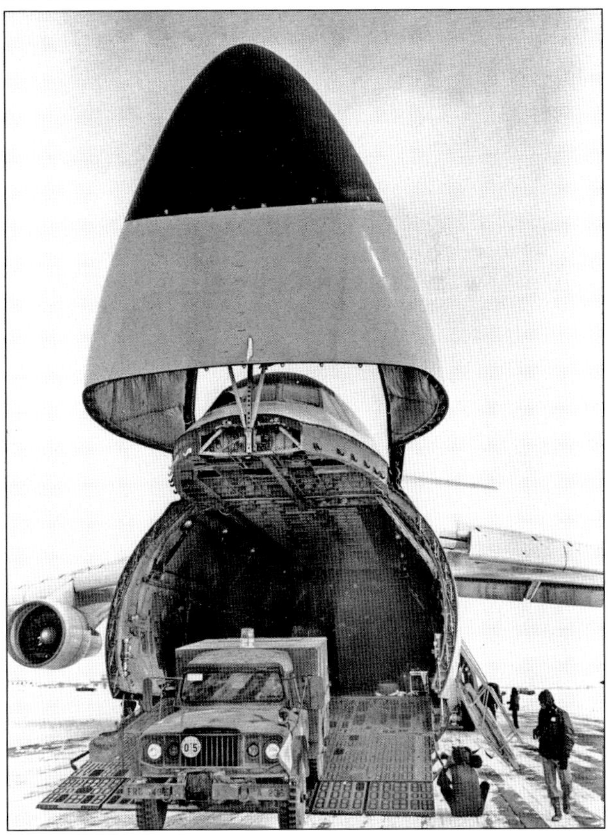

Tom Casey coordinated the work of the National Guard and the US Army Corps of Engineers to clear away the snow in the Buffalo-Niagara region. He felt that a disaster declaration might set a precedent that future presidents would be forced to live with. (BLBS.)

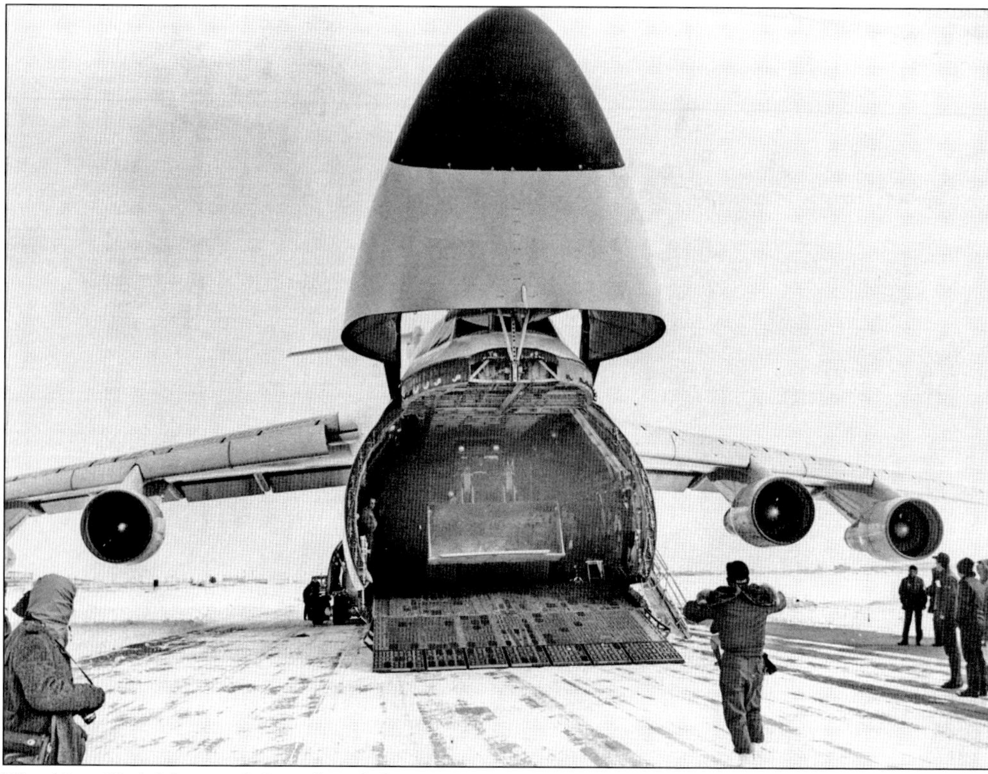

The New York National Guard and the US Army sent in equipment to assist citizens in Buffalo, Batavia, Watertown, and all towns and villages in between. (BLBS.)

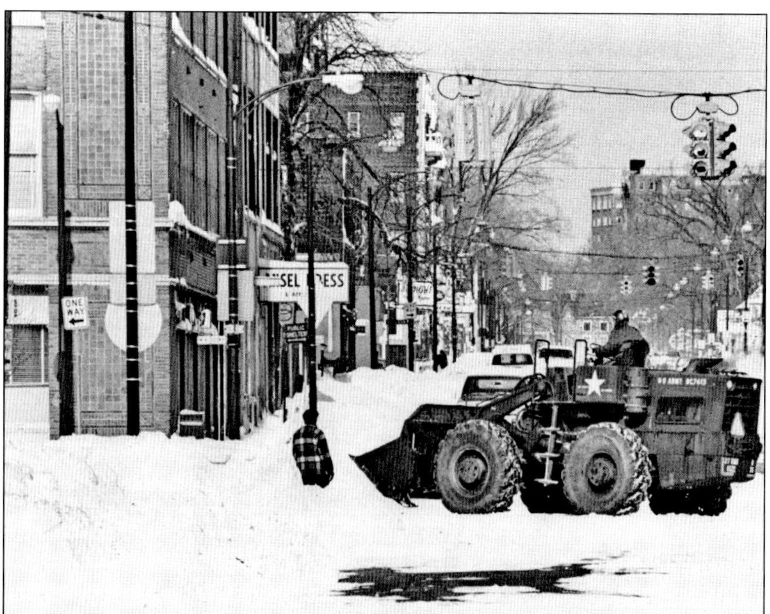

Military personnel won the praise and respect of the residents for their quick work dealing with the snow in Buffalo and beyond. (BLBS.)

Tom Casey brought an additional 300 troops from Fort Bragg, North Carolina, to assist the 500 National Guardsmen already serving in the area. The soldiers from Fort Bragg arrived on February 2, 1977, and remained in the area through most of February. (BLBS.)

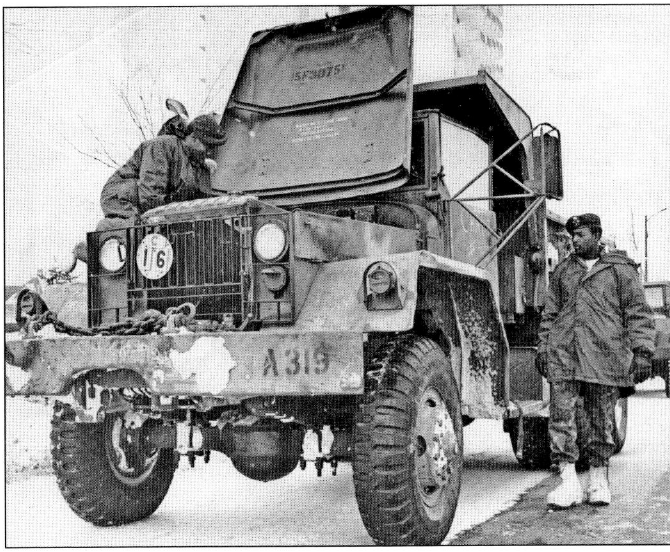

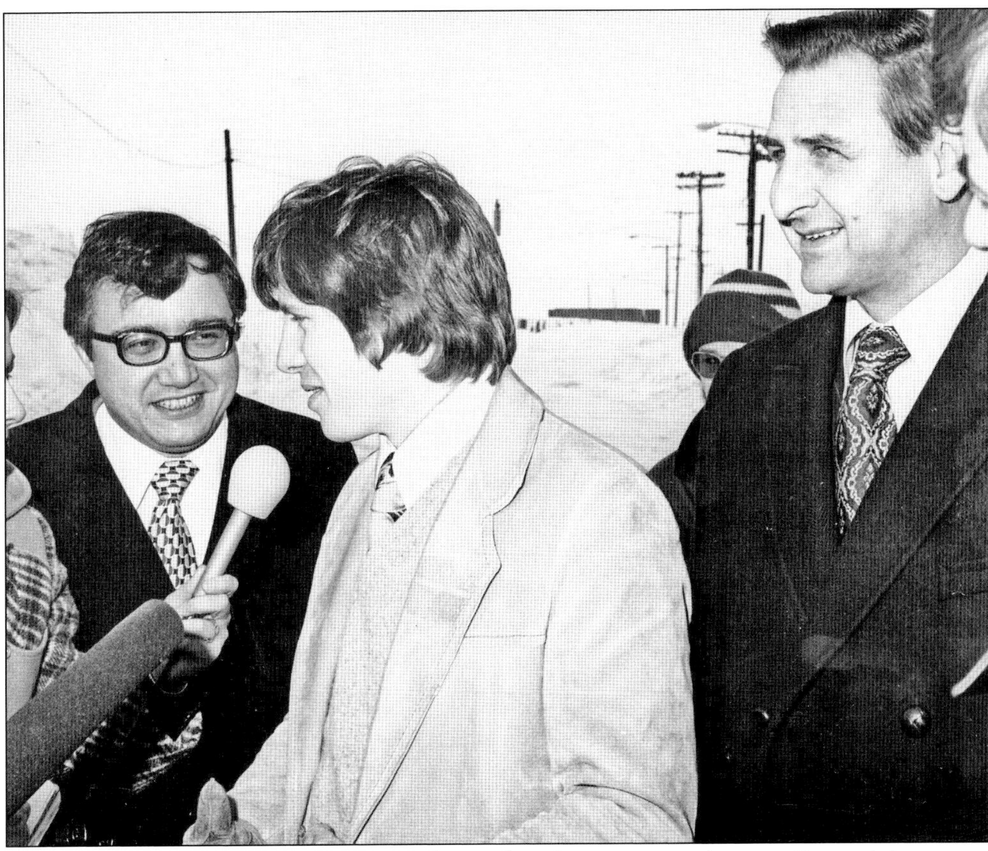

The local congressional delegation invited President Carter to tour the area. Carter did not come to Buffalo, but on February 4, 1977, his son James Earl "Chip" Carter III came to inspect the area. Pictured are, from left to right, Rep. John Lafalce, Chip Carter, and Rep. Henry Nowak. Although not pictured, Sen. Daniel Patrick Moynihan also made the trip to Buffalo. (BLBS.)

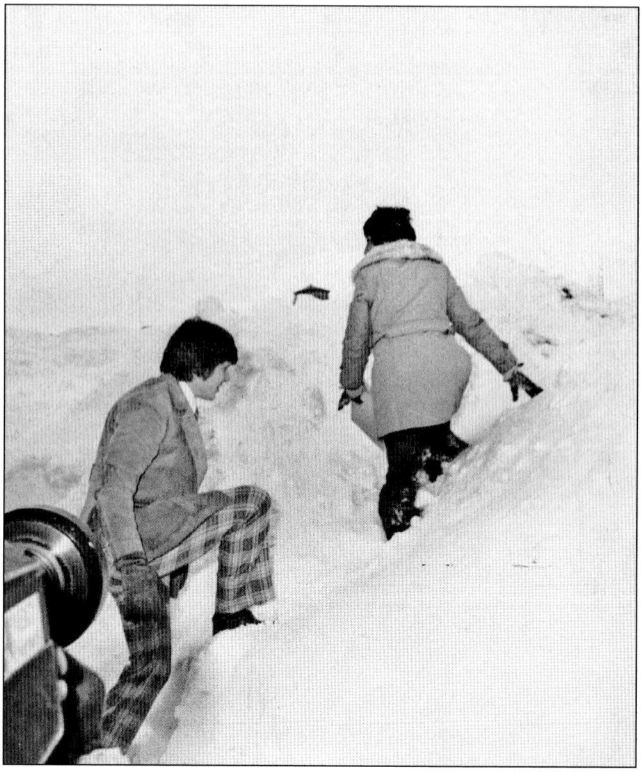

Chip Carter, pictured here with White House aide and former Rochester vice mayor Midge Costanza, remarked that he had never seen so much snow in his life. (BLBS.)

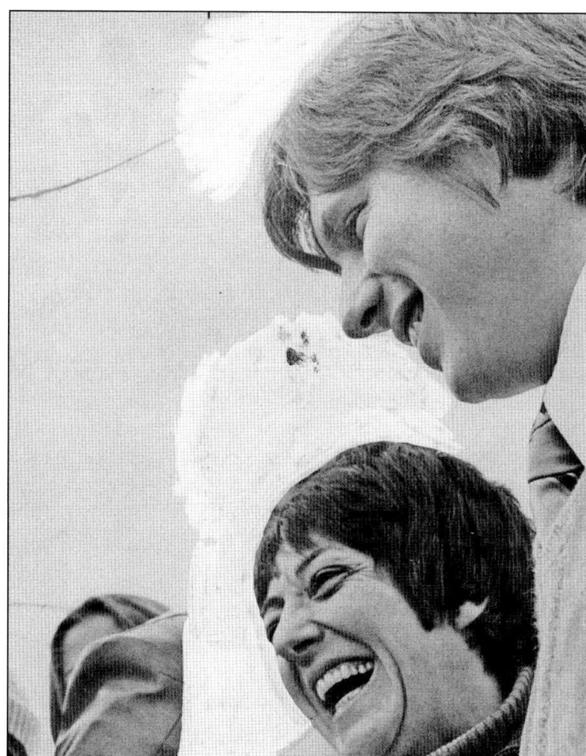

Chip Carter and Midge Costanza were charmed by the people of Buffalo. They met with elected officials and members of the business community. Behind the scenes, the powerful Democratic Party leader Joseph Crangle was also applying pressure to the White House delegation. This combination of persuasion and political pressure worked. On February 5, 1977, Pres. Jimmy Carter issued the first declaration of a major disaster for snow in US history. (BLBS.)

A federal disaster declaration meant that federal aid would be available to pay for the cleanup of the snow and to pay overtime for plow drivers or private contractors to assist in snow clearing operations. Businesses damaged by the storm could be reimbursed, and people who lost wages received unemployment insurance and food stamps. This declaration saved the City of Buffalo from bankruptcy. (BLBS.)

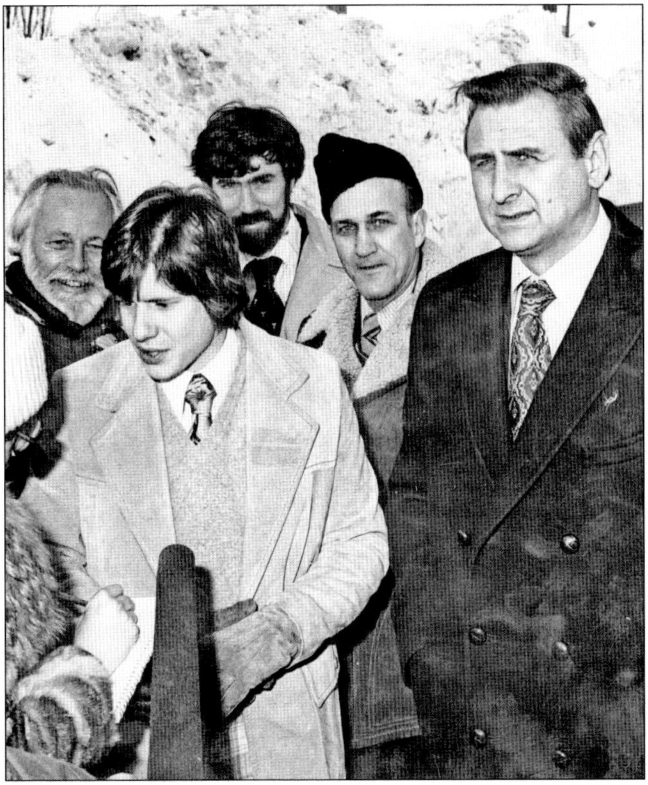

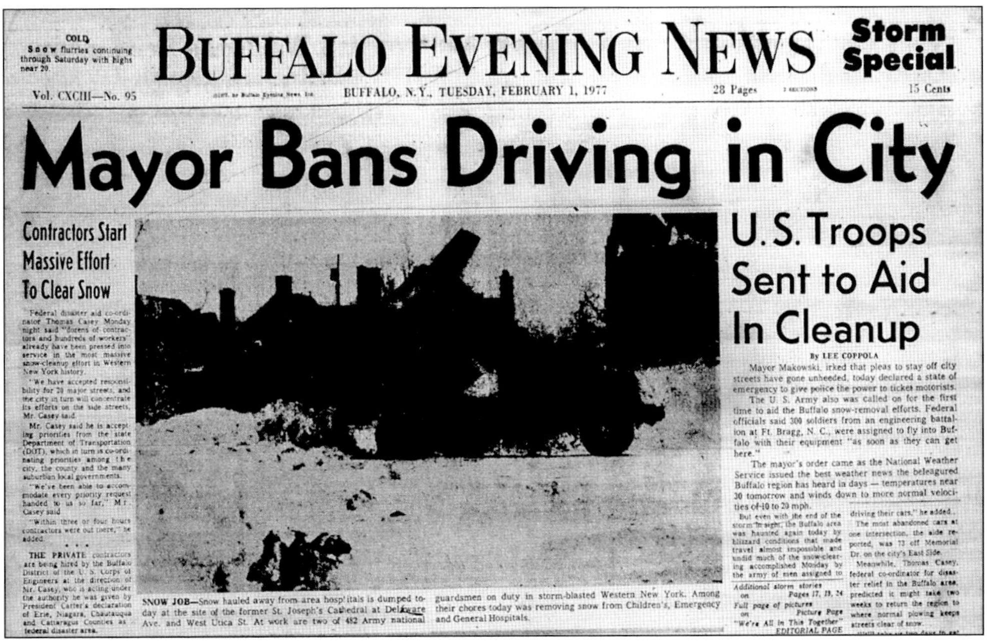

COLD
Snow flurries continuing through Saturday with highs near 20.

BUFFALO EVENING NEWS

Storm Special

Vol. CXCIII—No. 95 BUFFALO, N.Y., TUESDAY, FEBRUARY 1, 1977 28 Pages 15 Cents

Mayor Bans Driving in City

Contractors Start Massive Effort To Clear Snow

Federal disaster aid co-ordinator Thomas Casey Monday night said "dozens of contractors and hundreds of workers" already have been pressed into service in the most massive snow-cleanup effort in Western New York history.

"We have accepted responsibility for 20 major streets, and the city in turn will concentrate its efforts on the side streets, Mr. Casey said.

Mr. Casey said he is accepting priorities from the state Department of Transportation (DOT), which in turn is co-ordinating priorities among the city, the county and the many suburban local governments.

"We've been able to accommodate every priority request handed to us so far," Mr. Casey said.

"Within three or four hours contractors were out there," he added.

* * *

THE PRIVATE contractors are being hired by the Buffalo District of the U. S. Corps of Engineers at the direction of Mr. Casey, who is acting under the authority he was given by President Carter's declaration of Erie, Niagara, Chautauqua and Cattaraugus Counties as federal disaster area.

SNOW JOB—Snow hauled away from area hosp'itals is dumped today at the site of the former St. Joseph's Cathedral at Delaware Ave. and West Utica St. At work are two of 482 Army national guardsmen on duty in storm-blasted Western New York. Among their chores today was removing snow from Children's, Emergency and General Hospitals.

U.S. Troops Sent to Aid In Cleanup

By LEE COPPOLA

Mayor Makowski, irked that pleas to stay off city streets have gone unheeded, today declared a state of emergency to give police the power to ticket motorists.

The U. S. Army also was called on for the first time to aid the Buffalo snow-removal efforts. Federal officials said 300 soldiers from an engineering battalion at Ft. Bragg, N. C., were assigned to fly into Buffalo with their equipment "as soon as they can get here."

The mayor's order came as the National Weather Service issued the best weather news the beleagured Buffalo region has heard in days — temperatures near 30 tomorrow and winds down to more normal velocities of 10 to 20 mph.

But even with the end of the storm in sight, the Buffalo area was haunted again today by blizzard conditions that made travel almost impossible and undid much of the snow-clearing accomplished Monday by the army of men assigned to

Additional storm stories on Pages 17, 19, 24
Full page of pictures on Picture Page
"We're All In This Together" EDITORIAL PAGE

driving their cars," he added.

The most abandoned cars at one intersection, the aide reported, was 73 off Memorial Dr. on the city's East Side.

Meanwhile, Thomas Casey, federal co-ordinator for disaster relief in the Buffalo area, predicted it might take two weeks to return the region to where normal plowing keeps streets clear of snow.

The city had the equipment, but getting the streets cleared was quite another matter. On February 1, 1977, Mayor Makowski ordered a total driving ban for the city of Buffalo. The ban was imposed to allow abandoned cars to be towed and plows to get down and clear streets. (Author's collection.)

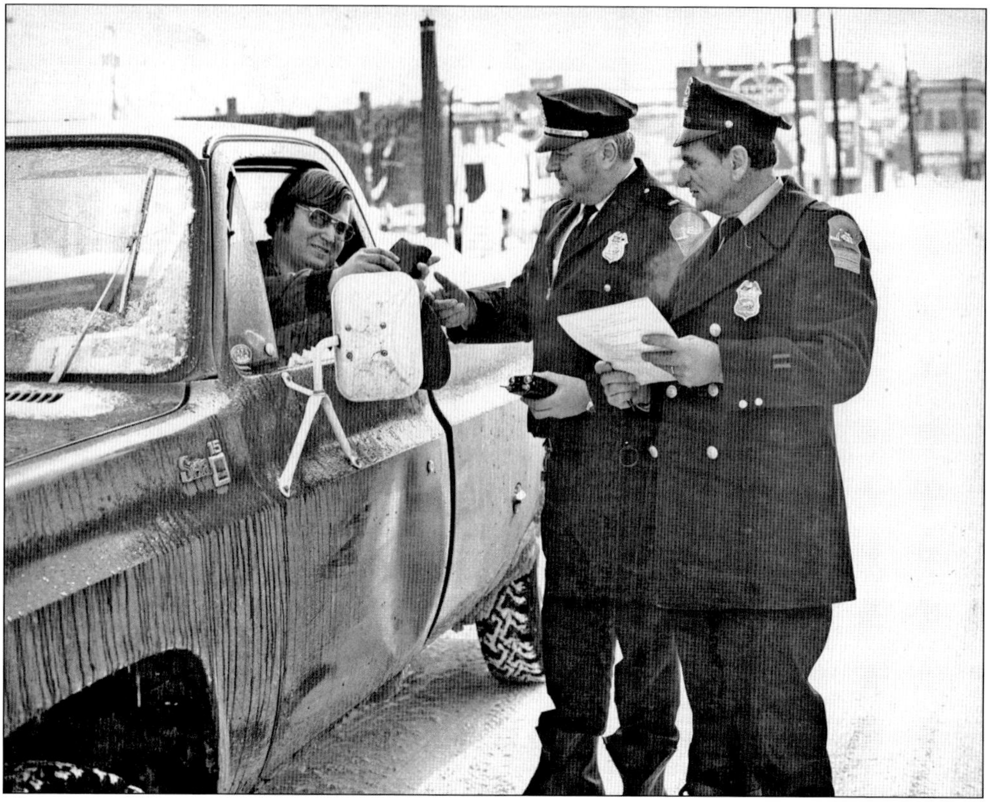

Tickets were issued to 97 people for failing to comply with the driving ban. The tickets included a fine of up to $500 and potential jail time of 90 days. (BLBS.)

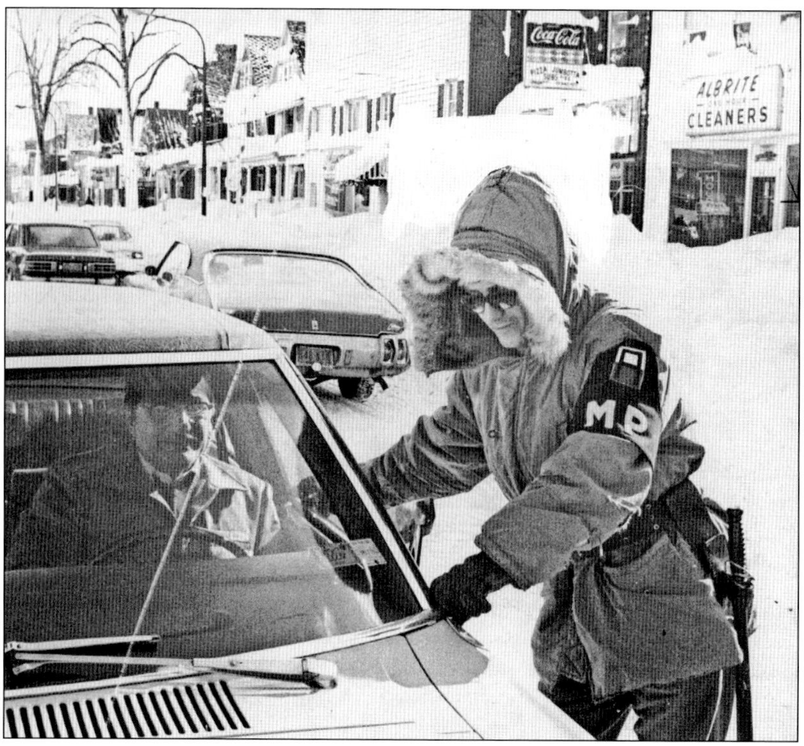

Military police helped enforce the traffic ban. (BLBS.)

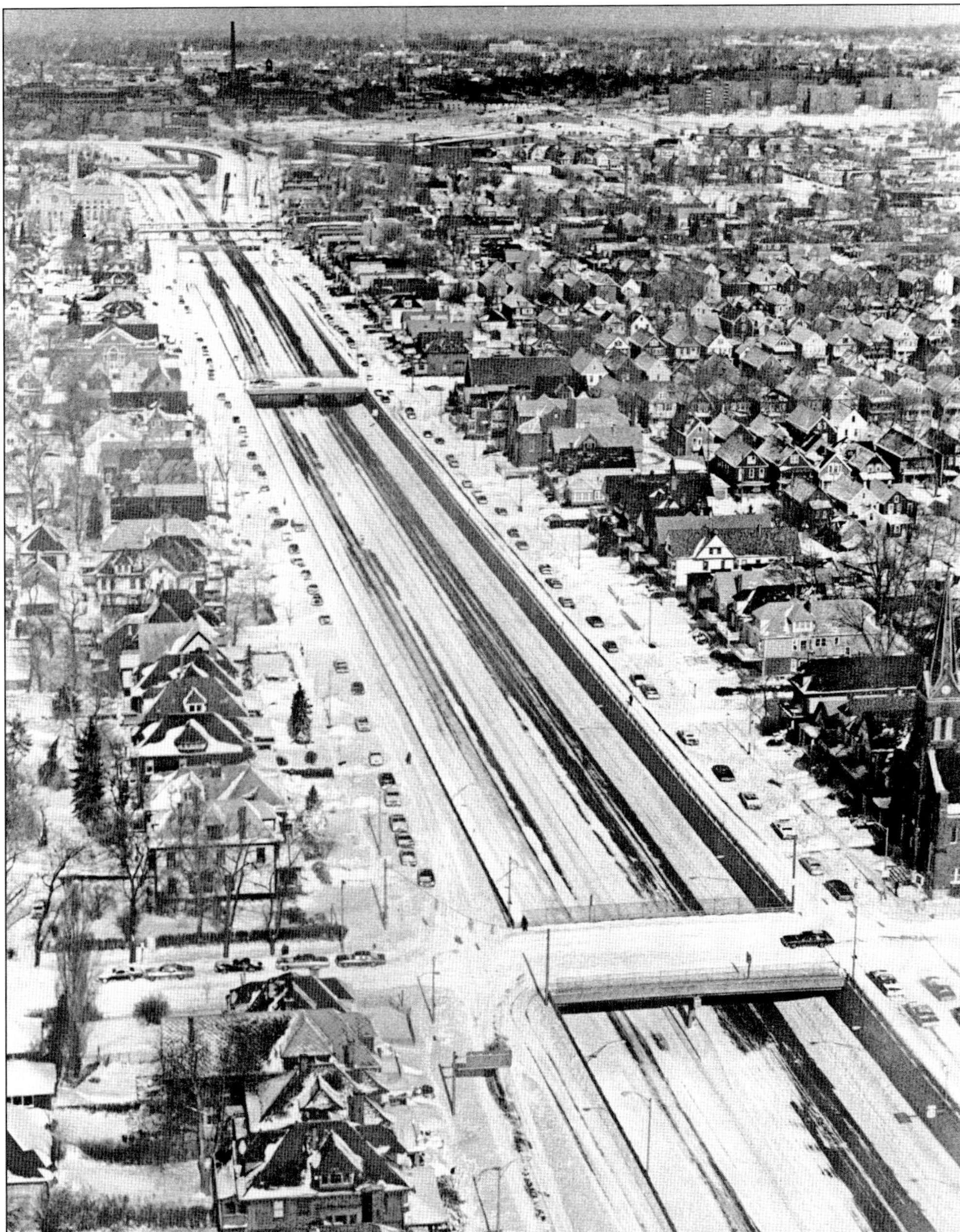

The driving ban was very effective and left the Kensington Expressway looking like an abandoned road. The expressway was built in the 1950s, when Buffalo was experiencing an economic boom and traffic congestion was becoming a problem for Buffalo's east side, especially along Humboldt Parkway, designed in the 1880s by the famous landscape architect Frederick Law Olmsted. Humboldt Parkway was to be the widest street in Buffalo and included two miles of green space. All of this was lost when New York Department of Transportation (DOT) officials and local leaders decided to alleviate traffic congestion on Buffalo's east side by building the Kensington Expressway, which destroyed the Humboldt Parkway and cut the neighborhood in half. (BLBS.)

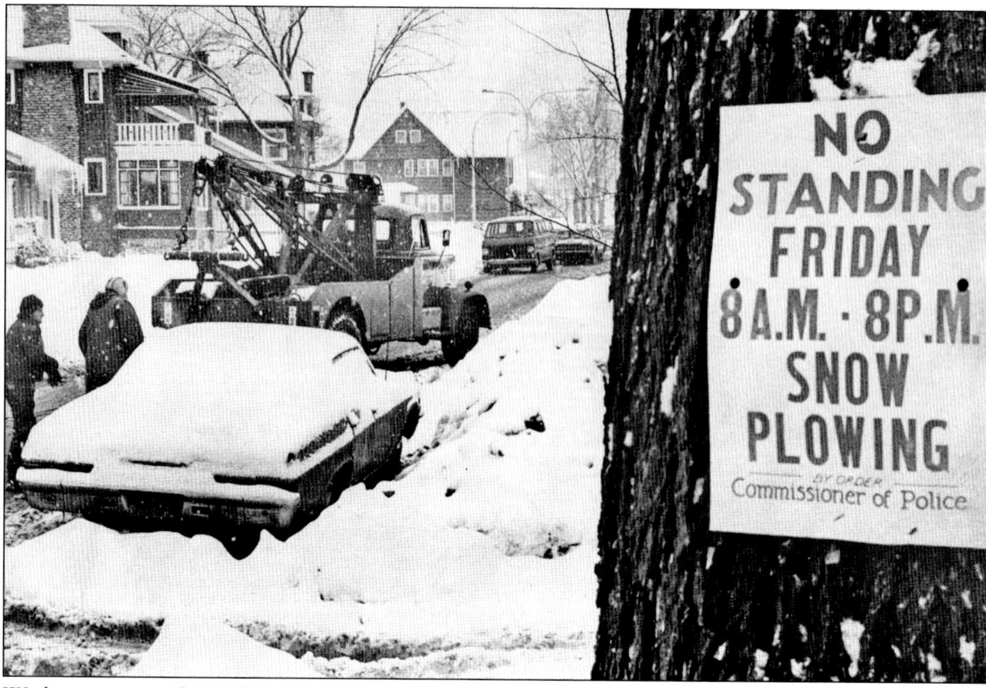

With assistance from the National Guard and Army and the travel ban, Buffalo finally got a handle on the illegally parked cars and began a massive towing operation to clear and reopen the streets. During the operation, however, thousands of cars were temporarily misplaced because of poor record keeping. (BLBS.)

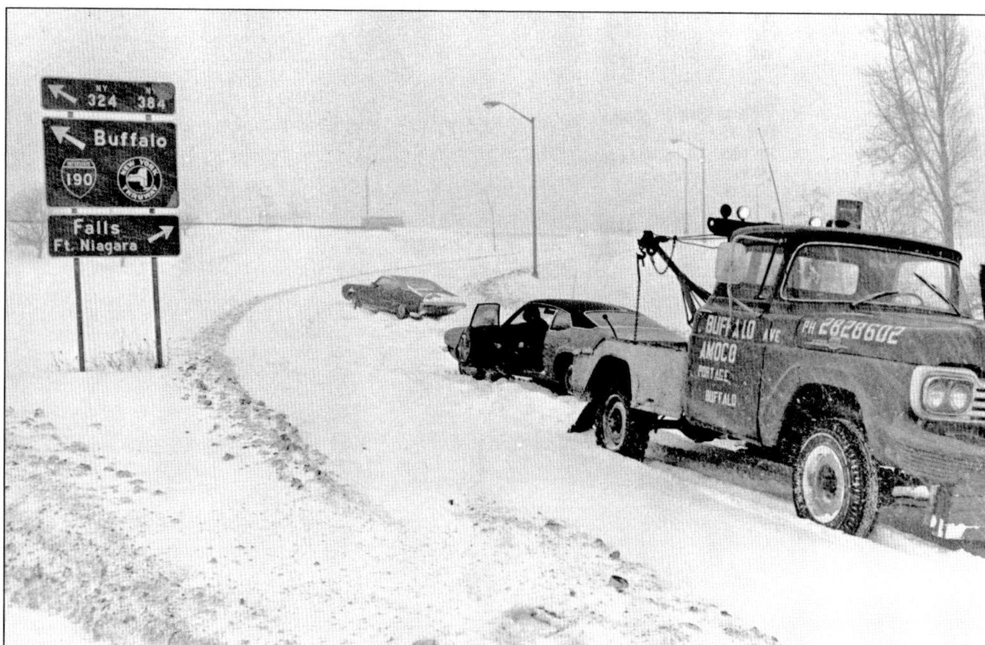

Abandoned cars littered the New York State Thruway and authorities had to hire private tow companies to assist in clearing them. Some citizens complained that they were overcharged by tow companies. (NFPL.)

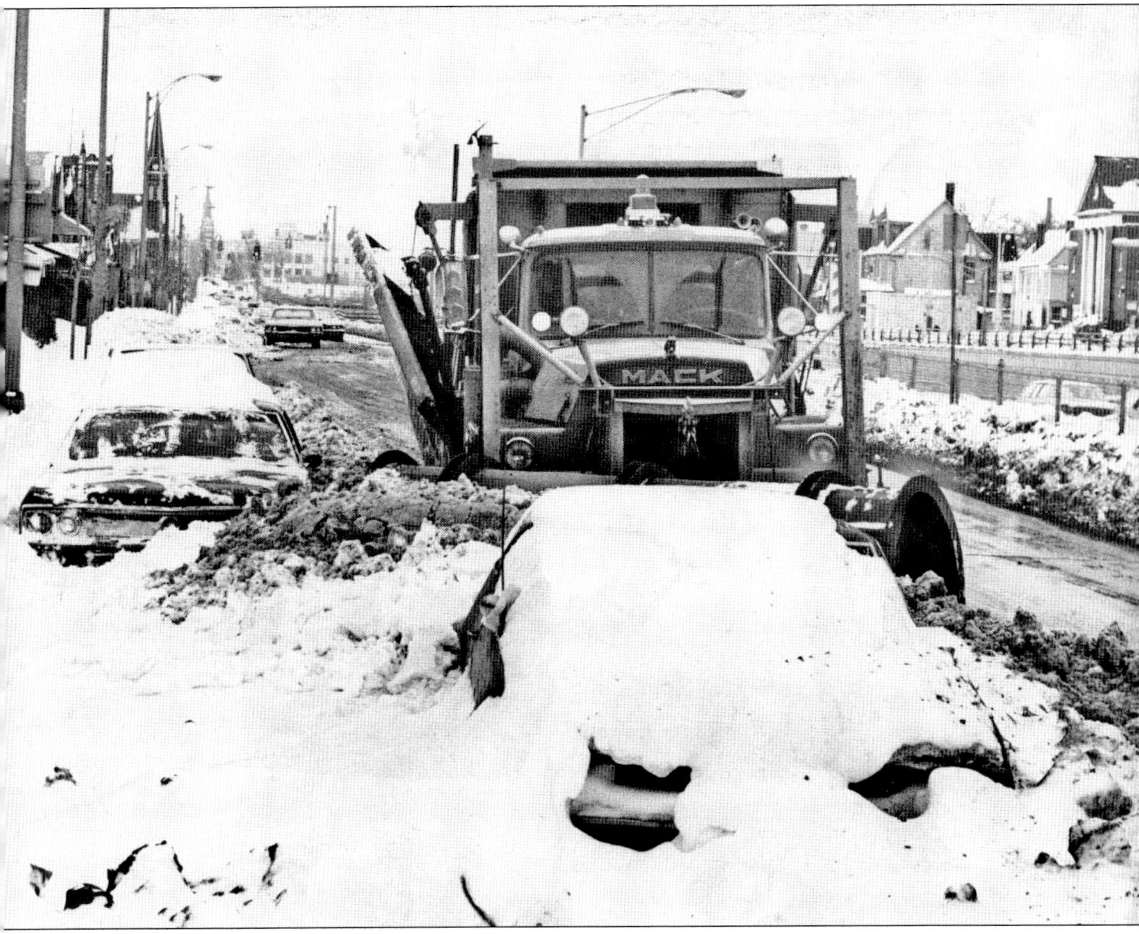

The cleanup process required patience and long hours. This plow driver is still dealing with cars blocking the road on Humboldt Parkway. Note how the expressway in the background cuts the city in half and divides the neighborhood. Parked cars have been the bane of public works officials since municipalities took on the responsibility of clearing away snow. Especially on the narrow streets of older cities like Buffalo, the parked cars make it impossible for plows to clear away all the snow from a neighborhood. Alternate street parking has been adopted in most cities to assist plows in clearing at least one side of a road on a regular basis. (BLBS.)

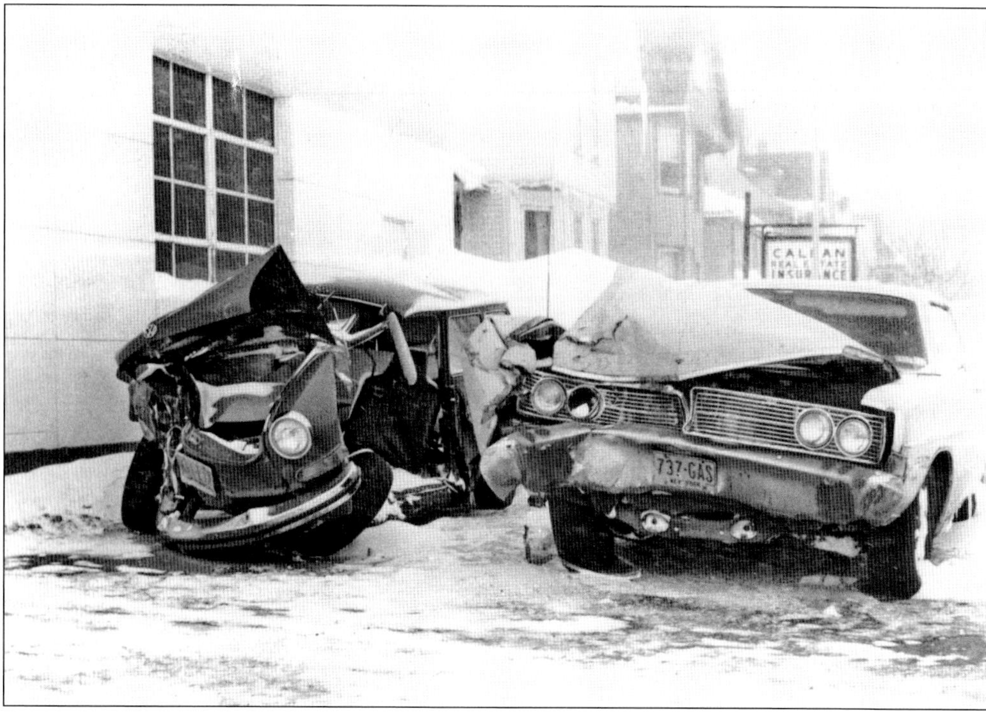

Hundreds of buried cars were damaged during cleanup operations. Sometimes, plows ran over them. In other cases, tow truck operators were not as careful with moving the automobiles as they might have been under normal circumstances. (GCHD.)

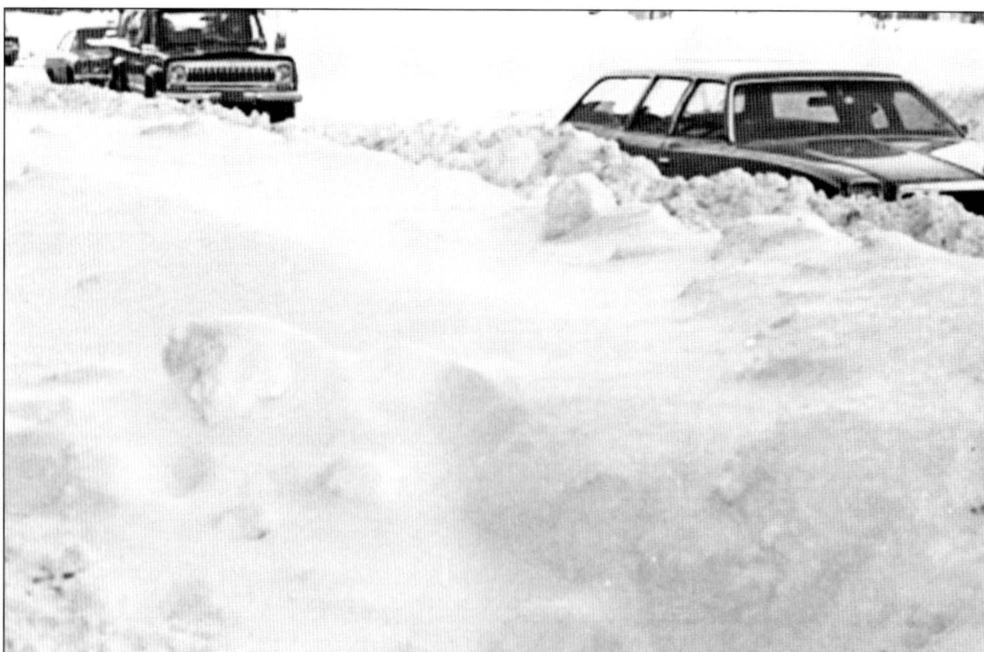

Two hundred miles away from Buffalo, in Watertown, officials suspended their driving ban on February 1. Drivers found themselves on roads with snow towering on each side of them. (WDT.)

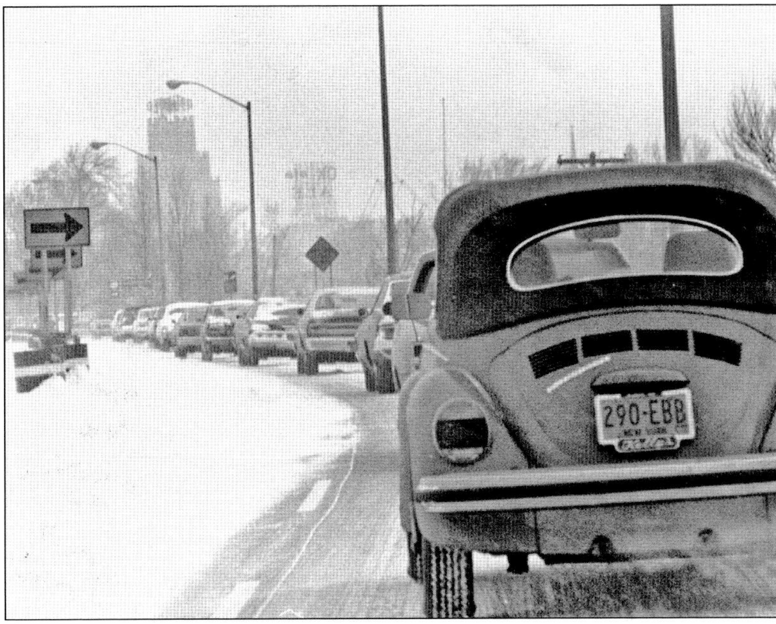

Once officials in Niagara Falls lifted the travel ban after the first week of February, roads became congested with individuals attempting to get to work or school, to run errands, or just to deal with the cabin fever they experienced when trapped indoors by the blizzard. (NFPL.)

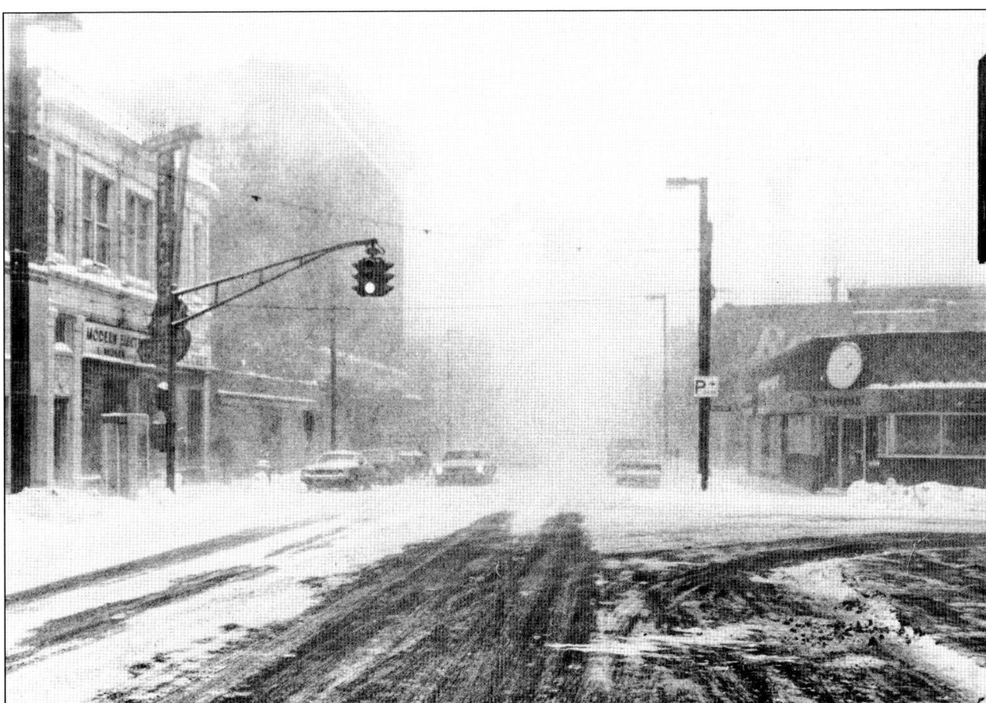

Travel in Niagara Falls and many other areas remained difficult, even after the driving ban was lifted. Wind-driven snow continued to cause limited visibility throughout the rest of the winter. (NFPL.)

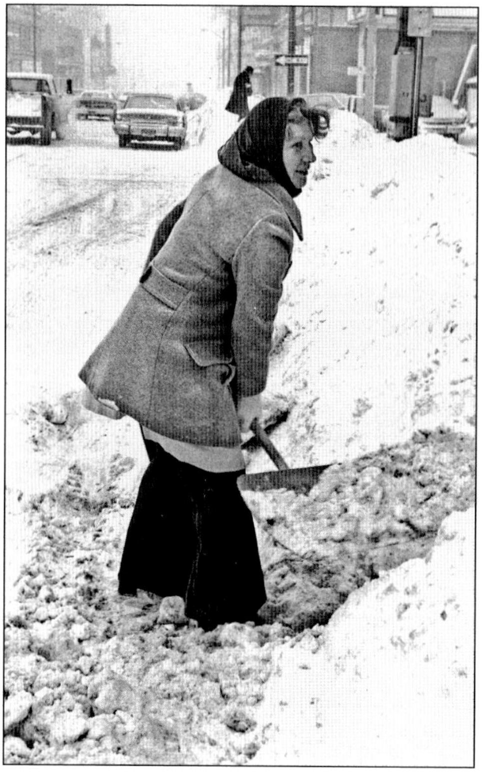

After the blizzard of 1977 ended, pedestrians found it difficult to get around. Clearing the roads was the primary goal for government officials. Clearing sidewalks was not as important. This woman in Niagara Falls works hard to clear the sidewalk in front of her store. (NFPL.)

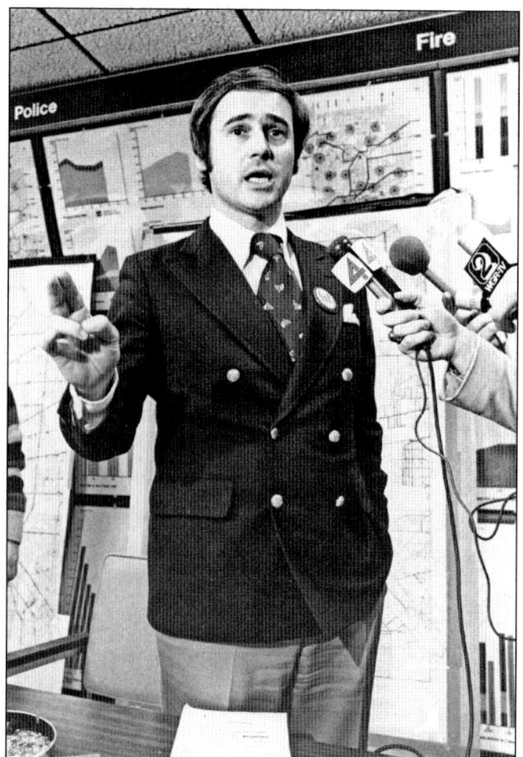

During the crisis created by the snowstorm, officials operated out of emergency management centers like this one in Buffalo. Due to financial constraints and a poor response to an ice storm that struck the region in March 1976, Erie County had opted in 1976 to close its civil defense office. (BLBS.)

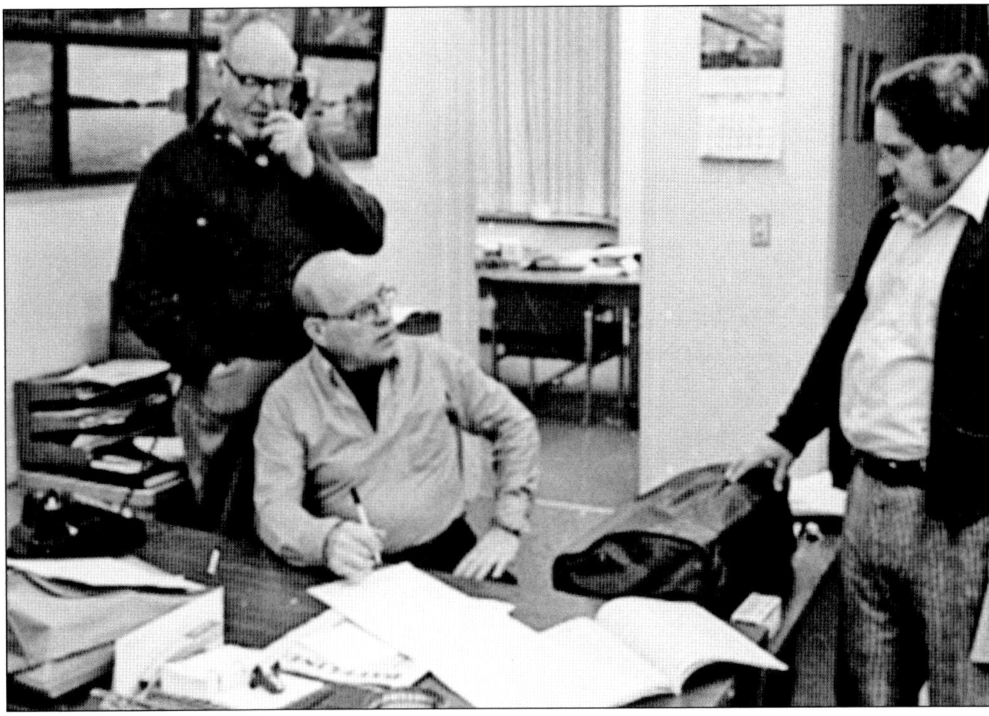

Jefferson County, New York, had an emergency management center to assist in coordinating the activities of the towns and villages in Northern New York. These cities were the hardest hit by the blizzard of 1977. (WDT.)

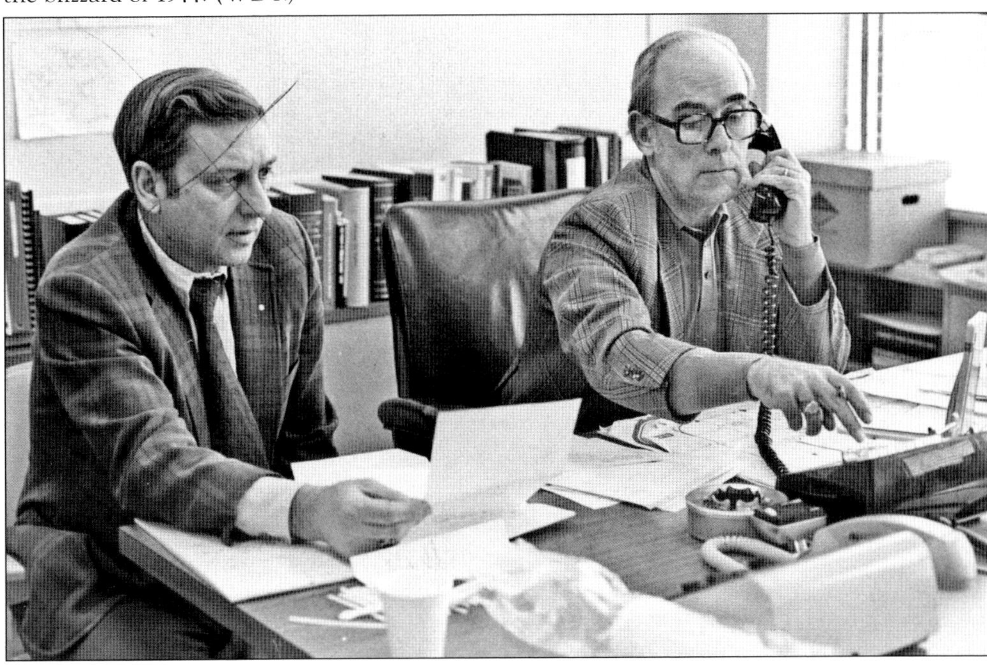

Niagara County emergency management leaders coordinated the work for cities like Niagara Falls and the many towns and villages located nearby. Kenneth Comeford, the Niagara County executive, said the storm caused $10 million in damage. (NFPL.)

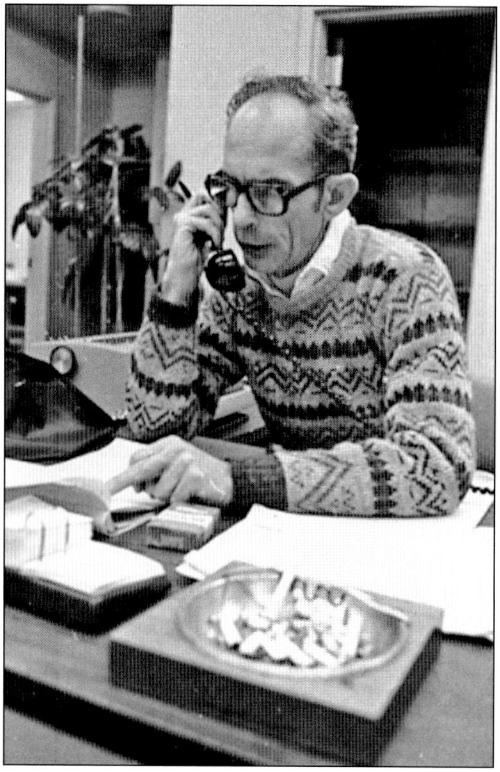

Donald Andrus spent a great deal of time on the phone coordinating the emergency work of officials working in Watertown. (WDT.)

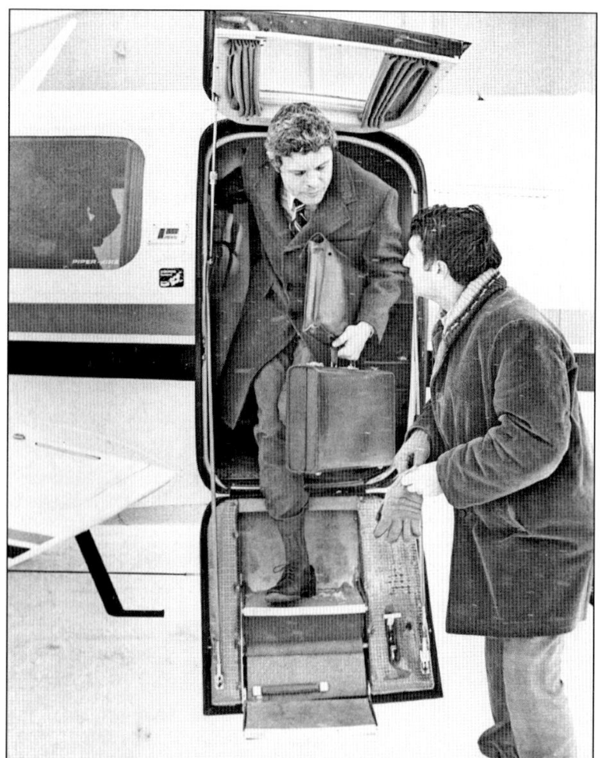

Erie County executive Edward "Ned" Regan, who was out of town when the blizzard struck, returned to Buffalo on January 30, 1977, and began to coordinate county response to the storm. County residents were less dependent on government assistance and, according to surveys taken at the time, were more satisfied with the Erie County response to the blizzard than that of the City of Buffalo, which was led by Stanley Makowski. (BLBS.)

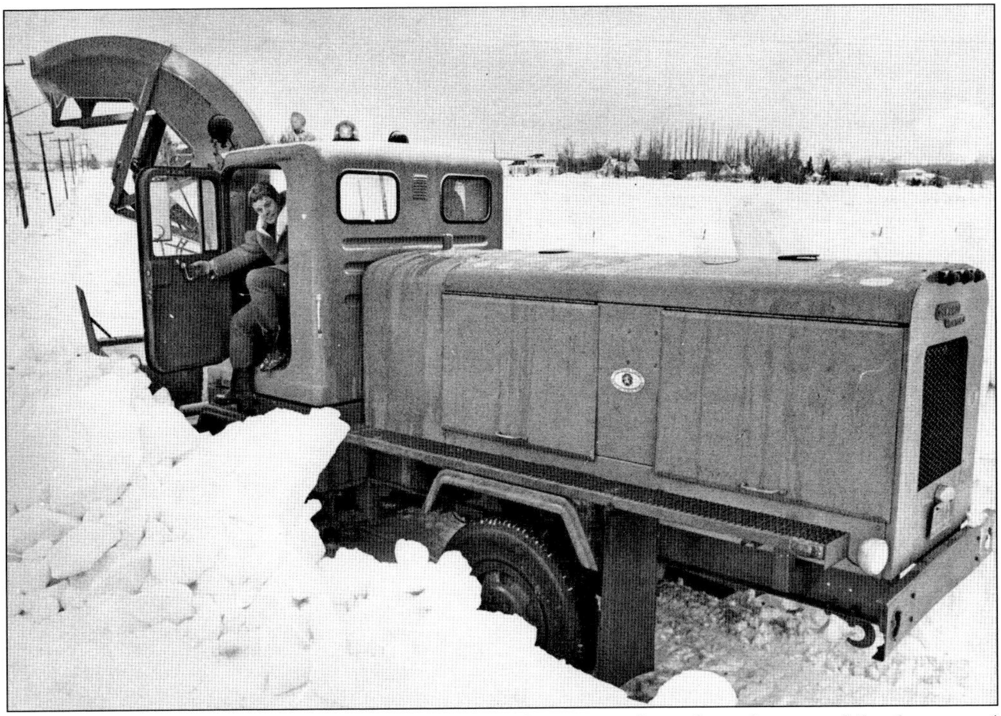

Erie County executive Ned Regan borrowed his wife's Jeep and conducted a tour of the devastated area. At one point, Regan tried to help county workers move a plow that was stuck in a snowdrift in Lancaster. (BLBS.)

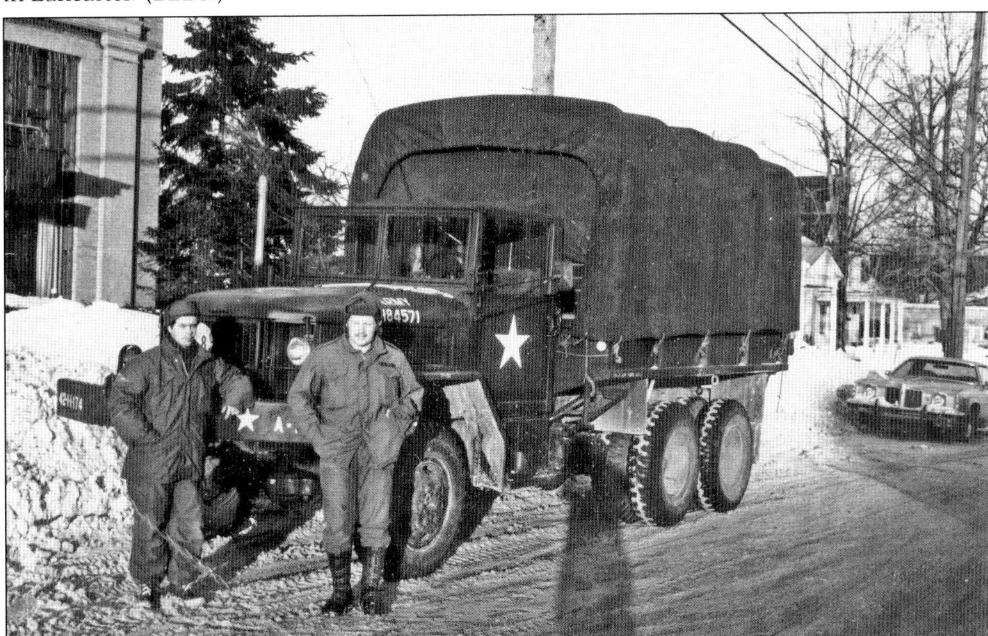

Officials in Erie County relied on the support of the US Army, which was in the area until February 8, 1977. These soldiers help out in the town of Alden, 22 miles outside of Buffalo. (Leonard A. Weisbeck Sr.)

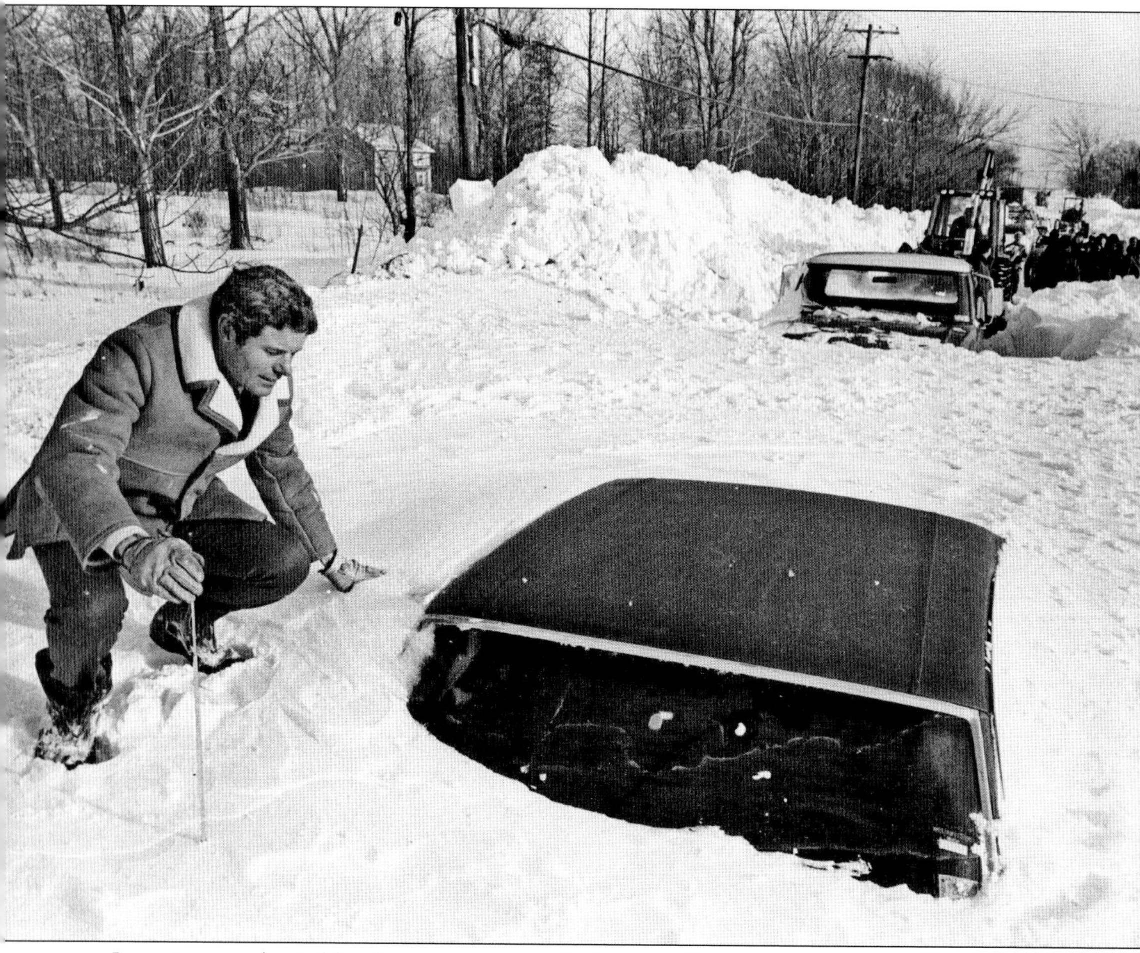

Locating cars buried by the storm was a priority to make sure no one was still trapped inside. Regan and others looked for antennas sticking out of the snow and then made sure that no one was in the car. Edward Van Buren "Ned" Regan was born and raised in Buffalo, and he was 43 years old at the time that the blizzard of 1977 struck. Regan had served on the Buffalo City Council before being elected the first county executive in Erie County in 1971. He served in that role until 1978, when he became the New York State comptroller, a position he held until 1993. At the end of his public career, he served as president of Baruch College (2000–2004). Regan died in 2014. (BLBS.)

Dozens of unsung heroes worked hard throughout the crisis. These included military personnel, fire and rescue workers, volunteers, and government officials who came into the Buffalo-Niagara region to aid residents in getting government assistance after the blizzard. (NFPL.)

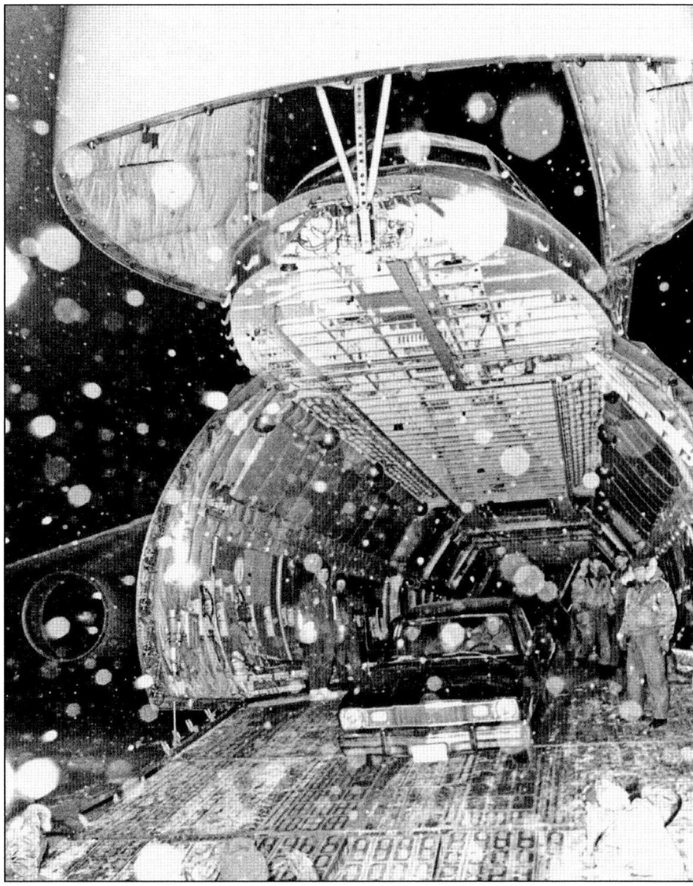

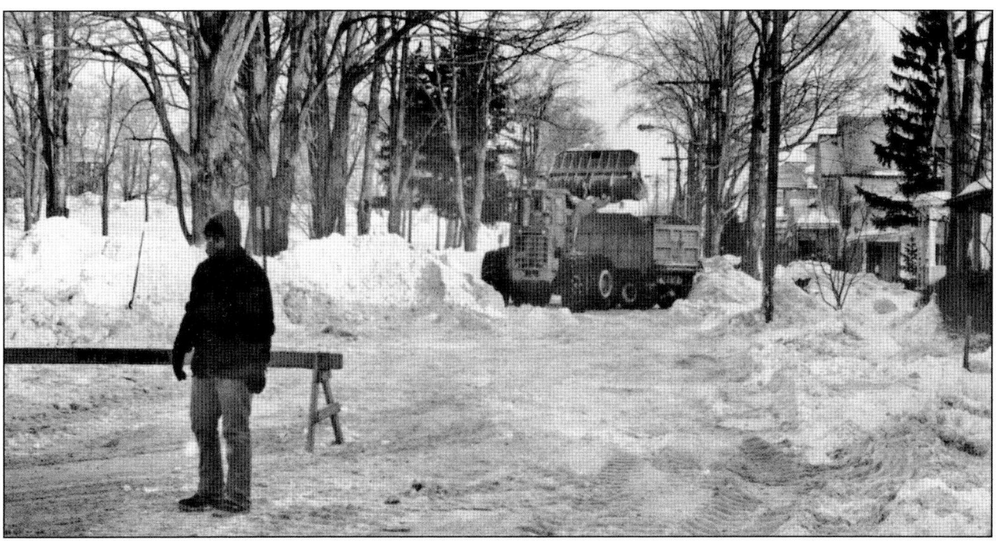

Some of the unsung heroes of the blizzard of 1977 included ordinary individuals who worked double or triple shifts to assist in snow removal operations. Working in the cold and wind, these public servants are clearing away snow from the road leading to the New York State School for the Blind in Batavia. (GCHD.)

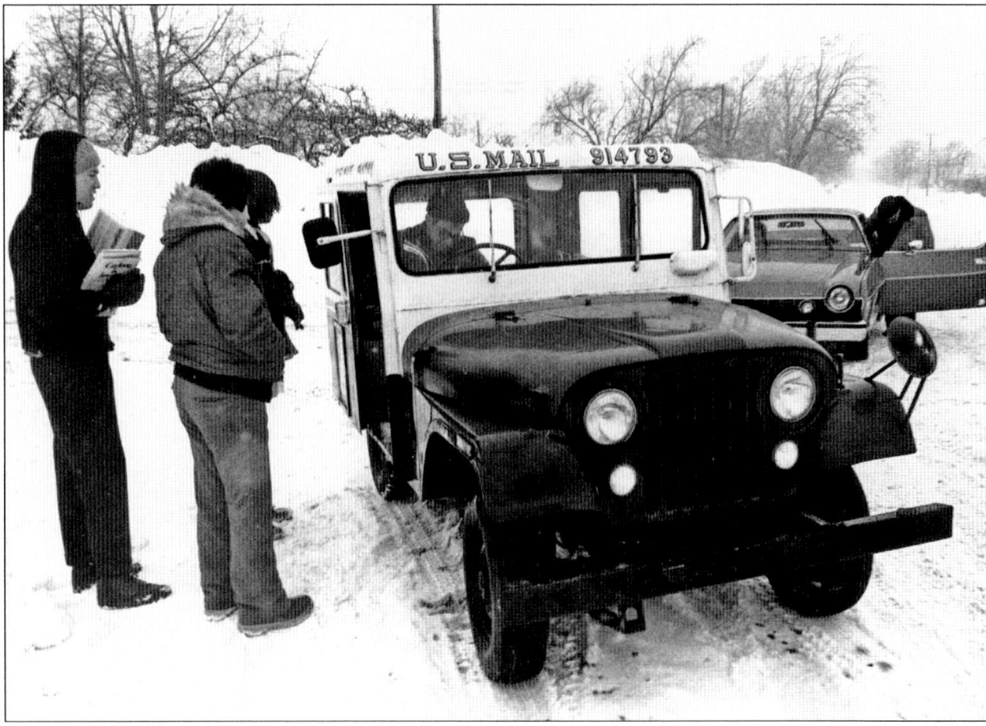

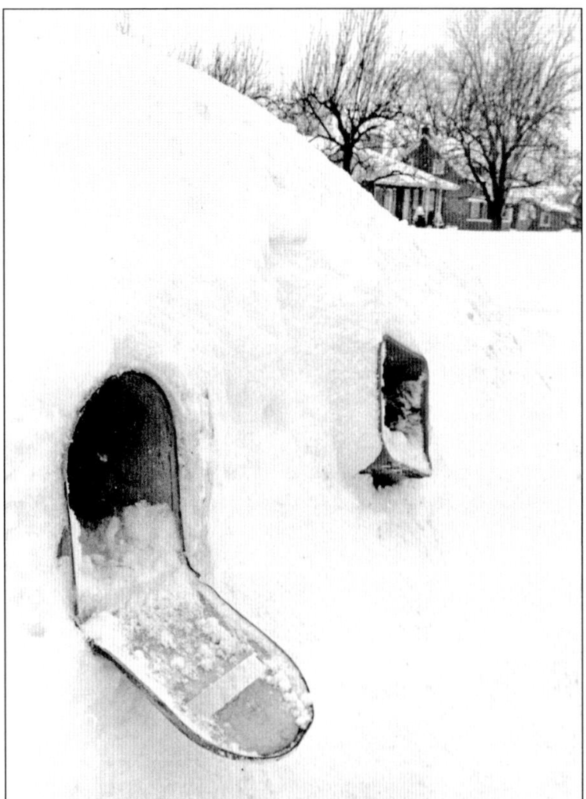

The US Postal Service was unable to deliver mail during the blizzard of 1977. Once the roads were open, postal workers went back to delivering the mail. In the age before cell phones, the Internet, or social media, mail meant social security checks, bills, greeting cards, and letters from family and friends. (NFPL.)

Postal workers persisted in their work despite the fact that finding a mailbox might be daunting. (NFPL.)

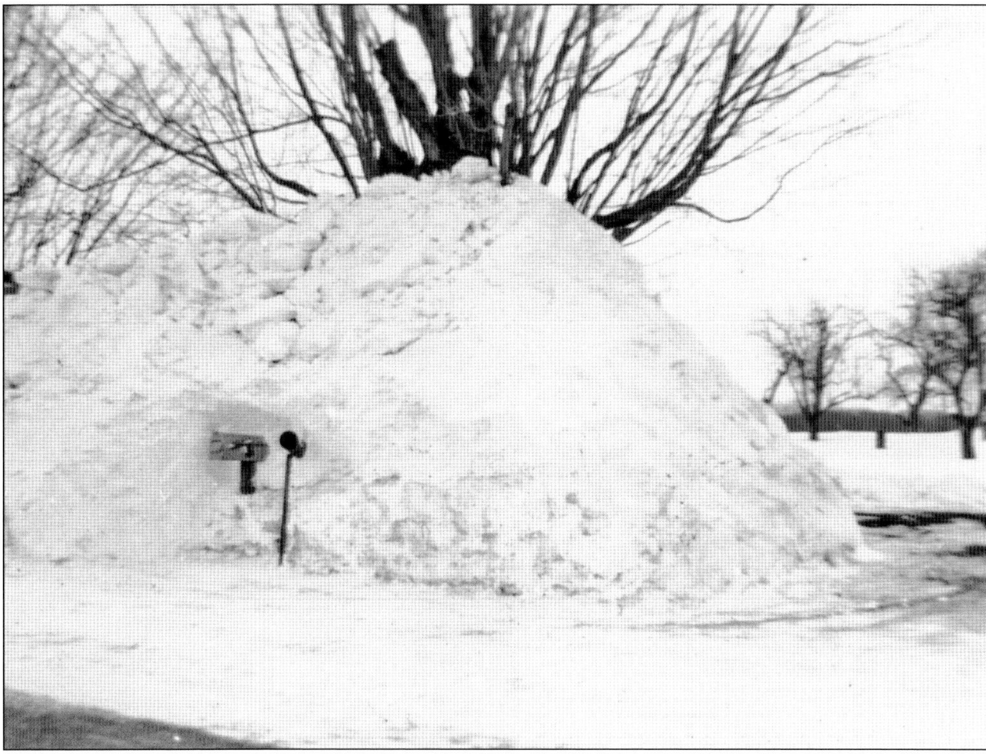

In some cases, finding the mailbox was easier than finding the house it belonged to, as this scene from Seven Springs Road in Batavia proves. (GCHD.)

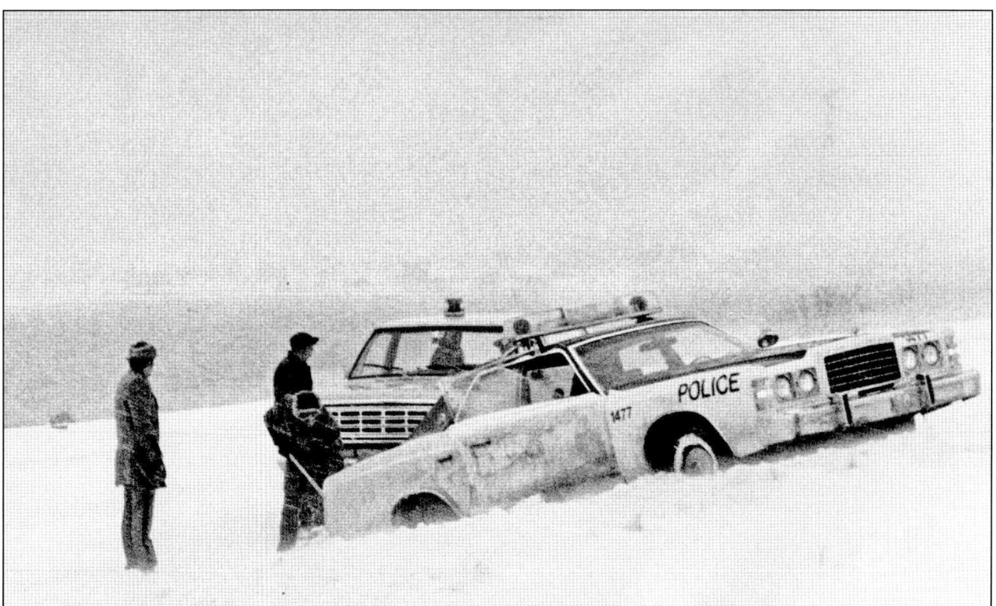

No matter what the weather, the police came out to assist the public, but sometimes the police were the ones who needed assistance. (NFPL.)

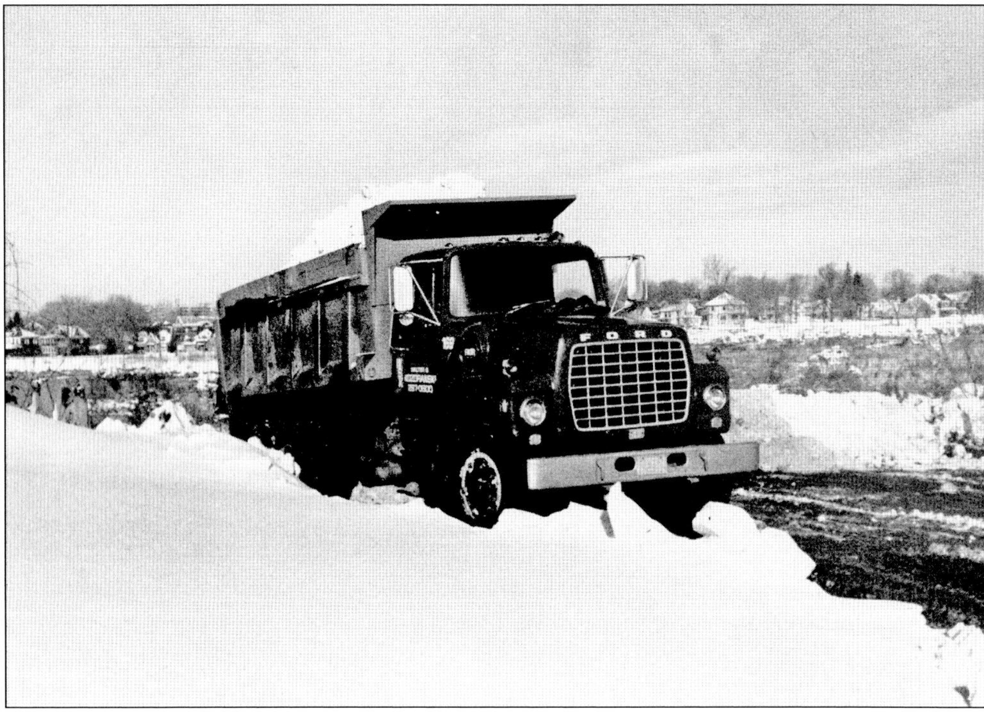

Long after the storm was over, public works employees hauled away the mountains of snow. (NFPL.)

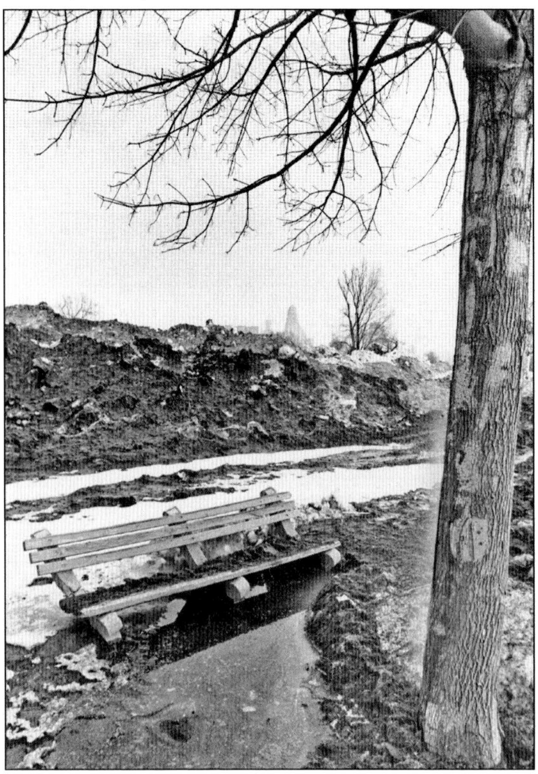
Long into spring, LaSalle Park in Buffalo held the grim deposit of snow, which contained dirt, car parts, road signs, and manhole covers. (BLBS.)

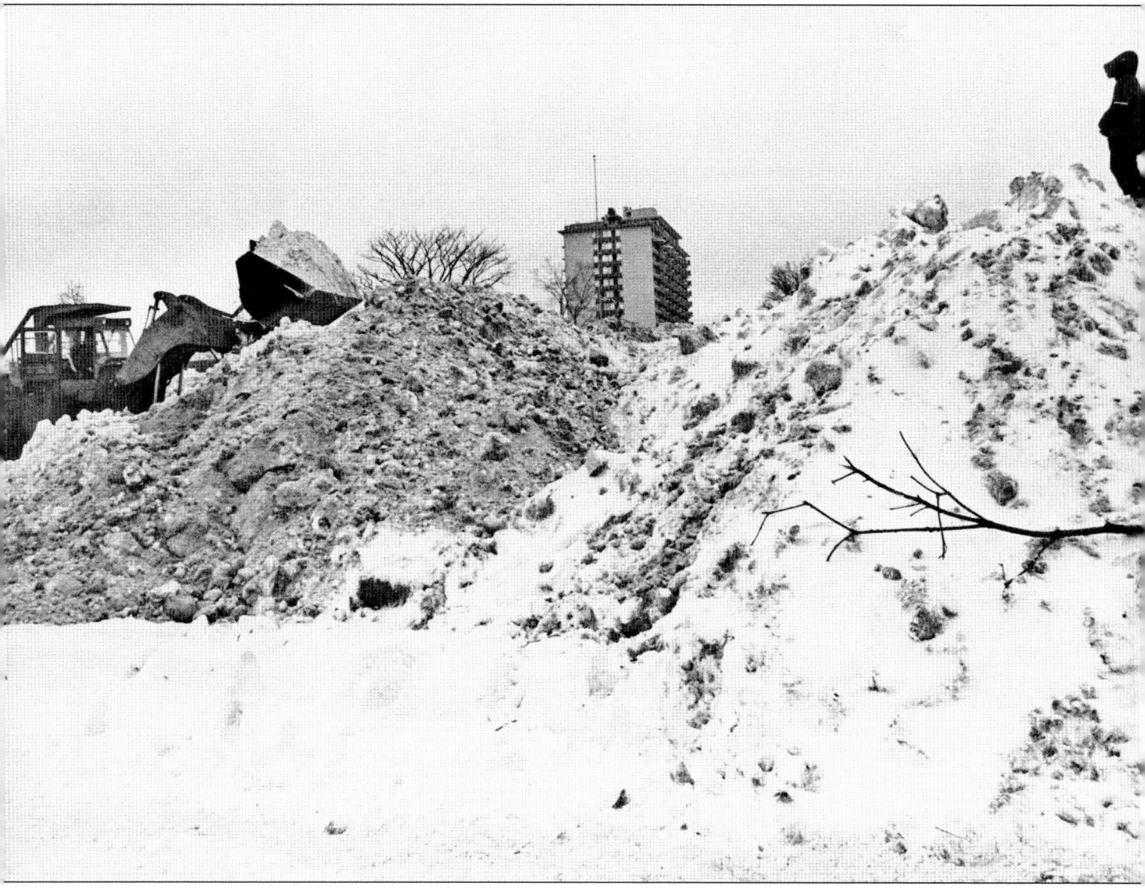

The snow is piled high as one person plays king of the mountain. Although such snow piles may have inspired the imaginations of children, they caused frustration for residents. Snow was dumped into city and county parks to get if off streets and out of parking lots. The snow acted as its own refrigerator and remained well into spring, which frustrated locals who could not use the parks because of the snow. Buffalo wanted the federal government to remove the snow, but Tom Casey balked. Sen. Daniel Patrick Moynihan intervened with the federal government, which provided financial assistance to the city so parks across Erie County could open by April 1977. (BLBS.)

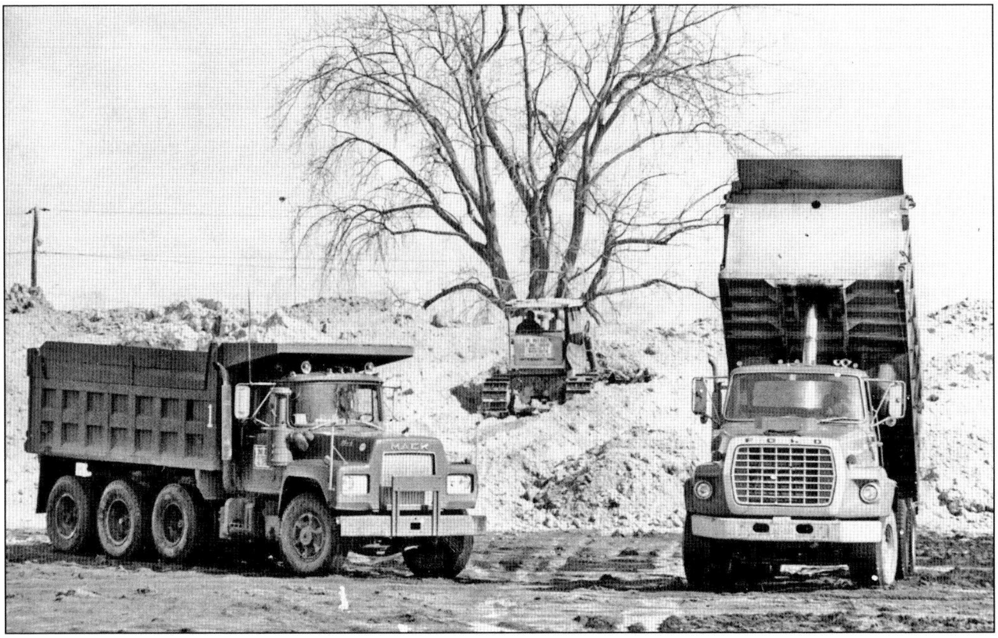

Highway workers delivered the snow to parks such as LaSalle Park in Buffalo, where it remained until the spring. LaSalle Park is named for René-Robert Cavelier, Sieur de La Salle, a 17th-century French explorer. LaSalle Park is located on the Buffalo waterfront, where the Niagara River meets Lake Erie. Ironically, the site of LaSalle Park was a dumping ground before it was turned into a 77-acre public park in the 1930s. (BLBS.)

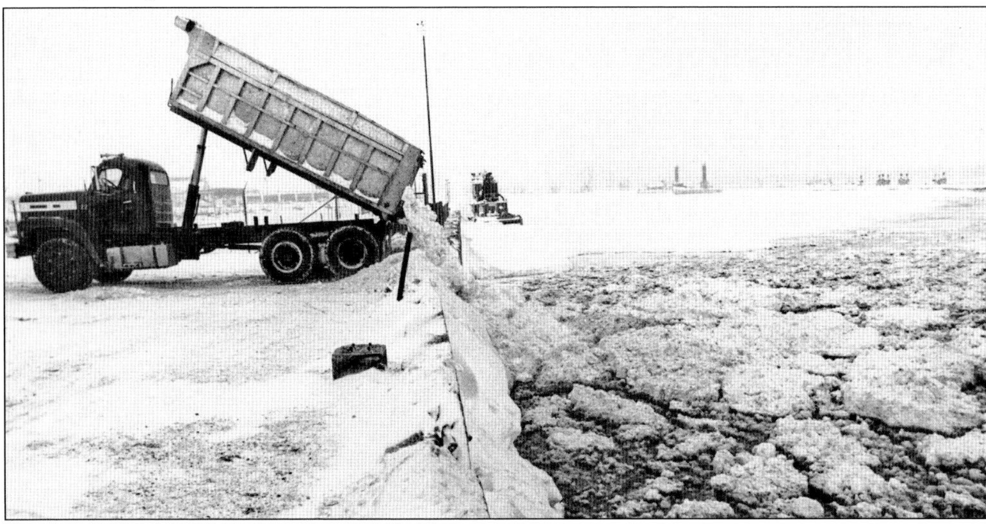

It may have been easier to dump the snow into the river, but this was not environmentally sound. After Rachel Carson's *Silent Spring* was published in 1962, Americans became more sensitive to the use of chemicals in groundwater. Many people were concerned about the harmful effects of road salt on plant and animal life. By 1977, some municipalities had banned road salt because of the effects inimical to roadside vegetation and potentially damaging to aquatic life. The snow collected from roadsides across Erie, Niagara, and Jefferson Counties contained dirt and objects that were considered pollutants. Buffalo was able to gain waivers to dump the snow due to the disaster declaration. (BLBS.)

Three

GETTING AROUND

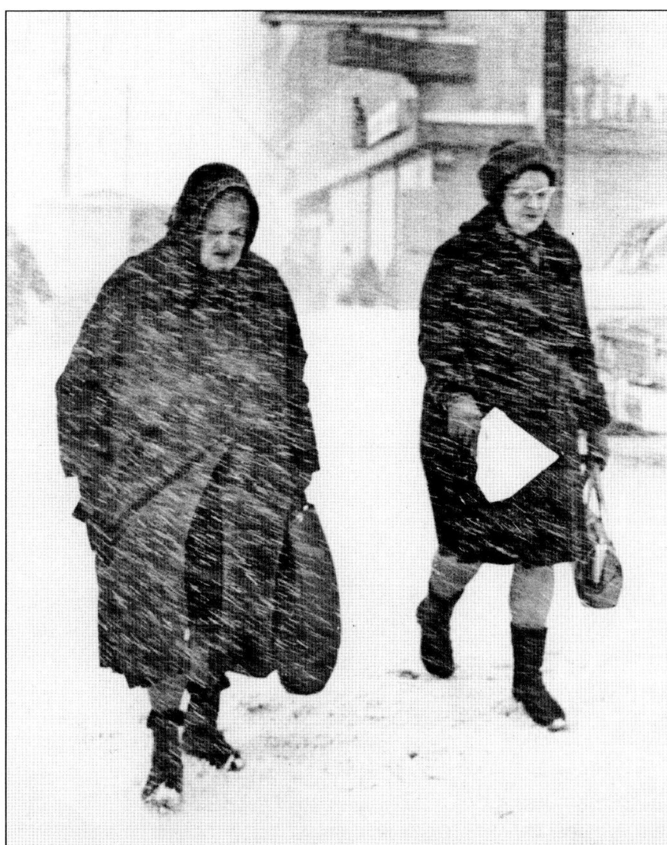

The blizzard of 1977 shut down the city of Buffalo from January 28 through February 1. A travel ban imposed on February 1, 1977, kept traffic off the roads. The ban was rescinded on February 3, only to be reimposed on February 4. The driving ban remained in effect through February 7. The ban, while necessary, presented a new set of challenges to the resilient people of Western New York. (BLBS.)

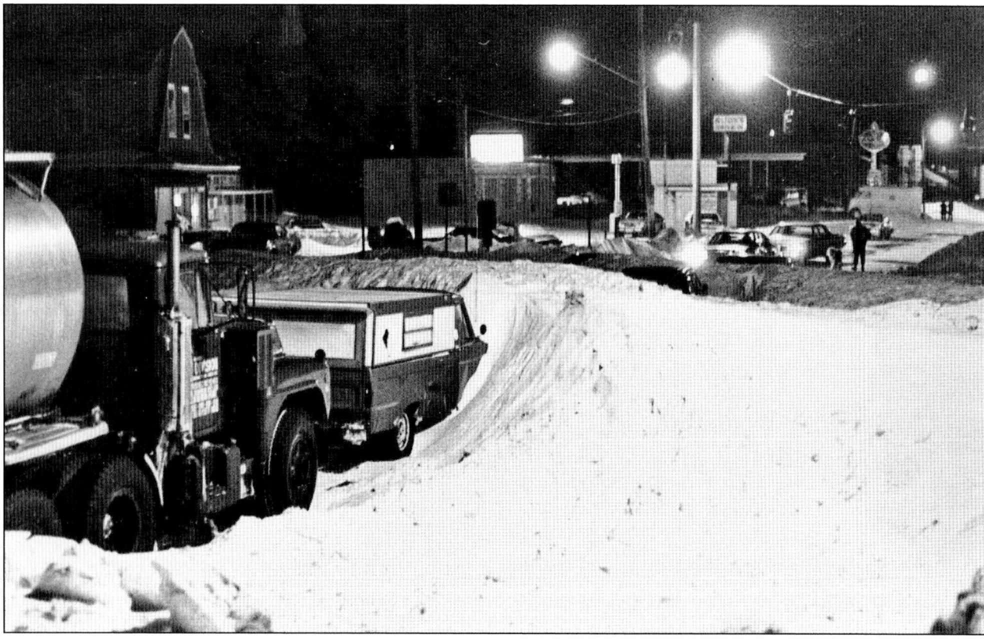

Drifting snow from the blizzard shut down roads, making travel impossible. (NFPL.)

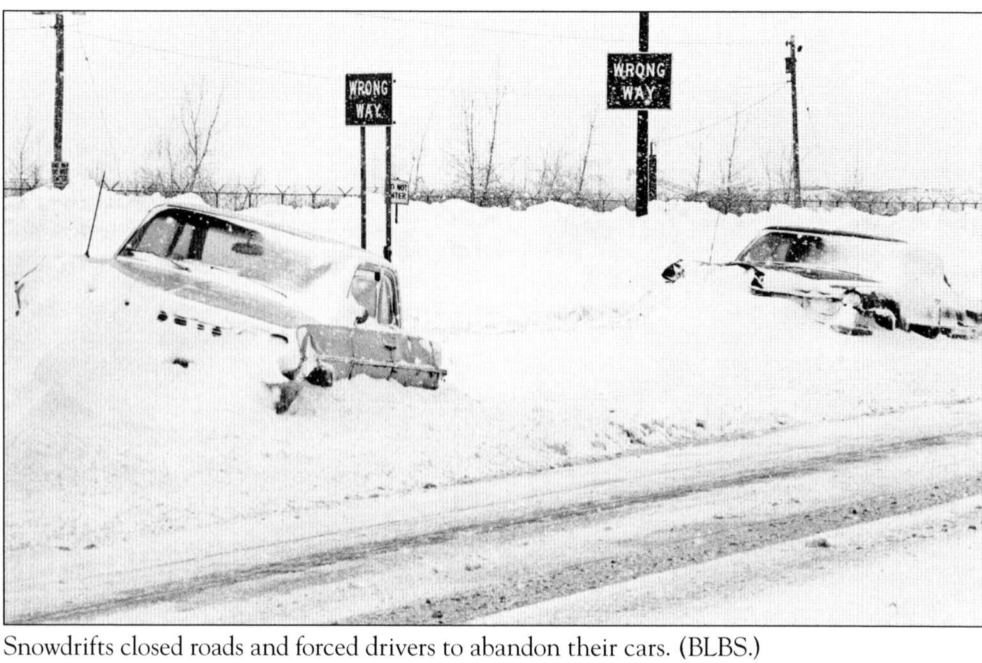

Snowdrifts closed roads and forced drivers to abandon their cars. (BLBS.)

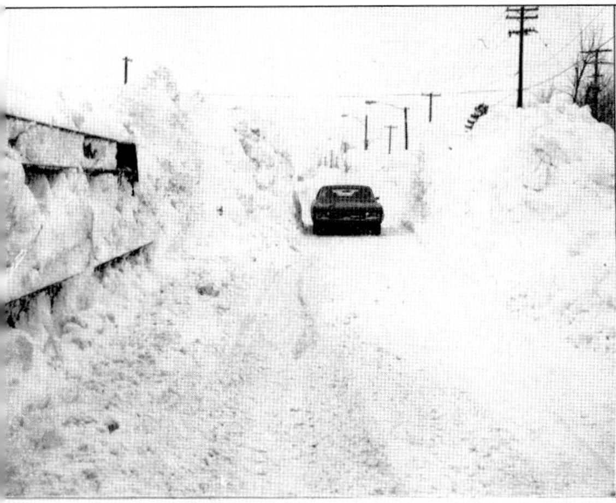

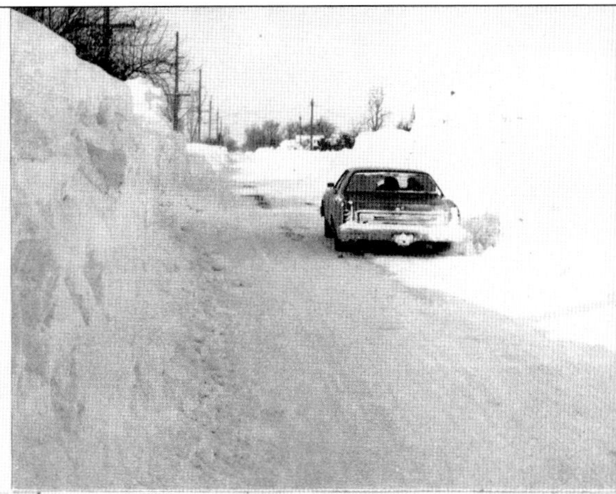

Walden Avenue near Erie County Home

Westwood Road had it's share of drifts

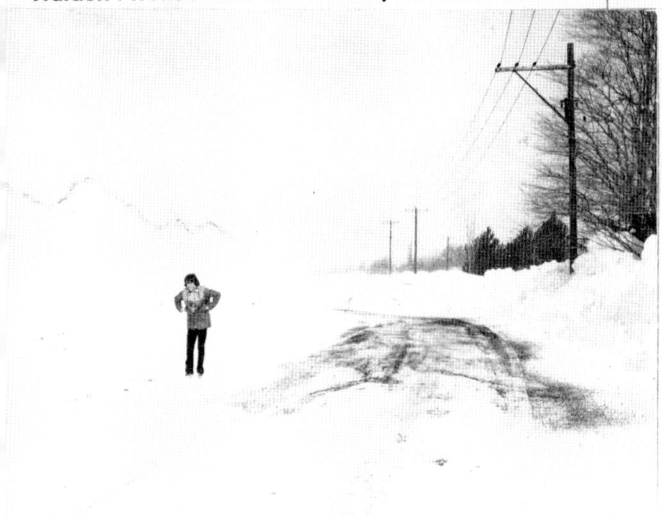

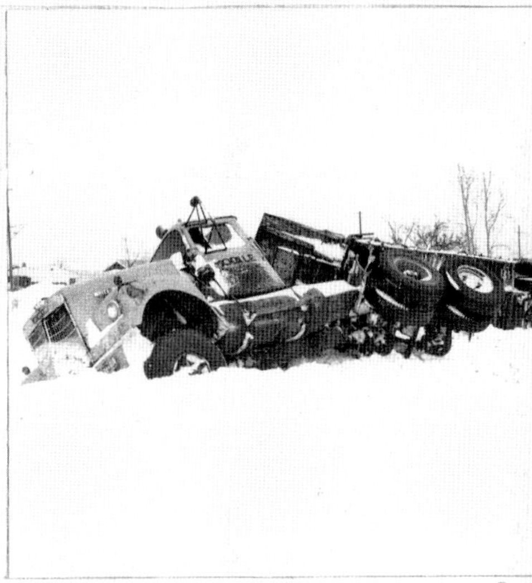

Three Rod Road gets dug out

Big truck on side, Walden Avenue near Ger

The Buffalo metropolitan region was a mess. Pictured here is Walden Avenue in Alden, where snowdrifts rose like walls around cars. Westwood Road in Lancaster was no better, as drifts dwarfed cars and made travel dicey. This image of Three Rod Road, which runs south from Alden into Marilla, shows how high the snow was compared to the unidentified woman standing in the road. The truck lies on its side near Walden Avenue and Genesee Street, a main thoroughfare for trucks traveling between the Rochester region and Buffalo. (Leonard A. Weisbeck Sr.)

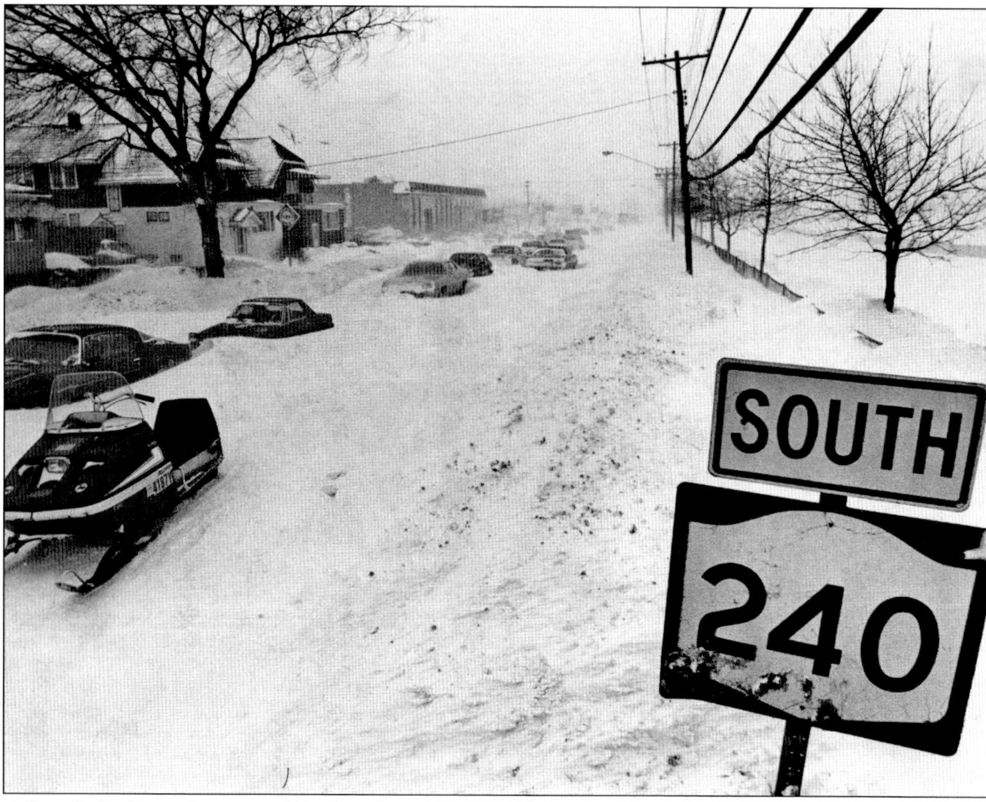

After drifts buried cars on Harlem Road in Cheektowaga, snowmobilers came along to make sure no one was trapped in his or her car. Their heroic efforts kept the number of deaths during the blizzard low. (BLBS.)

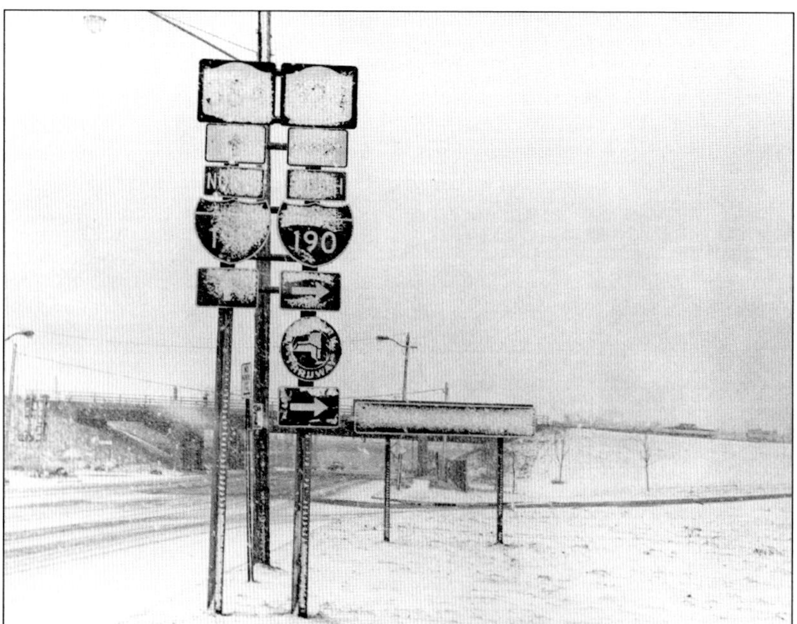

These signs tell the story. There was no thruway during the blizzard. Roads were closed in Buffalo, Niagara Falls, Batavia, and Watertown because of the snow. (NFPL.)

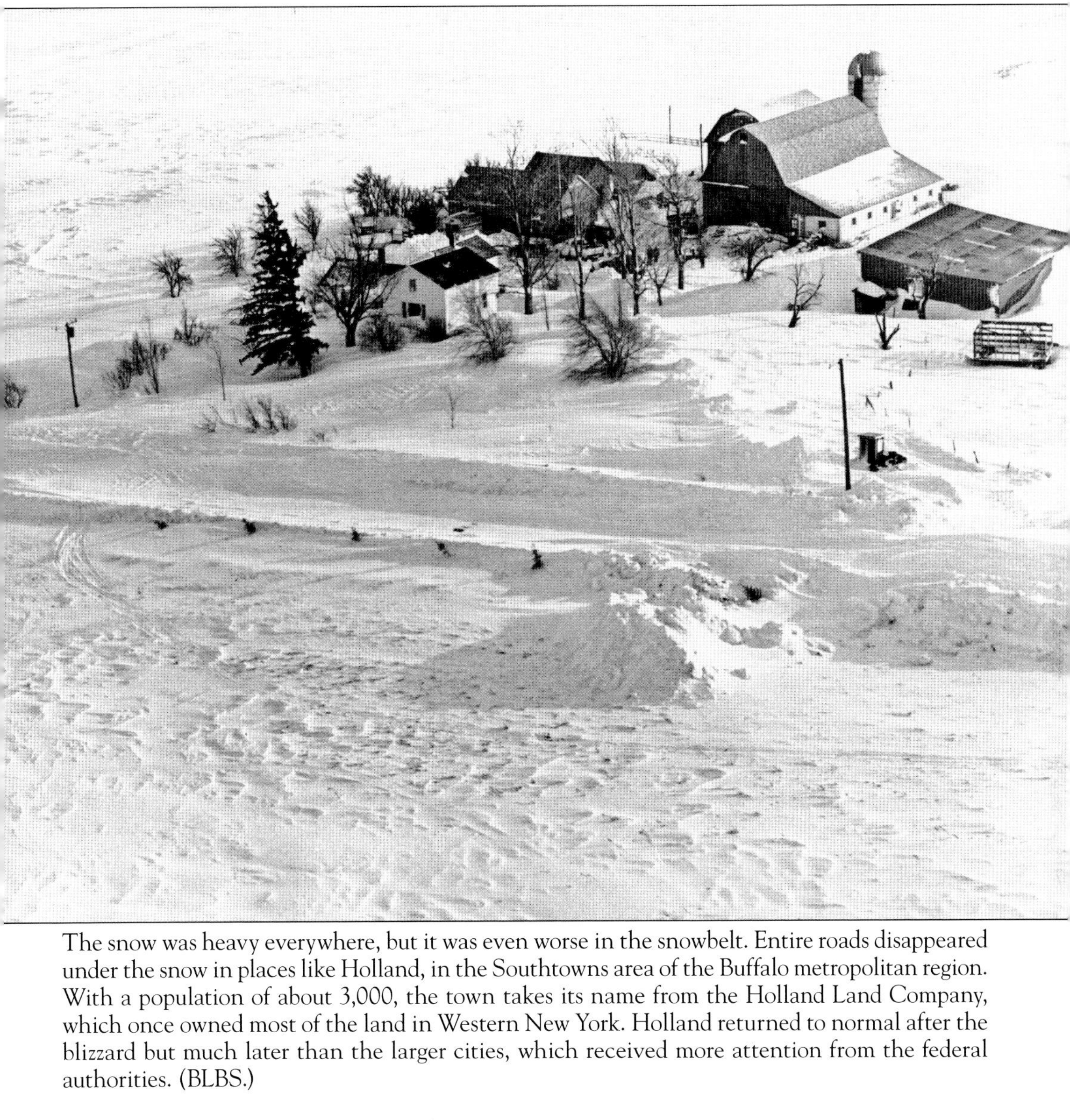

The snow was heavy everywhere, but it was even worse in the snowbelt. Entire roads disappeared under the snow in places like Holland, in the Southtowns area of the Buffalo metropolitan region. With a population of about 3,000, the town takes its name from the Holland Land Company, which once owned most of the land in Western New York. Holland returned to normal after the blizzard but much later than the larger cities, which received more attention from the federal authorities. (BLBS.)

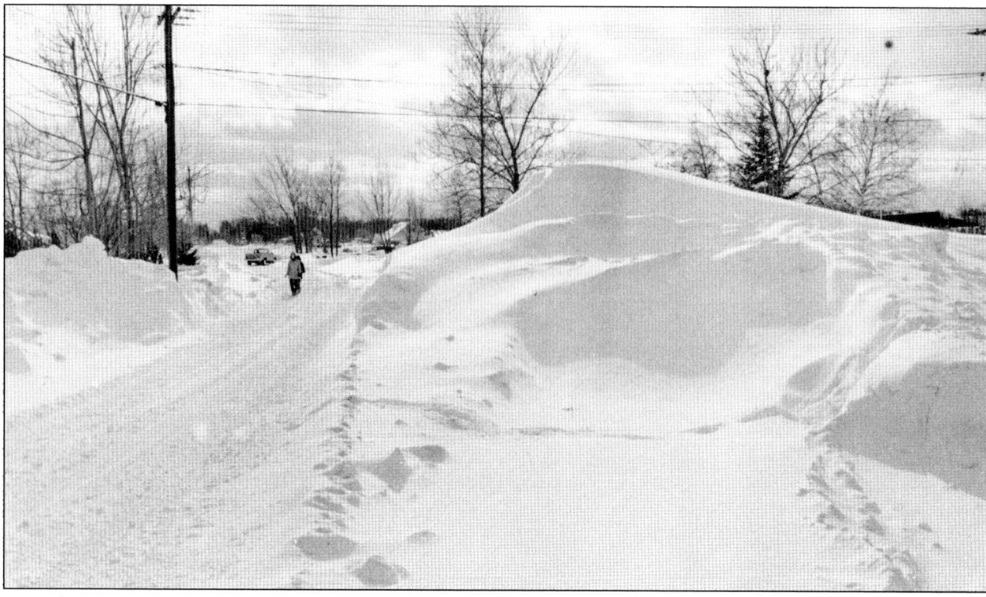

Conditions remained bad in Batavia, 45 miles east of Buffalo. State Street just south of the Thruway was buried beneath snow. (GCHD.)

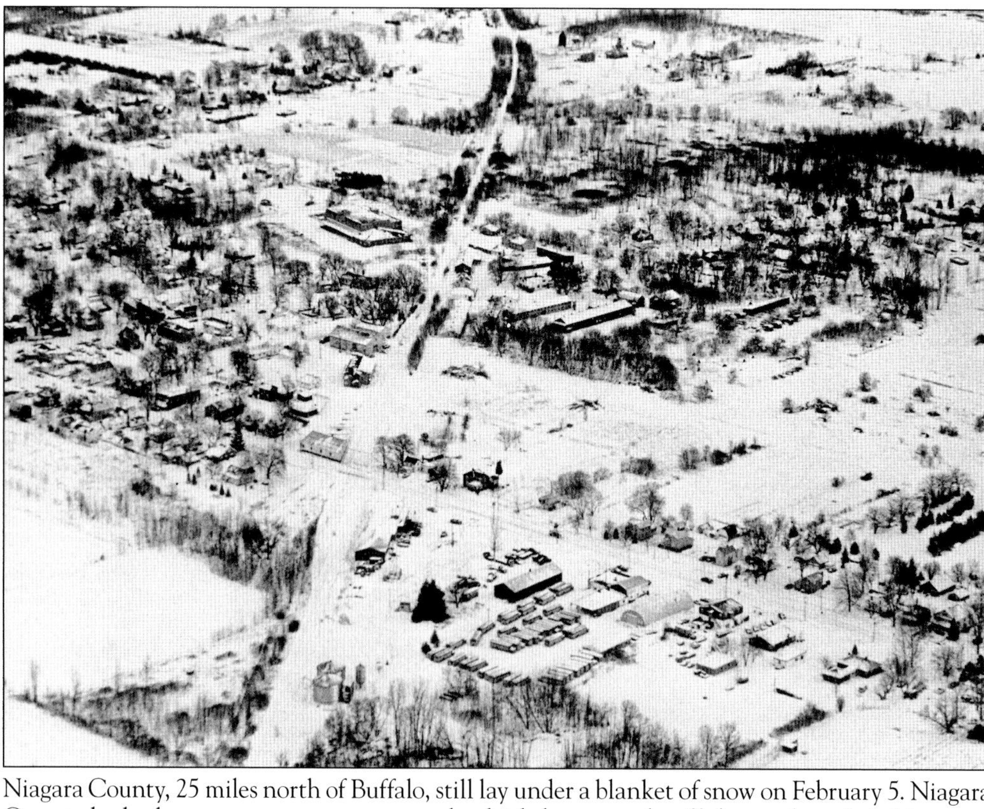

Niagara County, 25 miles north of Buffalo, still lay under a blanket of snow on February 5. Niagara County had a ban on nonemergency travel, which kept people off the roads and children out of school. Note the school buses covered by snow. The buses would remain dormant for at least another week. (NFPL.)

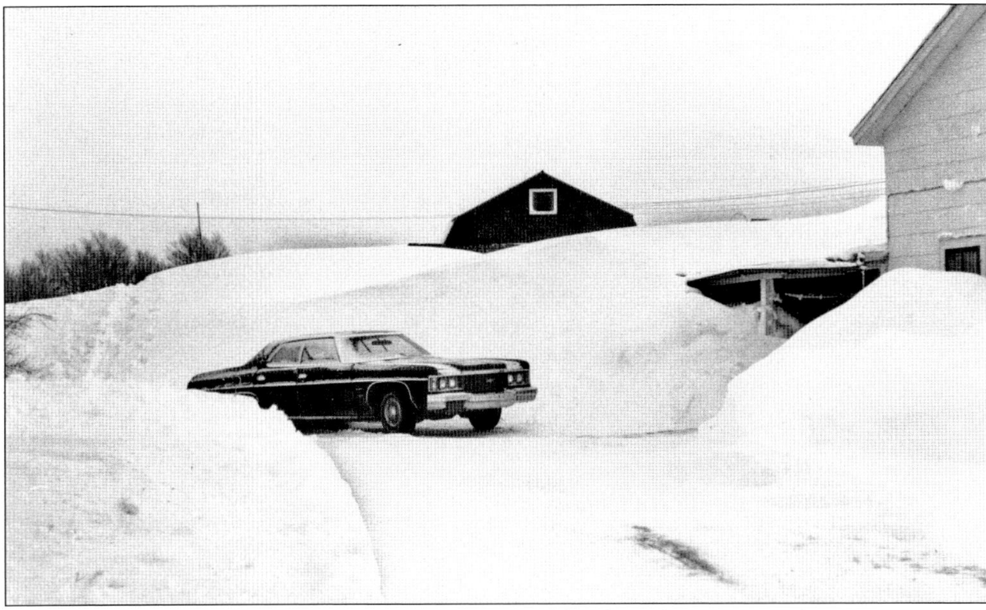

Three weeks after the blizzard struck, country farms like that of Norton Stockin on Route 39 in Smiths Corner, Wyoming County, still lay under drifts of snow. (BLBS.)

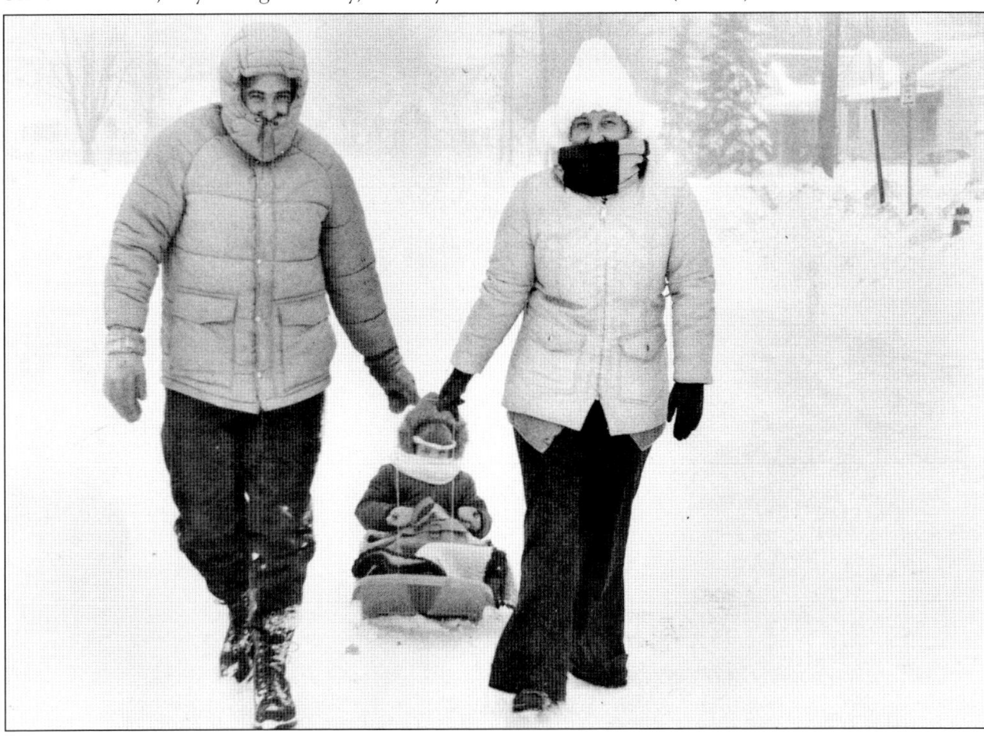

On January 31, 1977, this couple took their child for a sled ride. As one can see in this photograph, the cold and limited visibility persisted. On January 29, Buffalo had its coldest recorded temperature of the season at -7 degrees Fahrenheit. Perhaps the parents were having a bit of cabin fever and wanted to get out for a while, or they were eager to enjoy the "warm spell" as the temperature crept up into the double digits. (HST.)

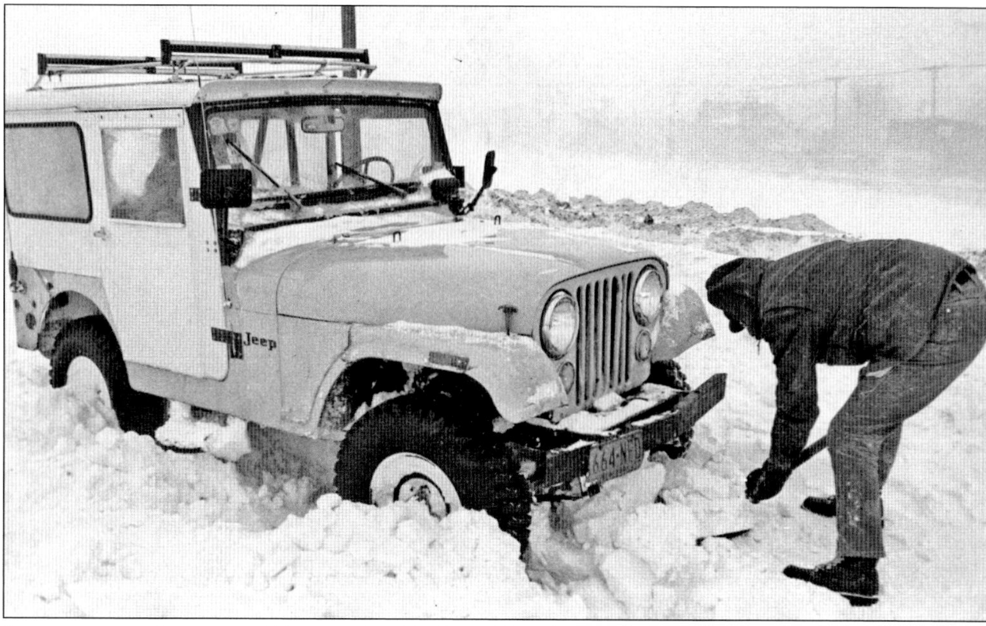

In response to the storm, Western New Yorkers, like this unidentified man from Niagara County, literally dug out their Jeeps. These and snowmobiles were some of the few vehicles that could handle the snow and drifts that covered the region. (NFPL.)

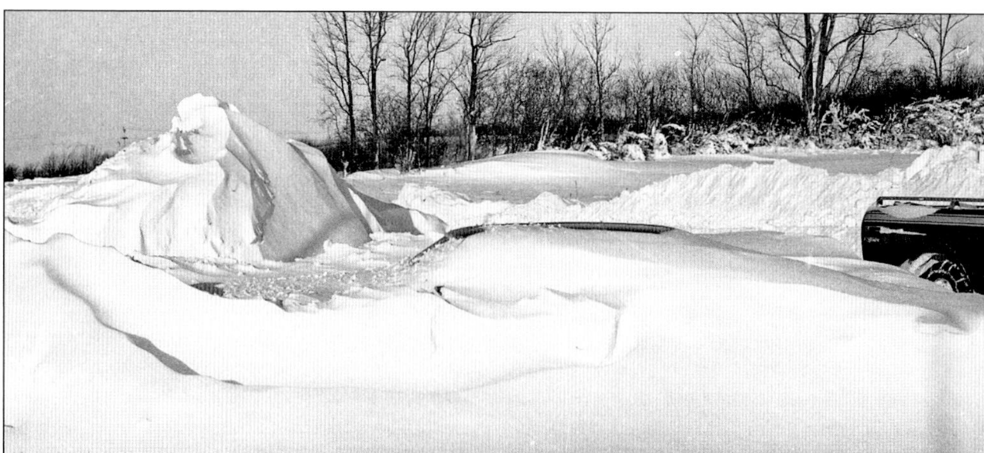

Automobiles were made useless by the storm. Rubber-tired vehicles require traction, which was not available once snow covered the roads. In 1977, most still had rear-wheel drive, which made it even more challenging to drive over snow. The outline of a car can be seen in the foreground. Hopefully, the owner was able to dig it out before a plow came along. (WDT.)

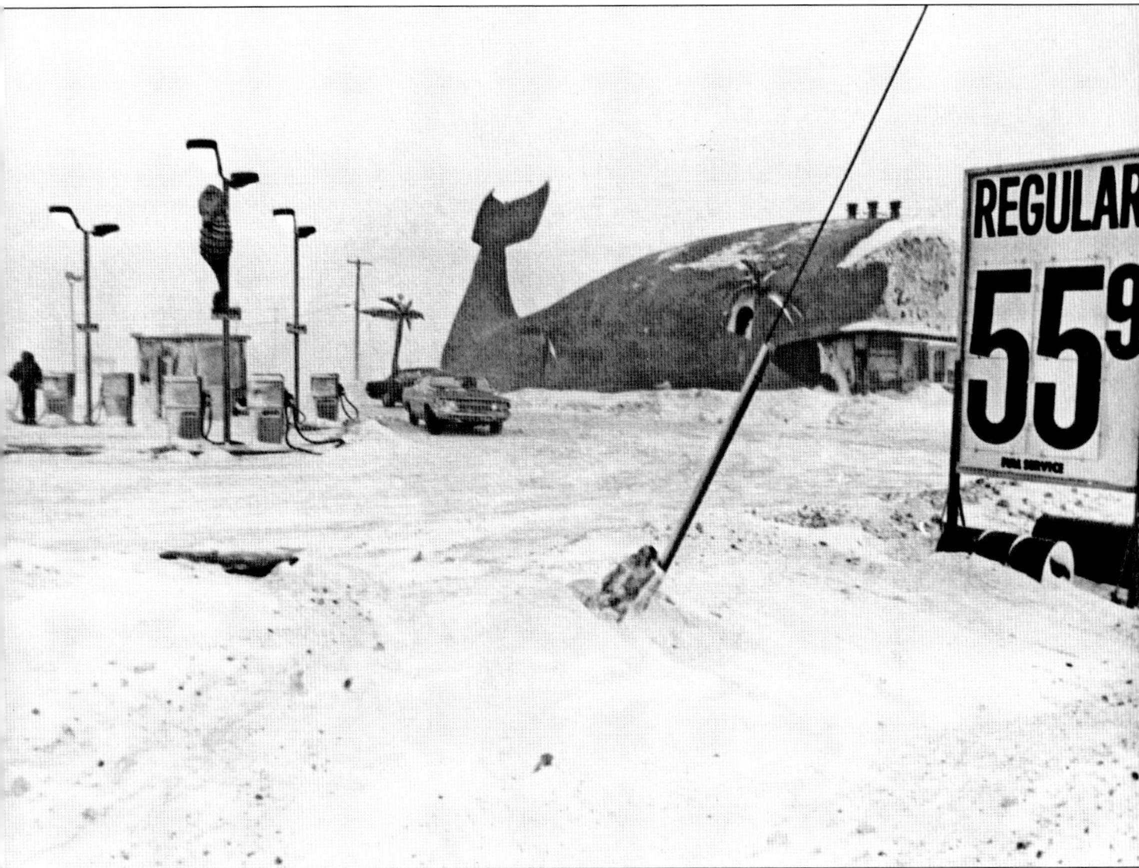

After the storm, drivers could clean off salt and dirty snow from their cars by going to the blue whale or "Willy the Whale" carwash on Young Street in the town of Tonawanda. The whale, 83 feet long, 22 feet high, and 30 feet wide, was a popular landmark when it first opened in 1973 but eventually was seen as an eyesore and was torn down in 1985. The gas prices of 55¢ a gallon represent the steady rise through the 1970s, and things got worse once gas was deregulated by President Carter in the late 1970s, when the price jumped to an average cost of 86¢ a gallon and then to over a dollar in 1980. (NFPL.)

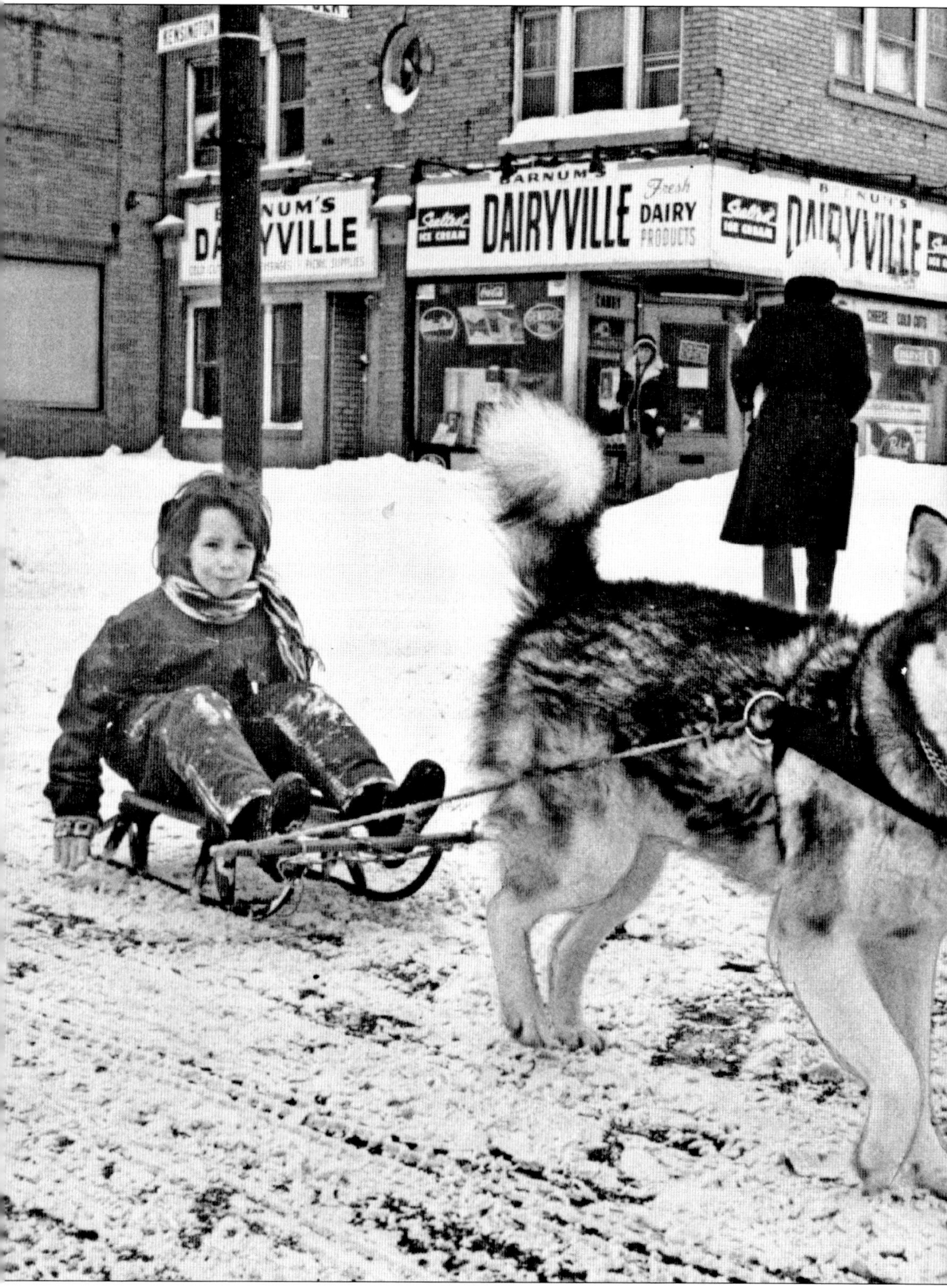
BARNUM'S
DAIRYVILLE
Fresh
DAIRY
PRODUCTS
Sealtest
ICE CREAM

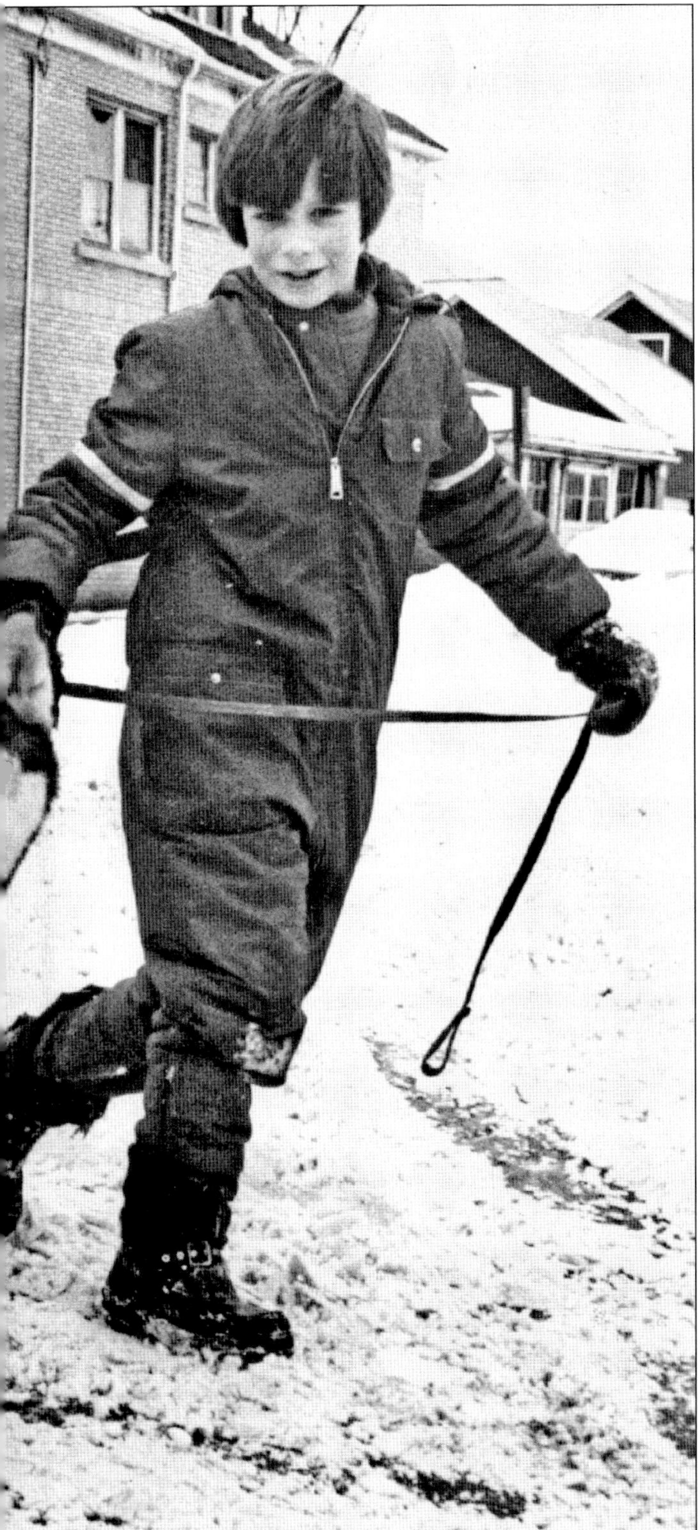

Because of the blizzard and then the driving ban imposed in Buffalo from February 1 to February 3 and then February 4 through February 8, city residents had to find alternative ways to get around. Dwayne and Kim Diparro of Kensington Avenue in Buffalo were clever enough to attach their sled to their malamute Tina, who mushed them to the Barnum's grocery store at Kensington Avenue and Suffolk Street. Sending children to the store without an adult was a regular feature of life in the 1970s. Also seen in the photograph are an unidentified woman and man standing outside the neighborhood grocery, which boasts that it sells milk, candy, and various inexpensive beers. (BLBS.)

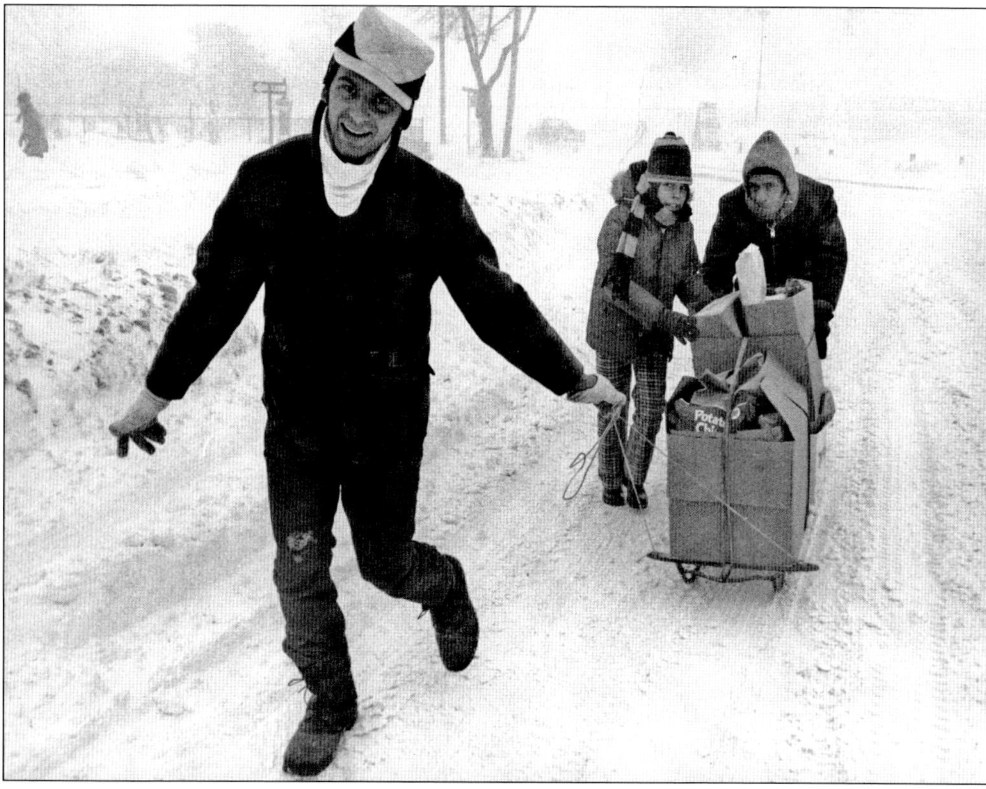

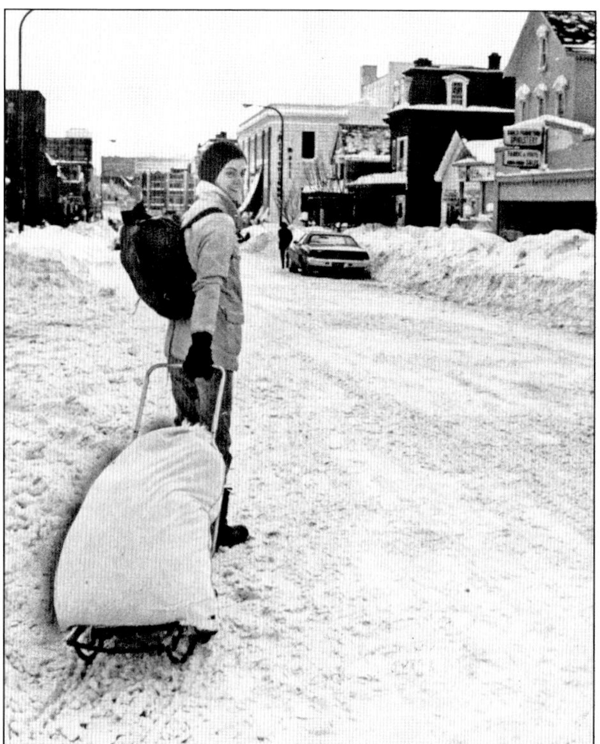

Teamwork between the Scozzafava and Spacone families allowed them to sled down to the Tops on Portage Avenue in Niagara Falls to get groceries for both families. This is one of the many examples of the way that the blizzard brought people together. (NFPL.)

The travel ban did not stop this woman on her way home from the Laundromat on Bidwell Parkway in Buffalo. Bidwell, another example of the influence of Frederick Law Olmsted on Buffalo, was designed as a broad street and green space that connects the park system in Buffalo to the neighborhoods. Many of the houses along Bidwell Parkway were built in the 1890s and early 1900s. (BLBS.)

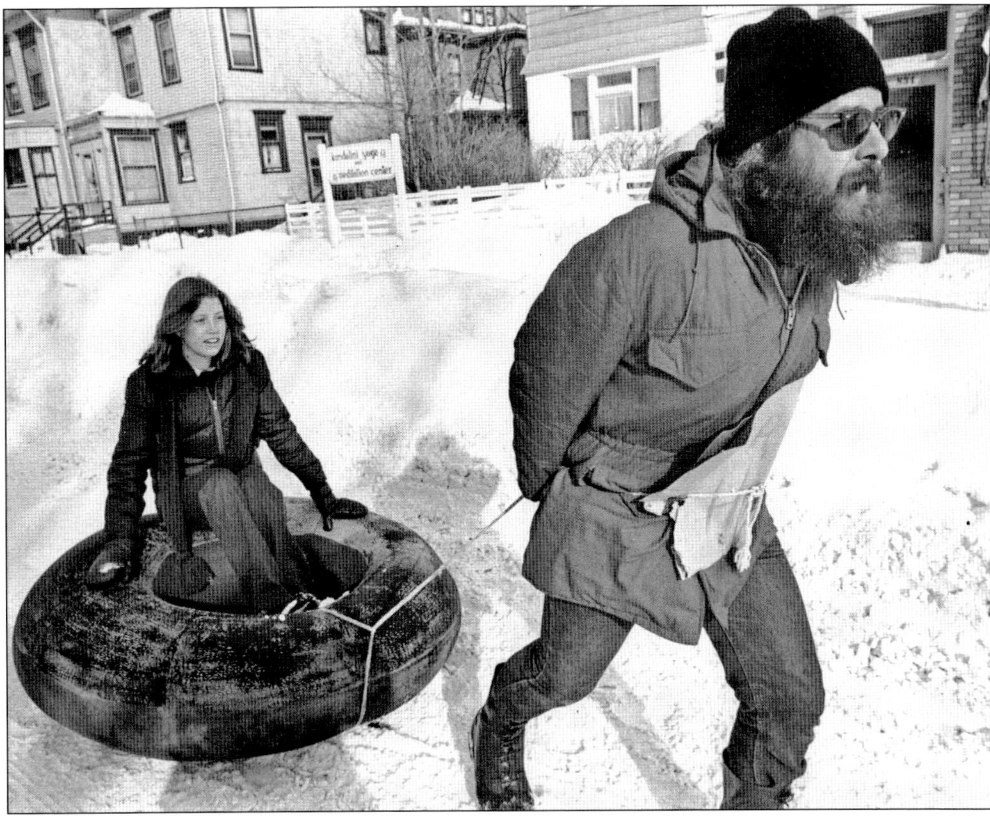

Tubing was another way to get around Buffalo during the driving ban. This young man gives his friend a ride on February 3, 1977. Note the yoga and meditation center in the background, an indication that the current interest in yoga is nothing new. (BLBS.)

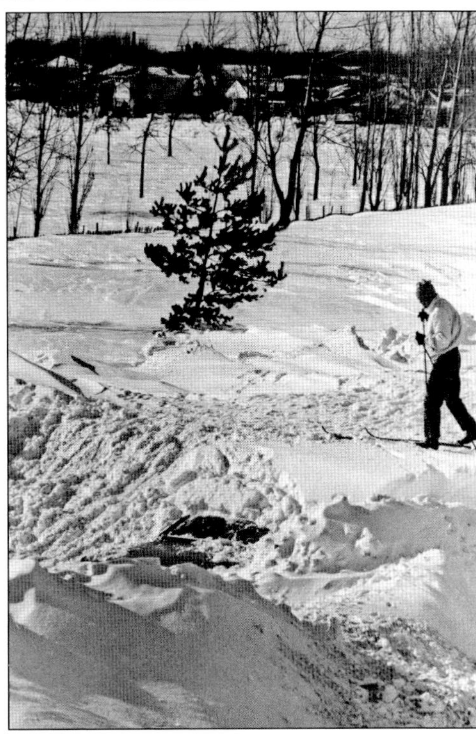

This cross-country skier is about to travel over a car covered in snow on Brompton Road in Tonawanda. Tonawanda is one of the Northtowns in the Buffalo metropolitan region. The Northtowns are usually spared the amount of snow dumped by lake-effect winds on the southern portion of Erie County. The blizzard evened things out, as the entire region saw snowdrifts of 15 to 30 feet. (HST.)

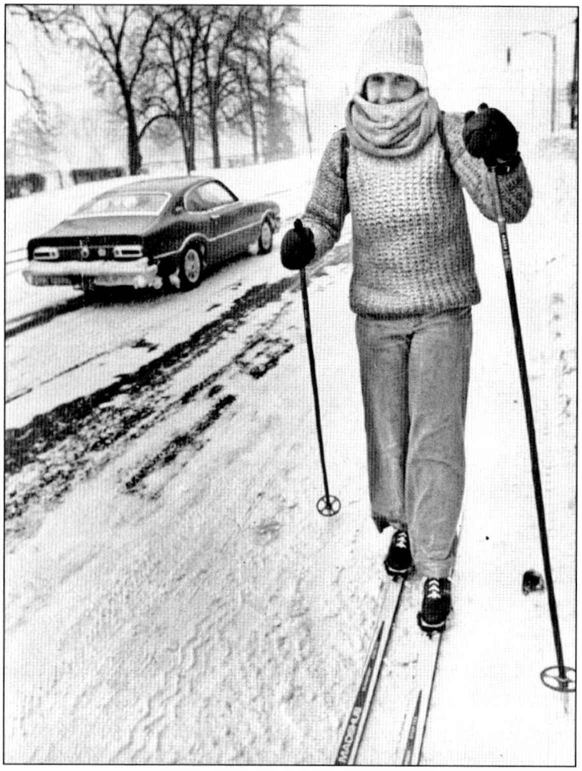

Marcia Greatrix, a registered nurse, skied her way to work at General Hospital in Buffalo. (BLBS.)

Why drive when one can ski? These workers return home on February 4, 1977. The city suffered congested traffic after the driving ban issued by Mayor Makowski was temporarily lifted. These savvy skiers walk down Main Street in Amherst, just east of Eggert Road in North Buffalo, also known as the Eggersville area. Ahead in the distance is Brunner's tavern, which is still a popular spot in the Buffalo area. (BLBS.)

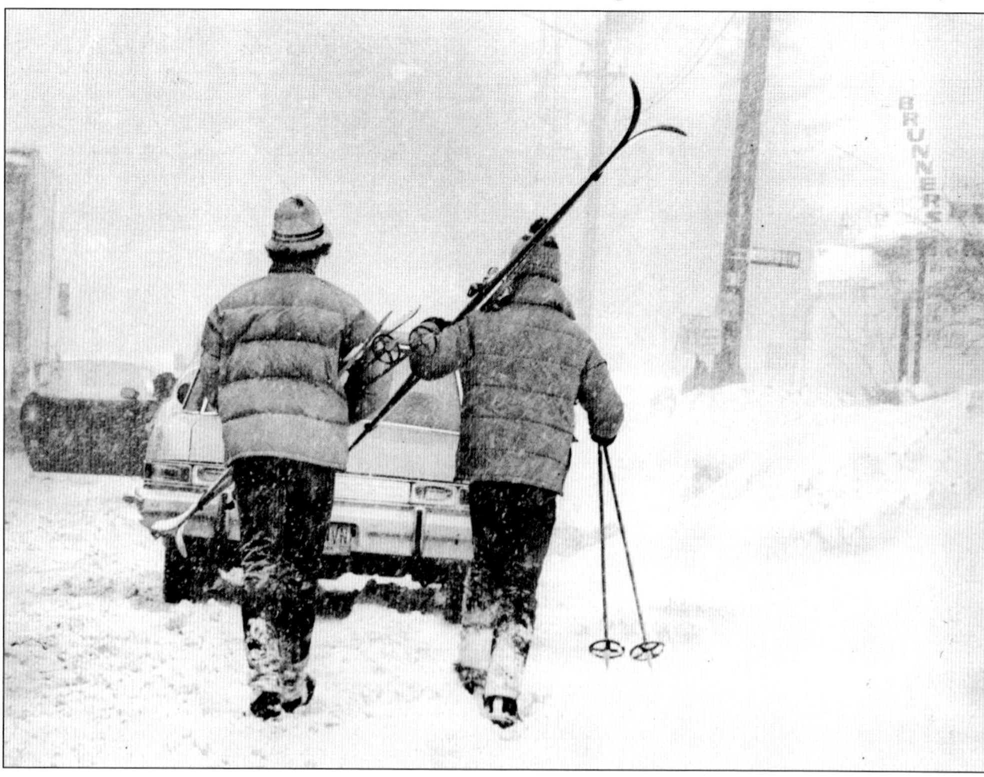

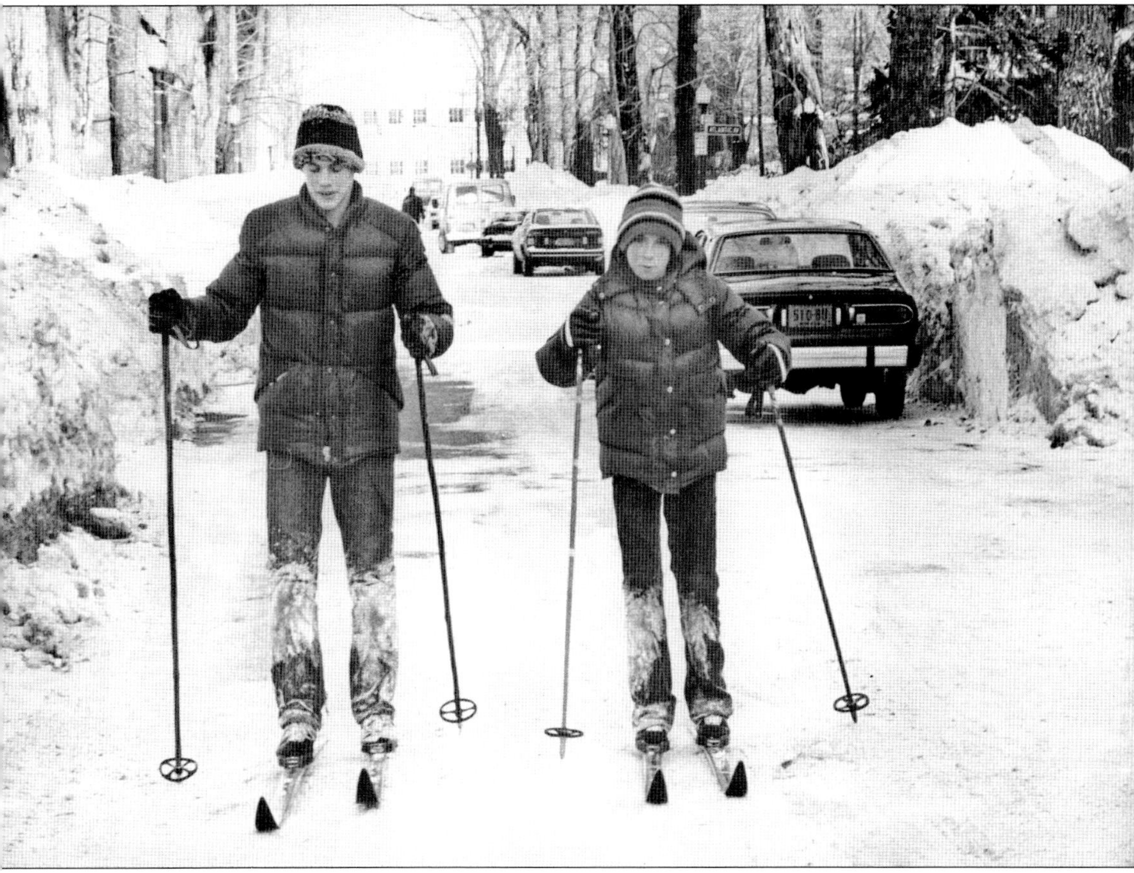

Streets remained a mess two weeks after the blizzard. On February 9, 1977, after the driving ban was lifted, the snowy streets enticed Jay DeCastro (left) and Andrew Muerer to put on their skis and head down Lexington Avenue, which runs between Delaware and Richmond Avenues in north Buffalo. (BLBS.)

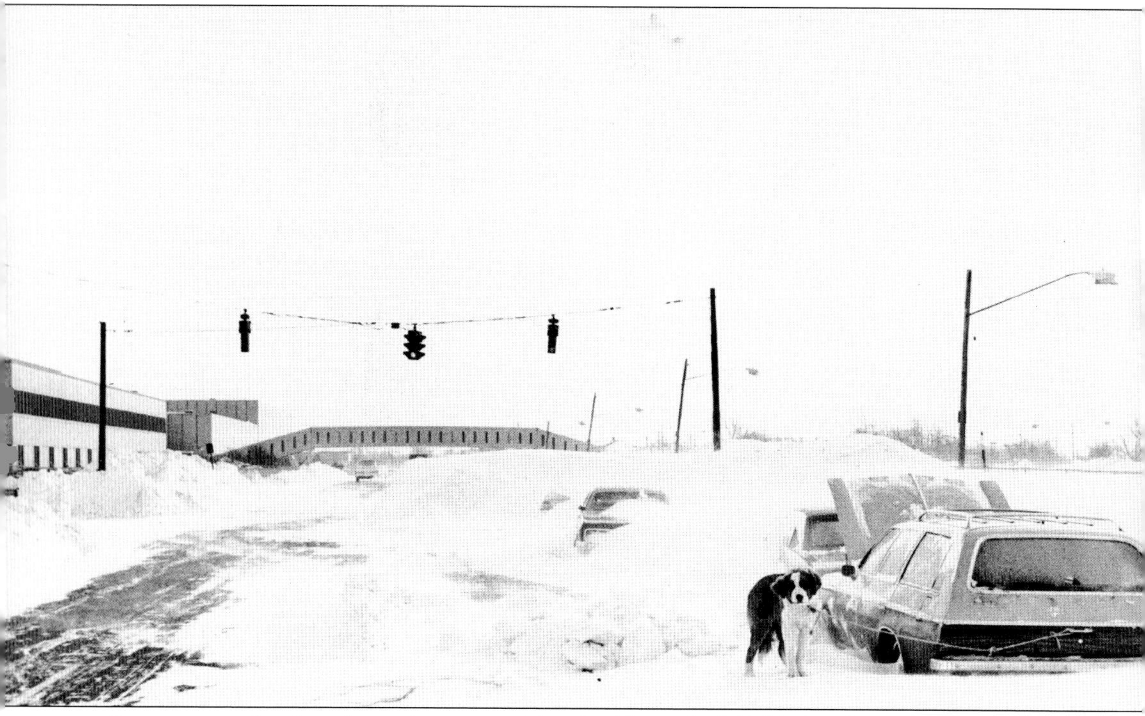

For anyone who feared another storm like the blizzard of 1977, this Saint Bernard, pictured tethered to a disabled station wagon, may have been the perfect companion. The legend of the Saint Bernard, perpetuated through Warner Bros. and Disney cartoons, was that these rescue dogs would appear with a small keg of whiskey or brandy around their necks to save those lost in Alpine snows. This is debatable, and some believe the kegs were a fictional embellishment to these rescue dogs. (BLBS.)

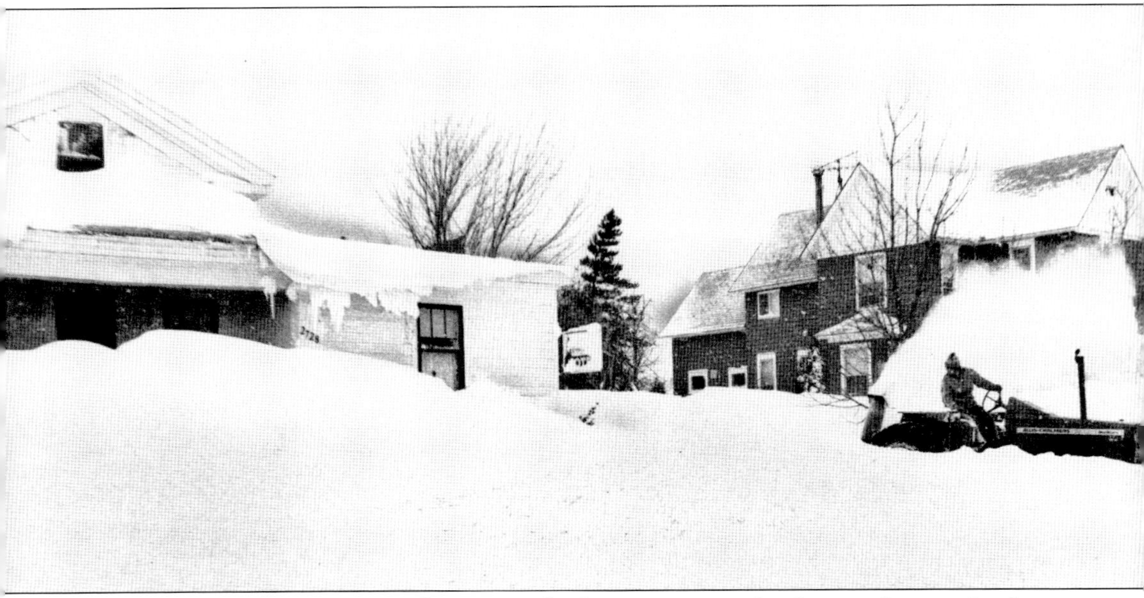

This man in Perry Center, New York, seems to be farming snow as he digs out from under the remnants of the blizzard around the Noble Buckland Evergreen Motel. The blizzard made quite an impression on Perry. The town's official book is written by native Patrick Brennan, who details his experience on a school bus during the blizzard. (BLBS.)

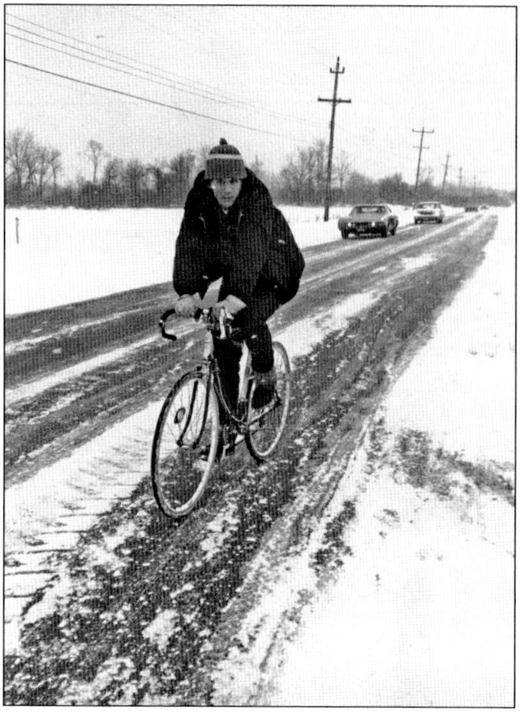

Bicycles were also useful when cars were banned from the roads. (NFPL.)

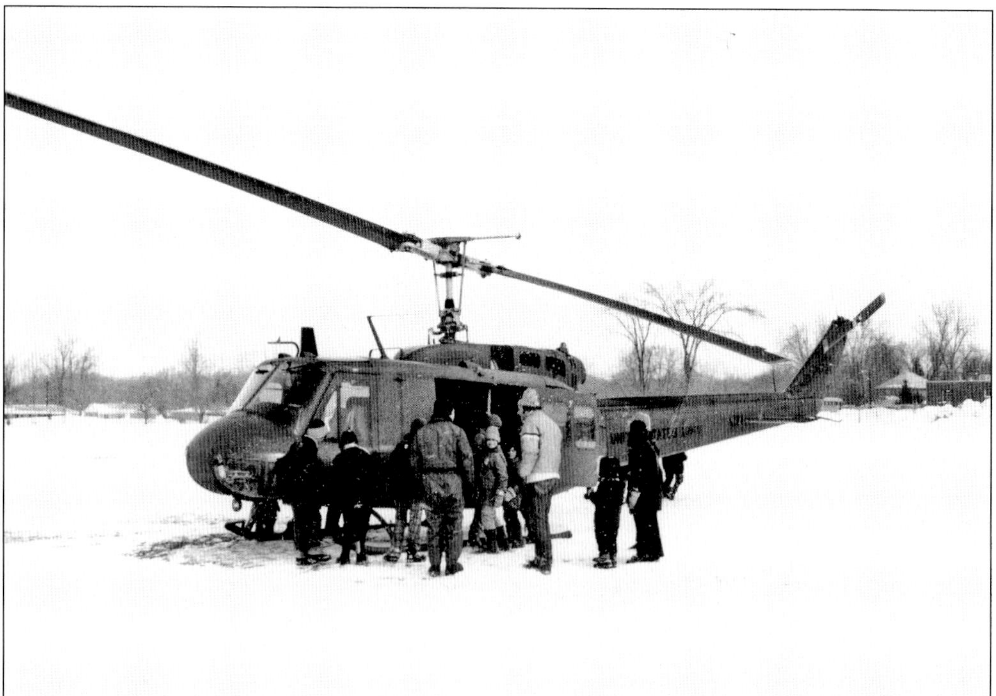

These children from Alden seem pretty excited about this helicopter, used by the Army National Guard in its search and rescue operations around Western New York in the aftermath of the blizzard. Helicopters were dispatched from the air base in Niagara Falls. (Leonard A. Weisbeck Sr.)

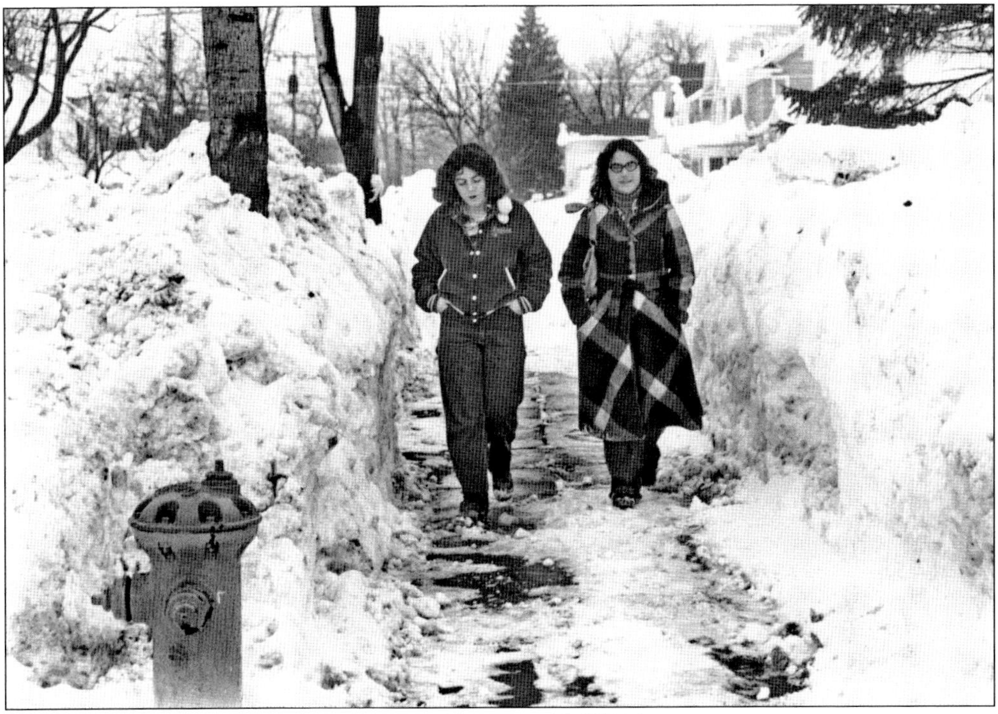

Walking was also one way to move around Batavia. (GCHD.)

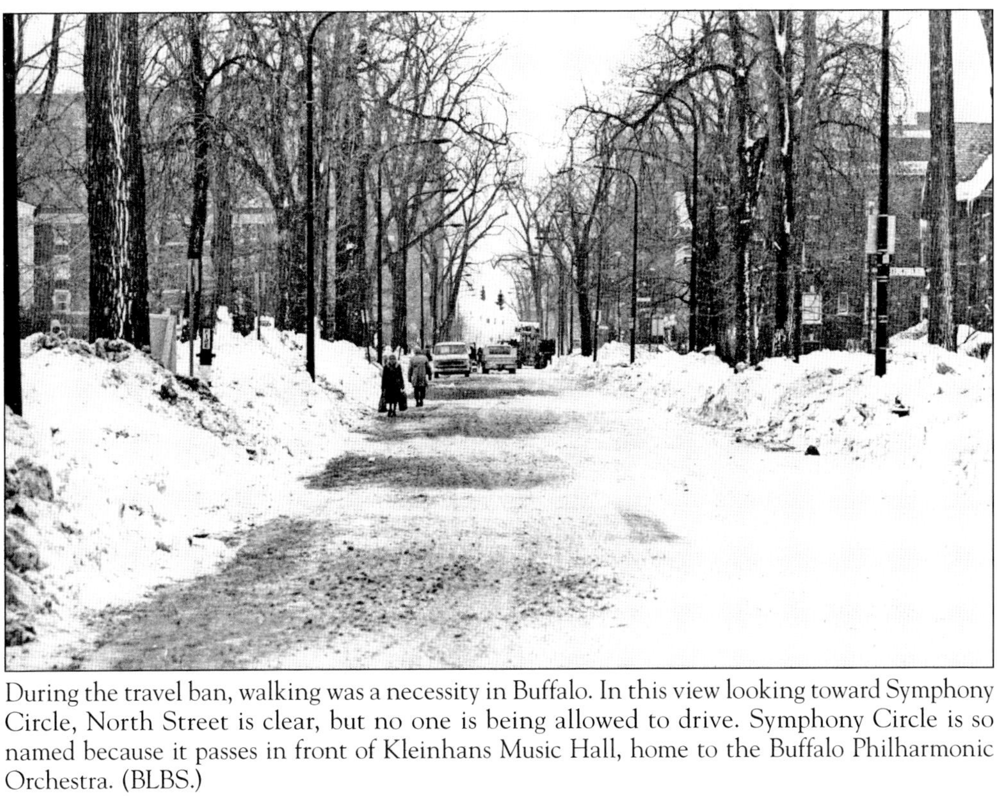

During the travel ban, walking was a necessity in Buffalo. In this view looking toward Symphony Circle, North Street is clear, but no one is being allowed to drive. Symphony Circle is so named because it passes in front of Kleinhans Music Hall, home to the Buffalo Philharmonic Orchestra. (BLBS.)

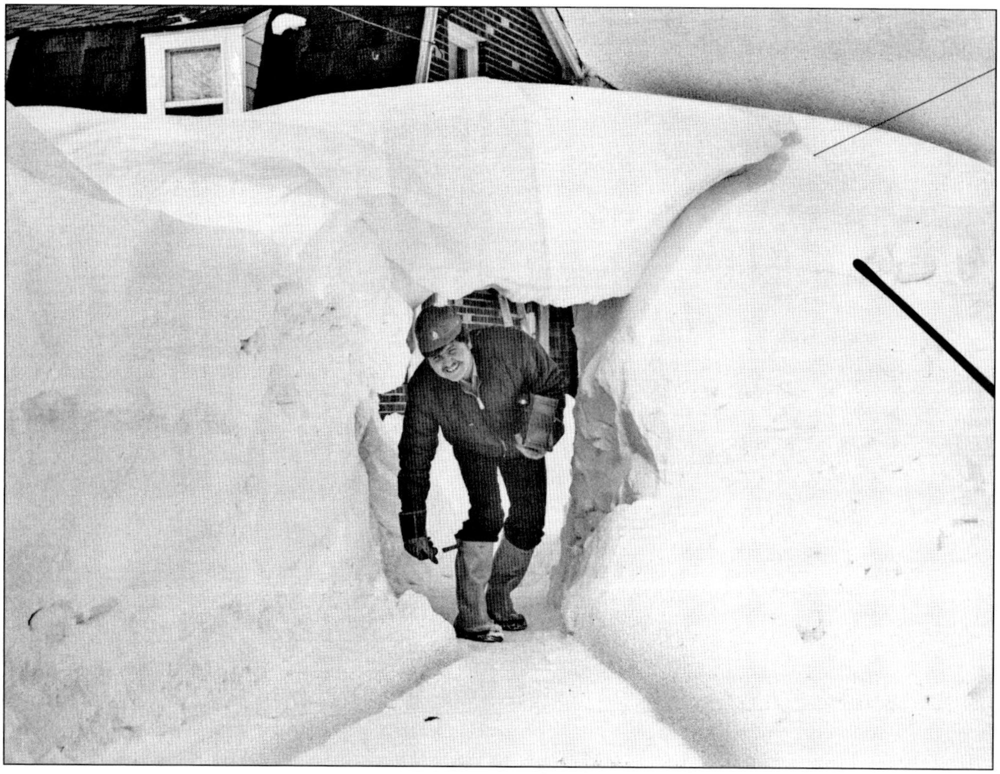

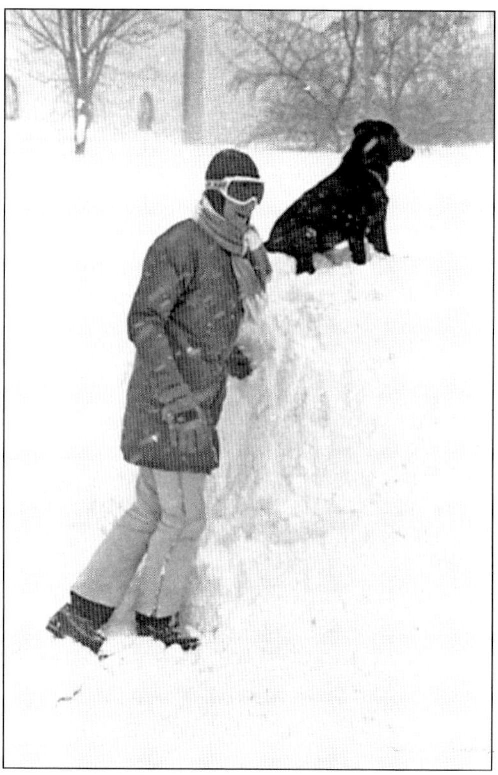

This meter reader is doing the best he can under the circumstances, ducking under and around the snow as he makes his way from house to house in Buffalo. (BLBS.)

Taking the dog for walk could lead one to new heights, as this unidentified man found out. (WDT.)

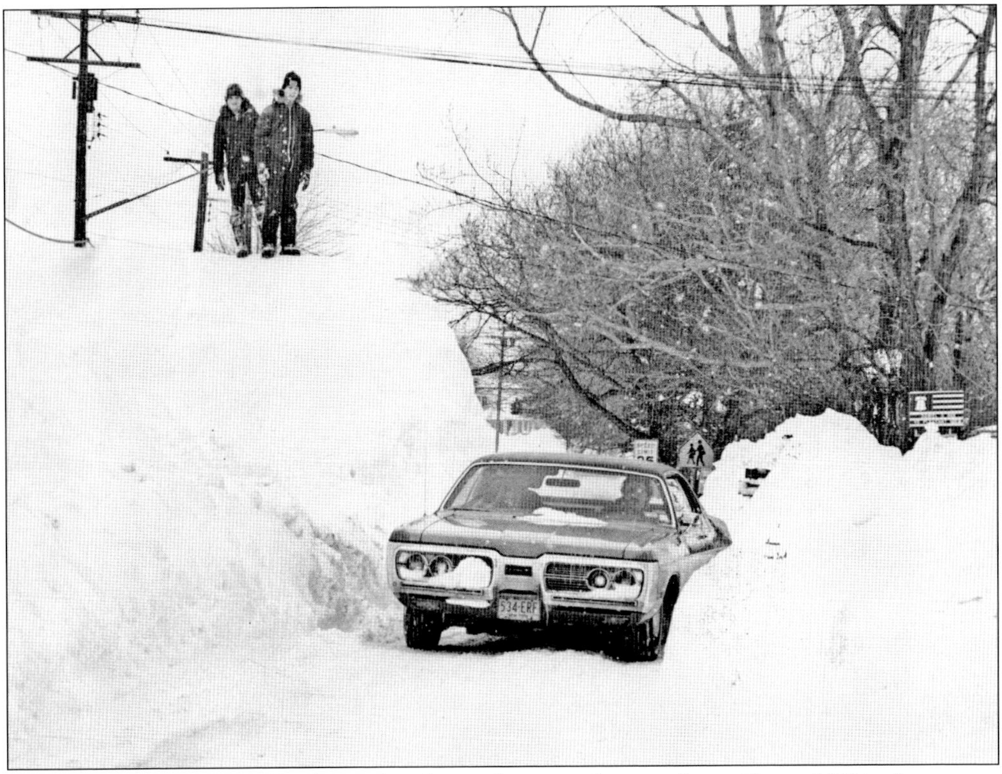

The snowdrifts remained high, as this driver discovered going down Harris Hill in Lancaster. Lancaster is a village in Erie County near Buffalo. According to some sources, Lancaster is named for a town in Massachusetts. (BLBS.)

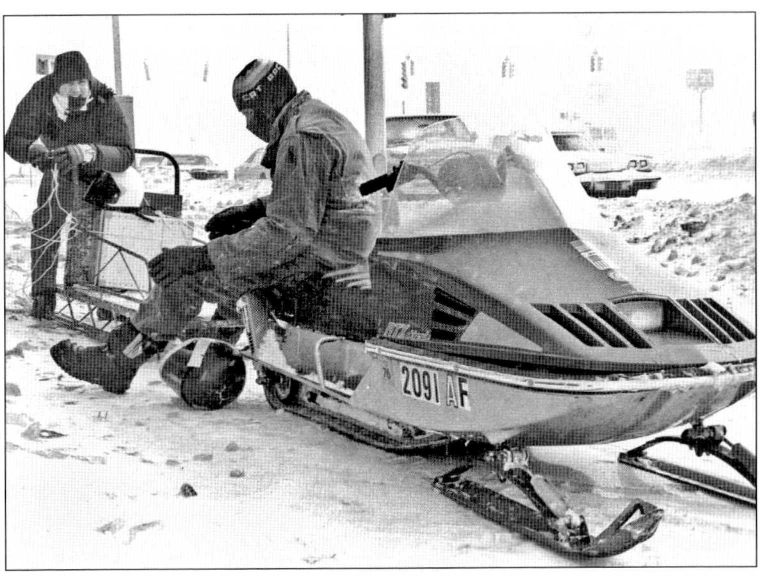

Snowmobiles were essential during the blizzard and afterward, and sales of snowmobiles went up during the driving ban. (NFPL.)

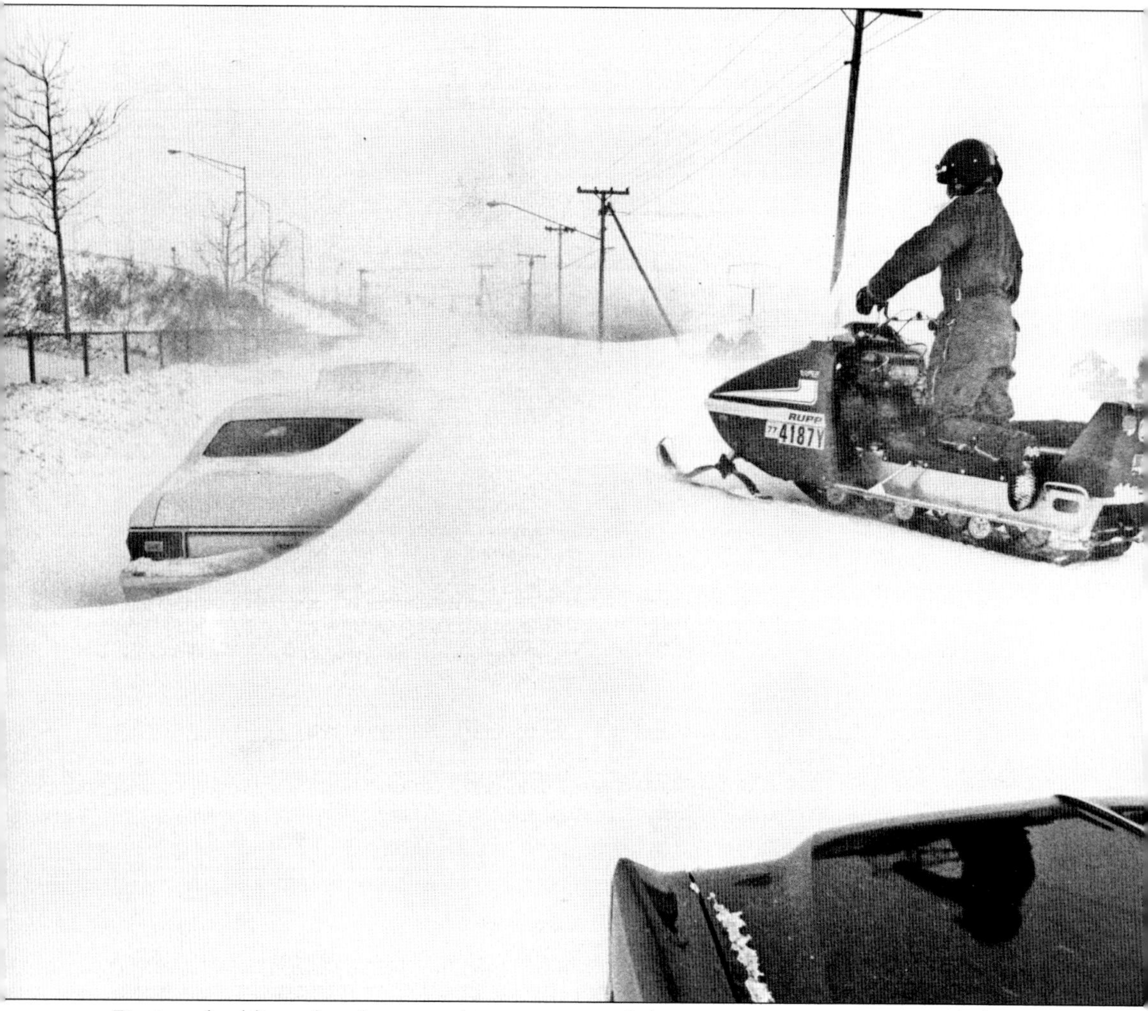

During the blizzard, volunteers driving snowmobiles went out to rescue stranded motorists. Pictured here are snowmobilers on Maryvale Drive between Pine Ridge Road and Harlem Road in the town of Cheektowaga. Cheektowaga is the second-largest town near Buffalo and lies just east of the city. The name comes from the Seneca phrase meaning "land of the crabapple." The Seneca Nation was part of the Haudenosaunee (Iroquois) Confederacy. (BLBS.)

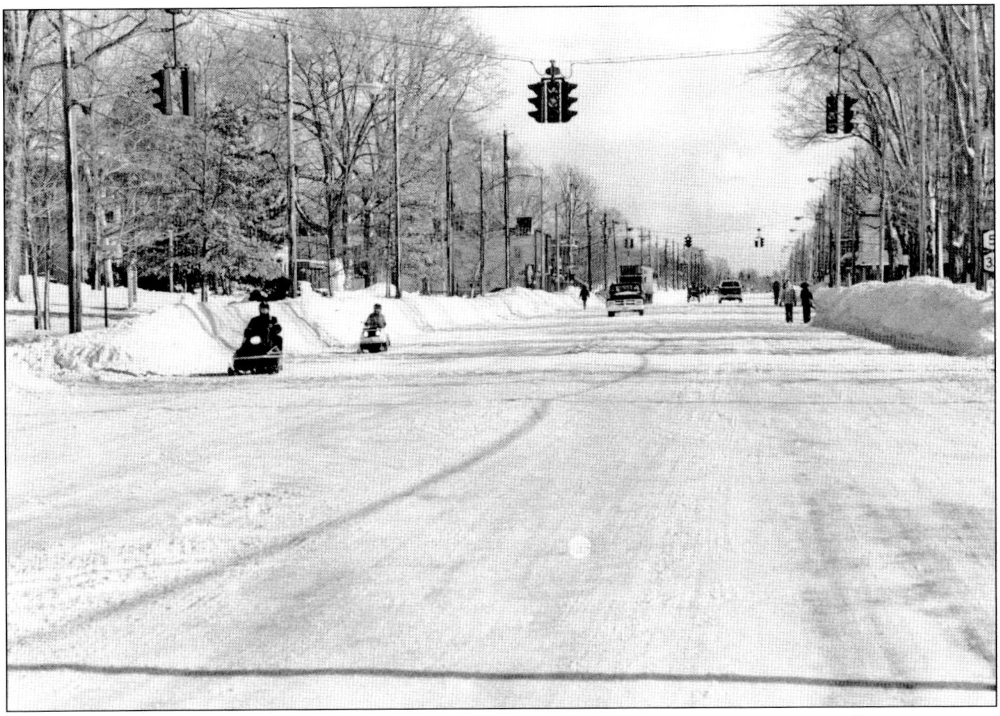

Traveling down Main Street near Ellicott Street in Batavia was a breeze on a snowmobile. (GCHD.)

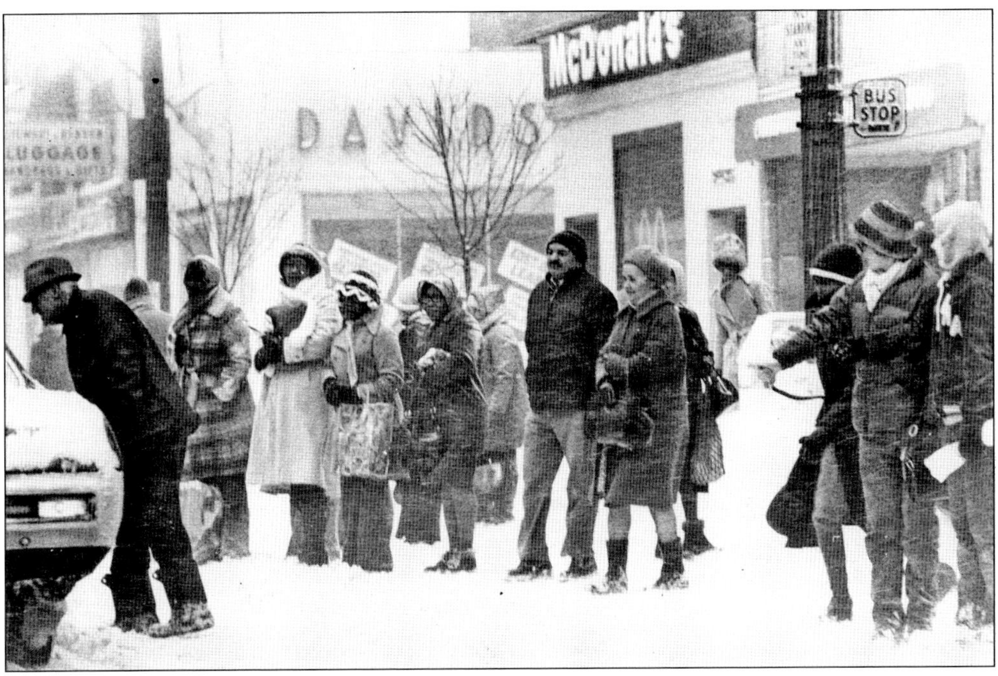

Most people who needed to get around during the storm and driving ban turned to public transportation. (BLBS.)

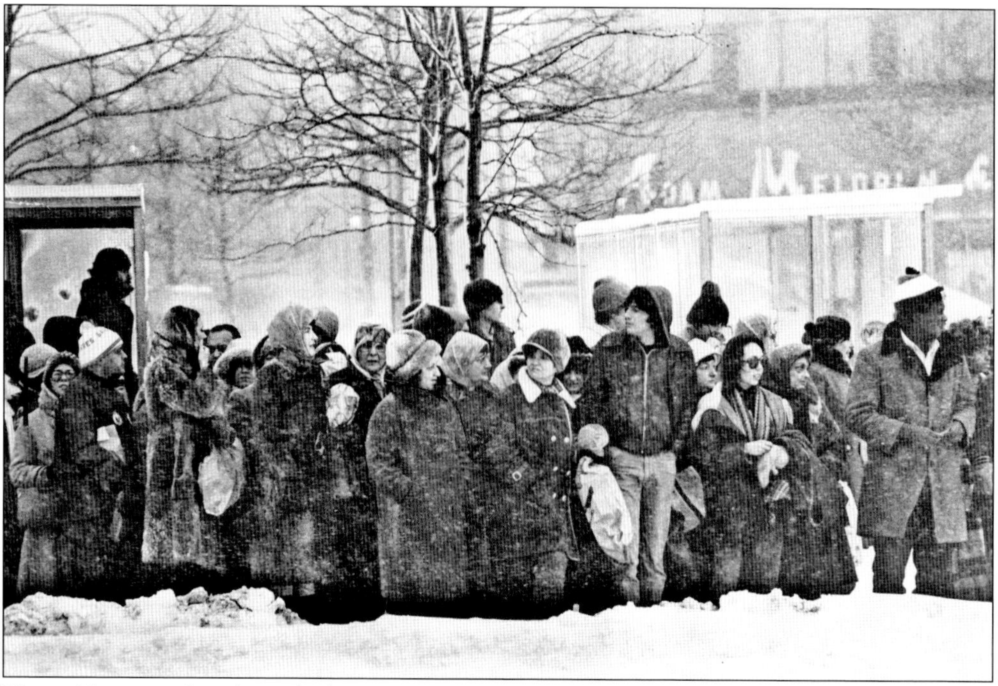

The cold persisted, making the long wait for a bus miserable for this group of riders at Main and Church Streets in Buffalo. (BLBS.)

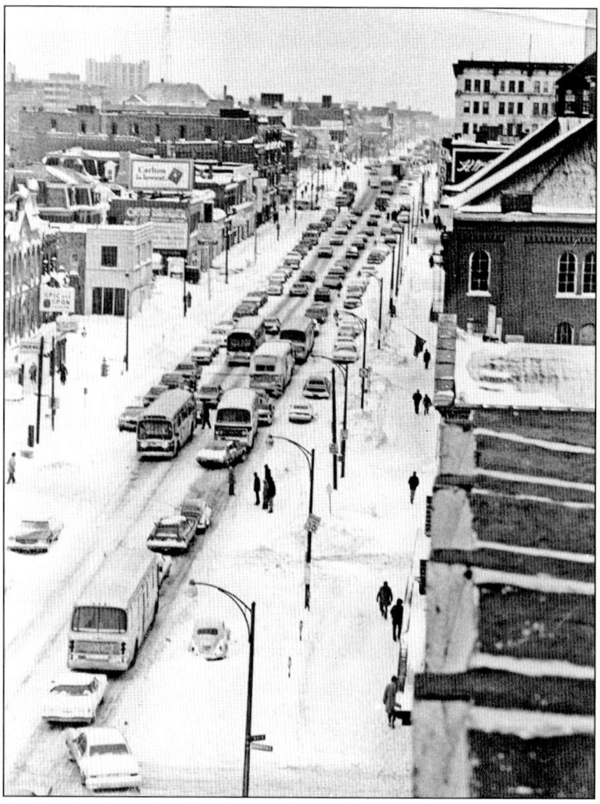

Even after the driving ban was lifted, streets in the city of Buffalo were often reduced to one lane in each direction, making for slow travel when someone wanted to make a left-hand turn. (BLBS.)

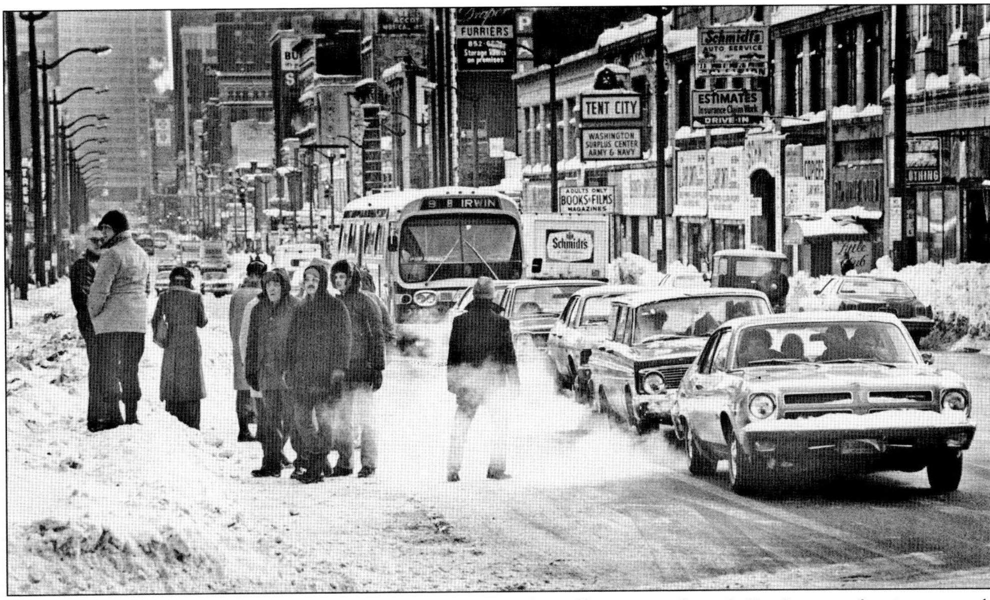

Walking in Buffalo was a challenge because city sidewalks were often full of snow, forcing people to walk in the street. (BLBS.)

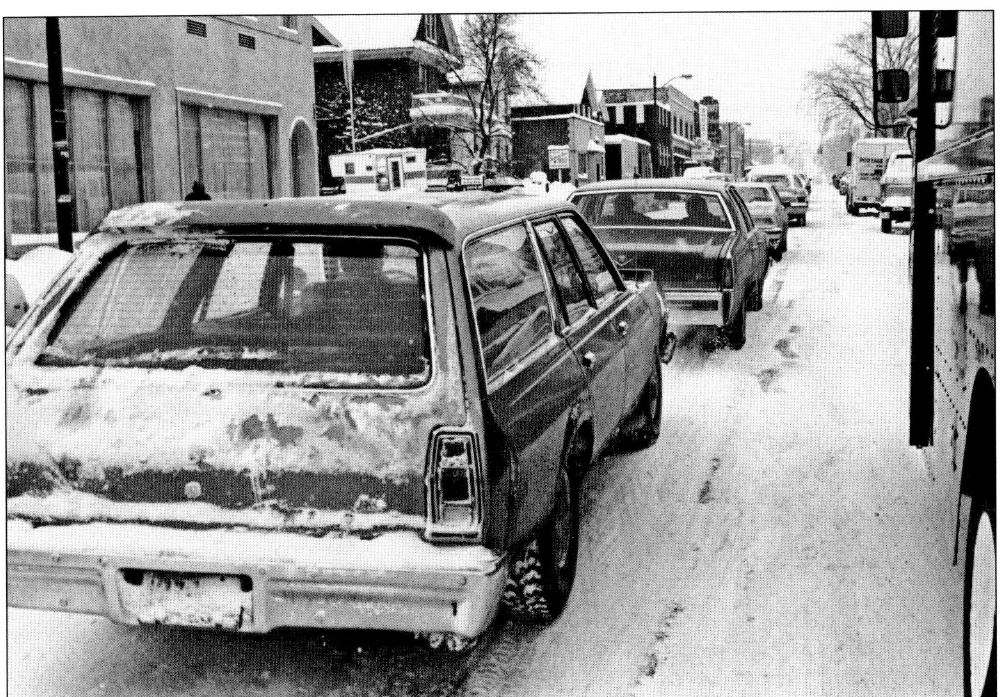
Niagara Falls also experienced slow travel after the blizzard. Once the driving ban was lifted, Third Street in Niagara Falls felt like a large parking lot. (NFPL.)

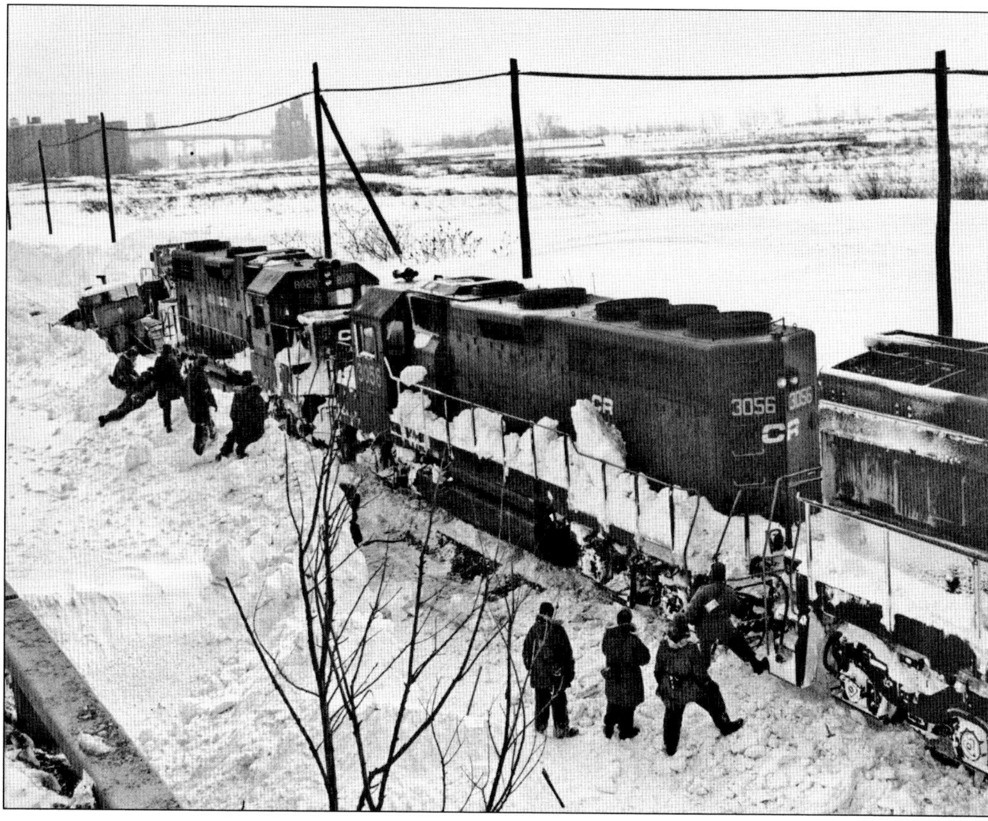

Moving freight into and out of Buffalo remained a problem for weeks after the blizzard. (BLBS.)

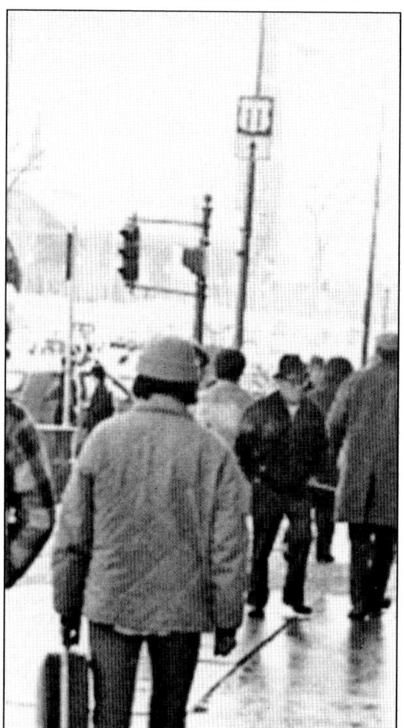

Signs that the storm and its impact were over can be seen as these pedestrians shop in downtown Watertown on February 4, 1977. (WDT.)

Four

HELPING HANDS

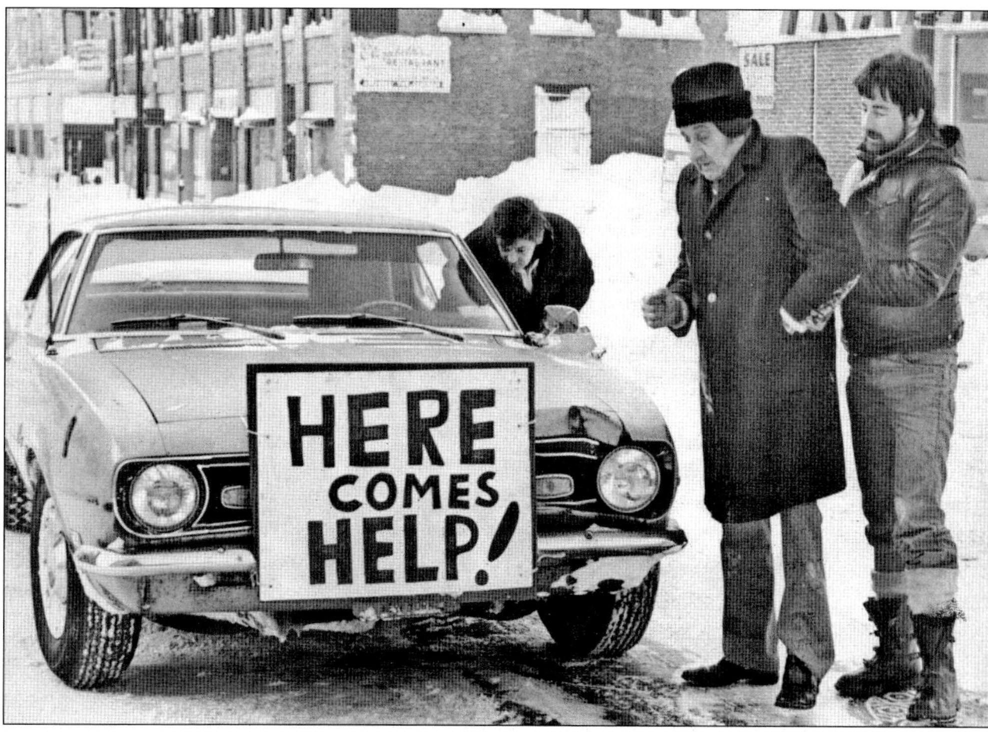

Dr. Jan Gutowski, seen here helping Ralph Lartanda into the car, was one of hundreds of people who helped their neighbors during the blizzard of 1977. Dr. Gutowski drove around helping individuals like Lartanda, who needed a ride from Pearl and West Huron Streets back to his home. Gutowski spent several days looking for ways to help the people of Buffalo and helped start people's cars, rescued freezing motorists from stalled cars, and drove pedestrians home or to shelters. (BLBS.)

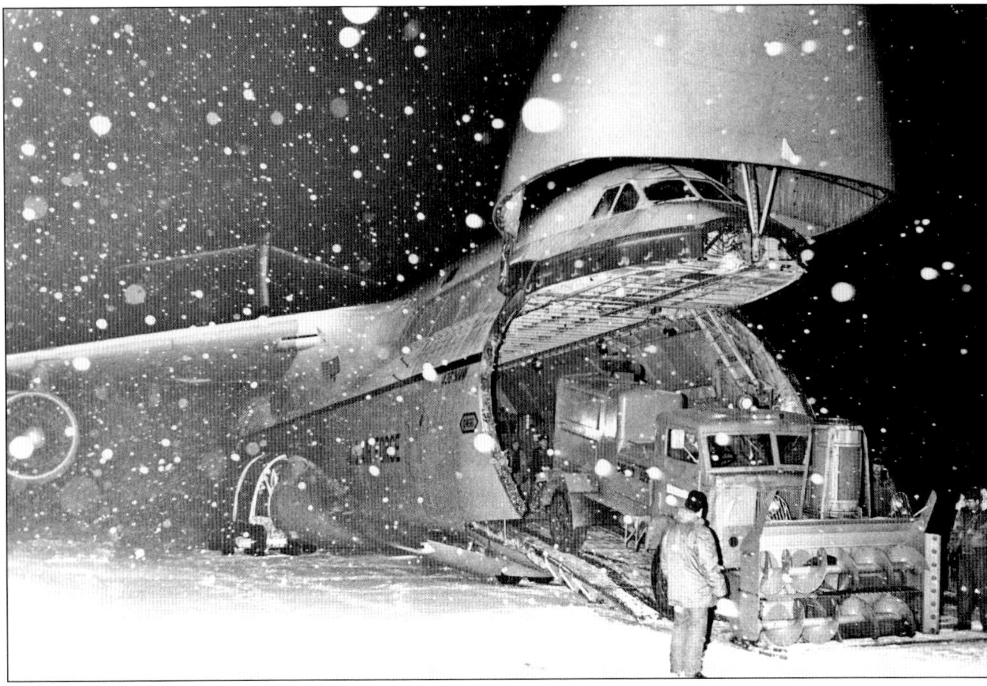

The US Army helped out during the crisis by sending in 300 airborne engineers from Fort Bragg along with snow-fighting equipment from various locations. The troops had to land at Niagara Falls International Airport and plow their way to Buffalo to aid the stricken city. (NFPL.)

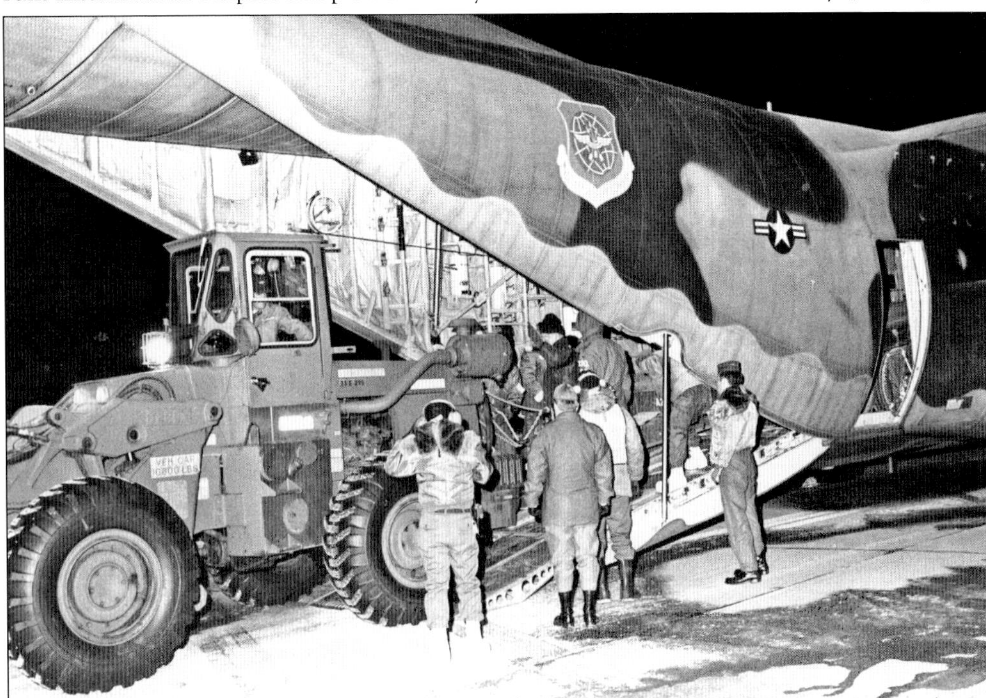

Troops flew into Niagara Falls International Airport at 3:00 a.m. on February 2 to assist with the winter weather cleanup. (NFPL.)

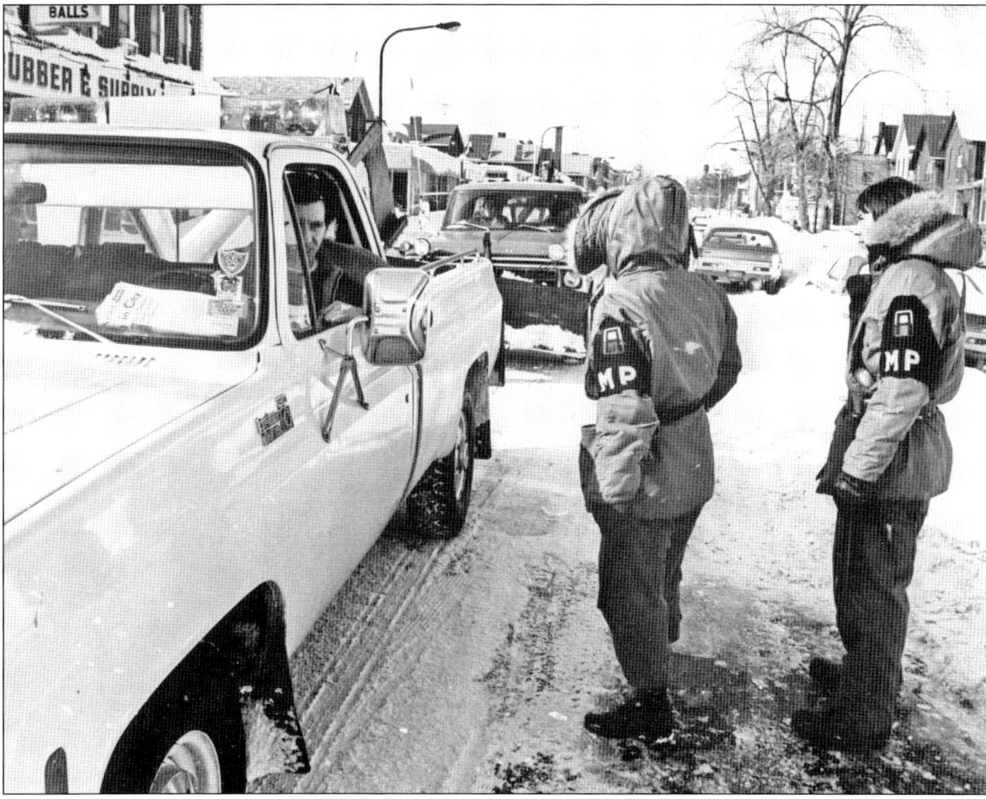

Along with engineers, the Army and National Guard sent in military police (MPs), who helped enforce the driving ban. (BLBS.)

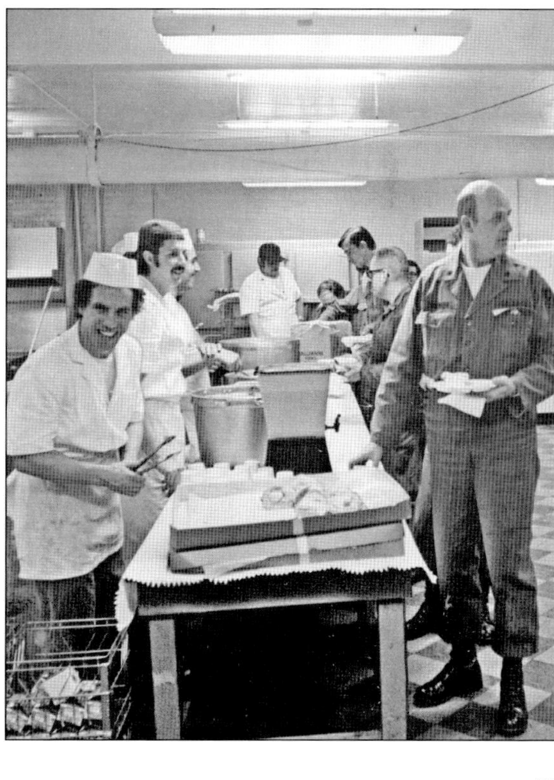

National Guard units operating out of downtown Buffalo stop for a meal in between missions. Five hundred guardsmen from the 152nd Engineering Battalion, 221st Engineering Battalion, and 42nd Aviation Battalion assisted residents throughout Western and Northern New York until February 10, 1977. (BLBS.)

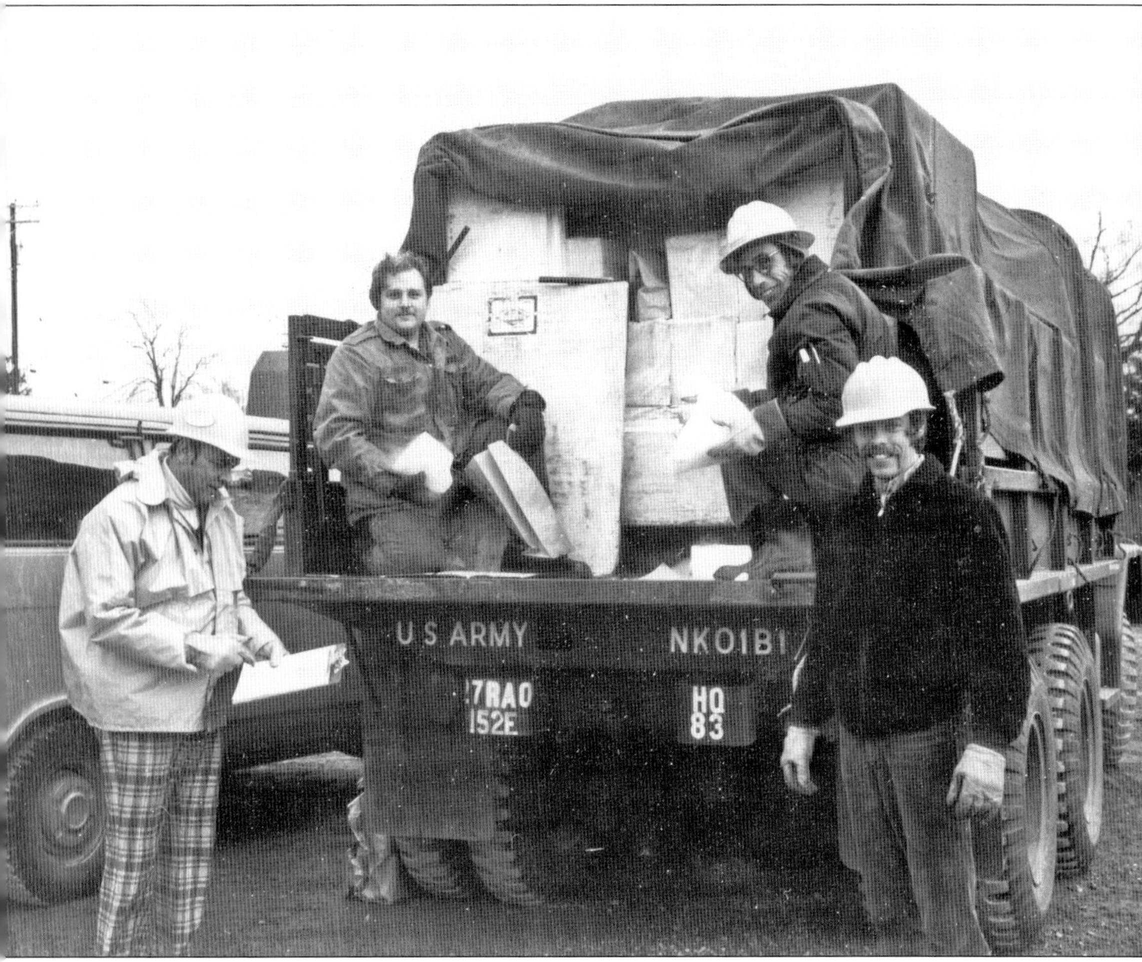

US Army and National Guard units helped deliver food in Alden. Food was scarce in many outlying and rural areas, since normal shipments could not arrive from outside the blizzard zone. Food in local grocery stores was depleted within days. (Leonard A. Weisbeck Sr.)

Long hours and cold weather took its toll on the military personnel, who show exhaustion in this picture. (NFPL.)

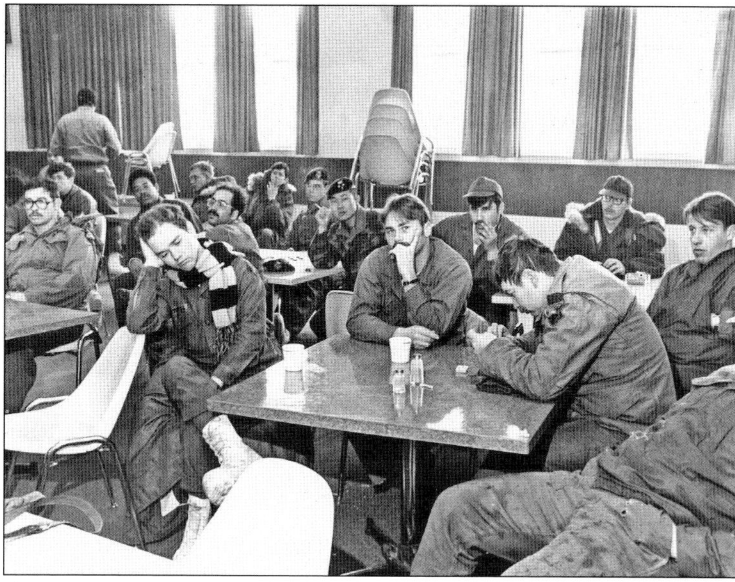

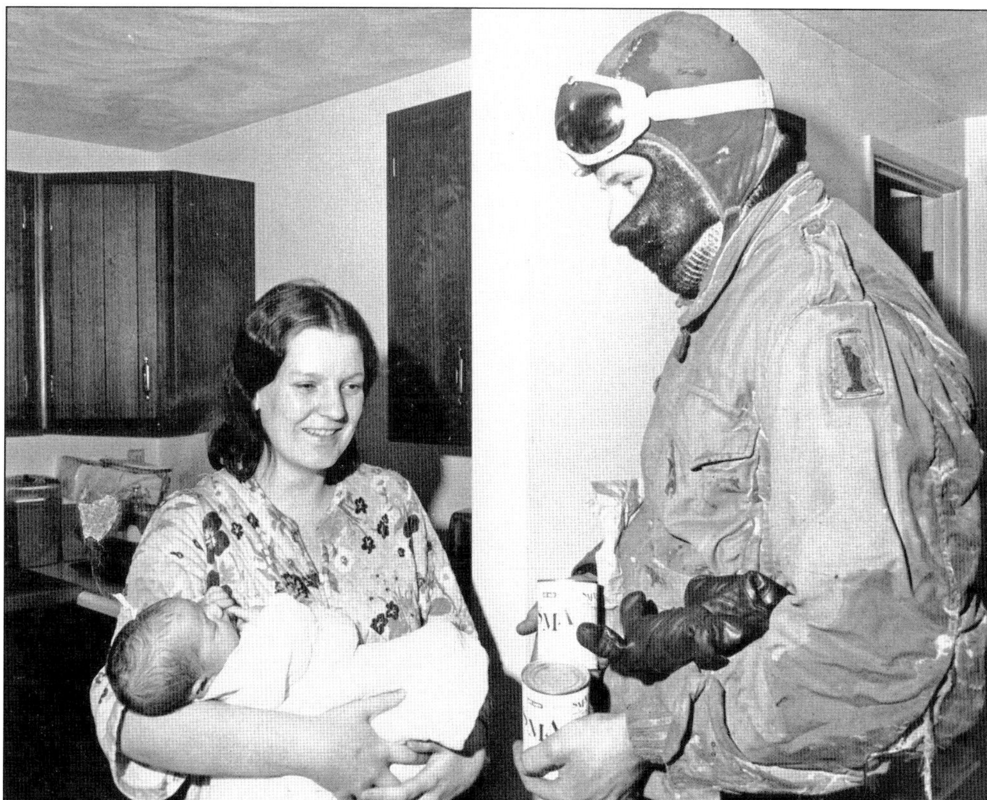

Another army was operating during the crisis—the Salvation Army. Here, Richard Messing delivers formula by snowmobile to Dorothy Trunto for her three-and-a-half-week-old daughter, Jacklyn Marie. Mr. Trunto was snowed in at the NiTec Paper Company and could not be there to assist his family. In Western New York, the Salvation Army fed 67,000 people, issued clothes to 4,500 people, and housed 851 people for six days starting on January 28, 1977. (NFPL.)

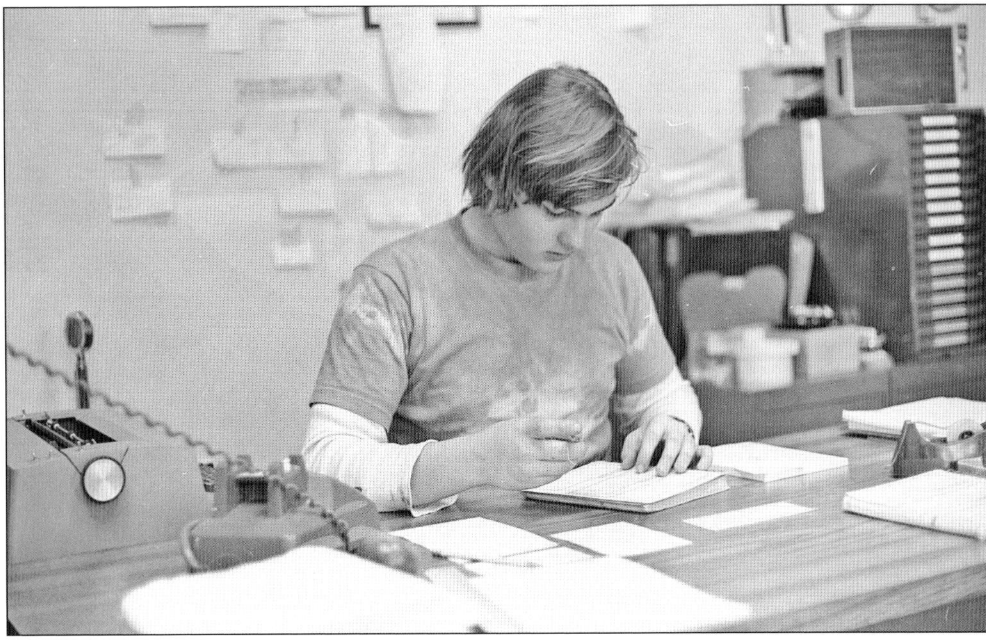

The American Red Cross was another organization that helped citizens in Western and Northern New York. The Red Cross conducted snowmobile rescue missions, provided food and shelter to those stranded by the storm, and fed hundreds of people through its mobile kitchens. (WDT.)

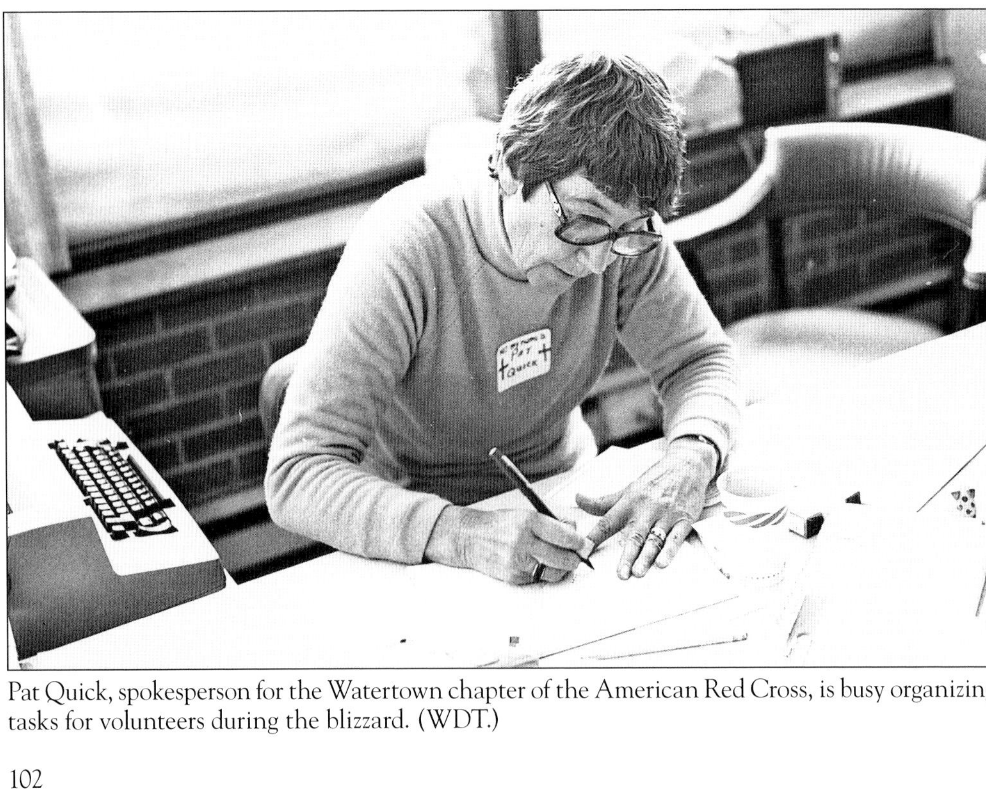

Pat Quick, spokesperson for the Watertown chapter of the American Red Cross, is busy organizing tasks for volunteers during the blizzard. (WDT.)

Police and fire crews made many emergency runs. Here, they prepare for a rescue near Niagara Falls. Firefighters in Niagara Falls had a tough time of it on January 28 and January 29, when they battled two separate blazes in that city that sent 20 firemen to the hospital for treatment. (NFPL.)

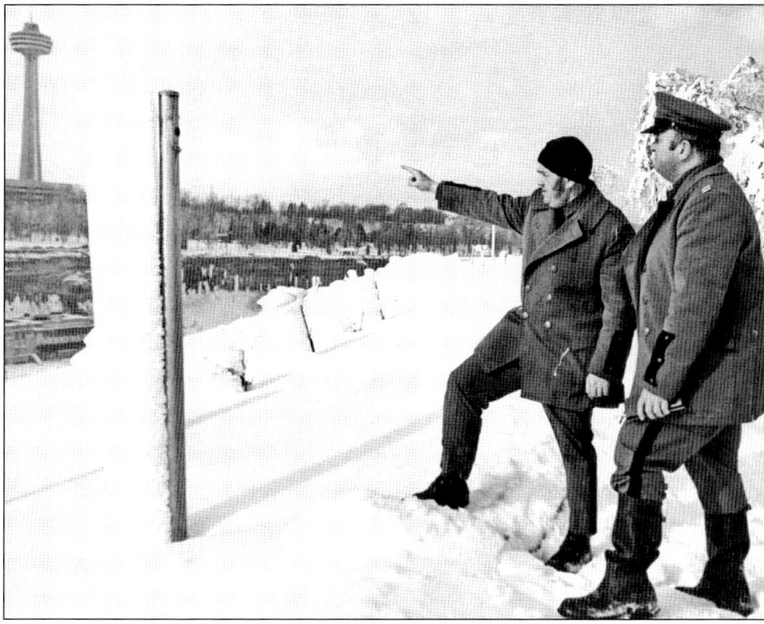

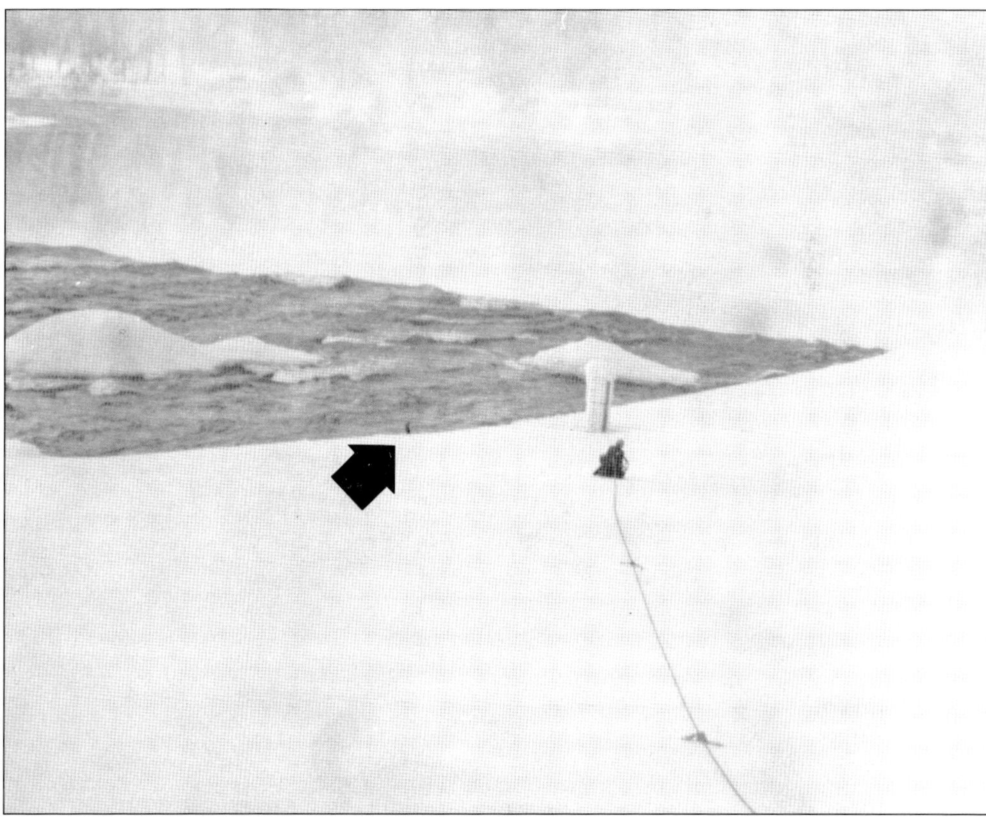

Slowly, the rescuers make their way to this individual trapped near the water. (NFPL.)

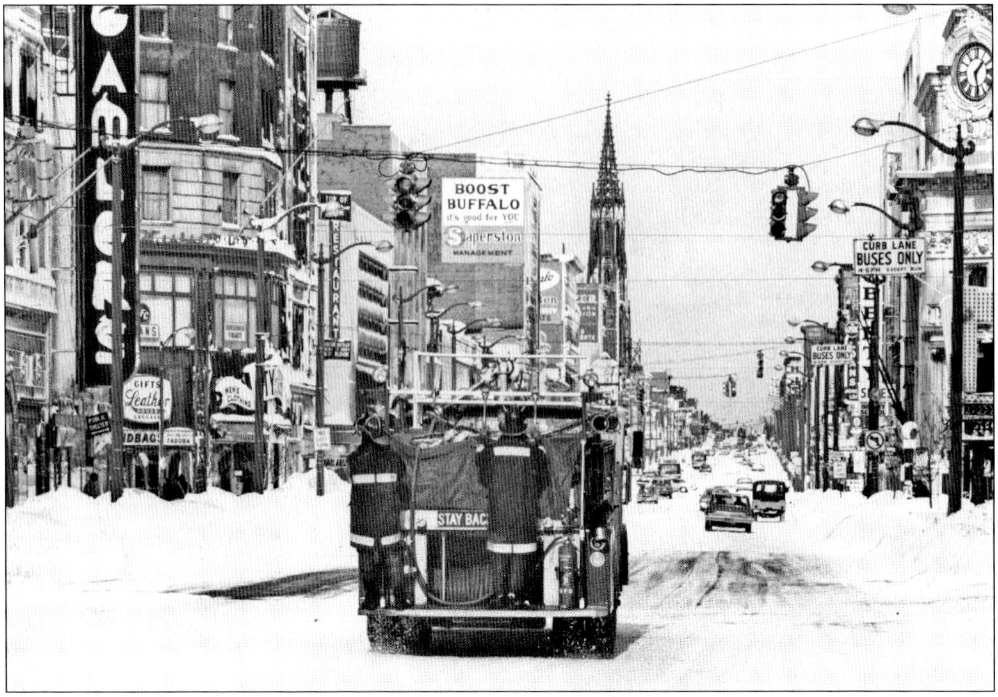

Fire crews were on call throughout the ordeal and well after. They rescued stranded motorists, sheltered people, and continued to fight fires, many of which were caused by faulty use of home heating appliances. The Buffalo Fire Department answered 1,570 emergency calls from January 28 through February 1. (BLBS.)

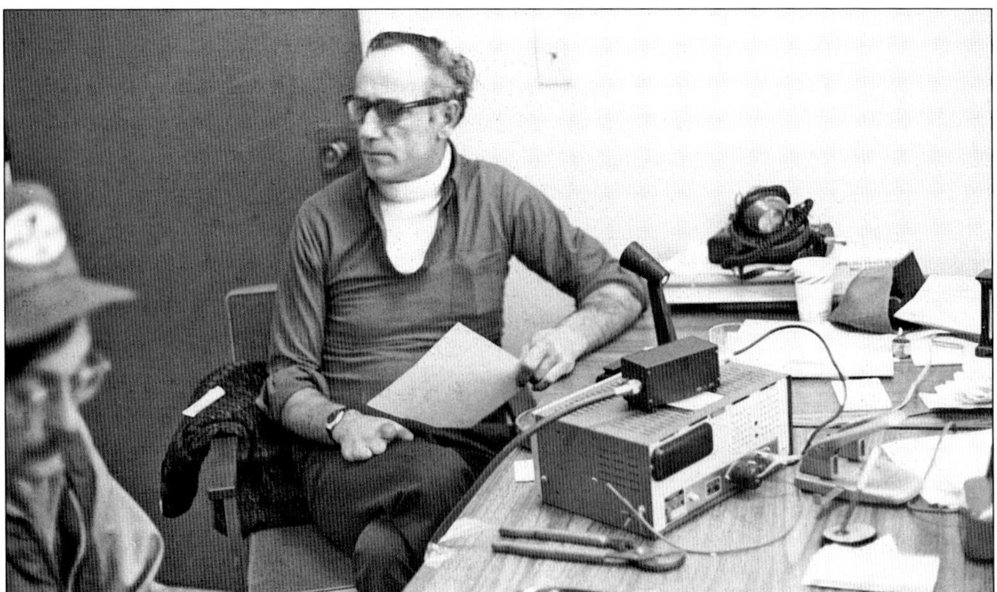

CB operators were integral to search and rescue operations throughout the crisis. Many volunteers were part of the REACT community (Radio Emergency Associated Communication Teams). They received messages and dispatched four-wheel-drive vehicles and snowmobiles to assist during the blizzard. (WDT.)

Commercial and noncommercial radio stations also played a critical role in allowing people to call in and ask for help or let people know where they were. People used the radio like a bulletin board during the crisis. Some radio personnel, like Danny Neaverth of Buffalo, were singled out for their essential contribution during the weather emergency. (WDT.)

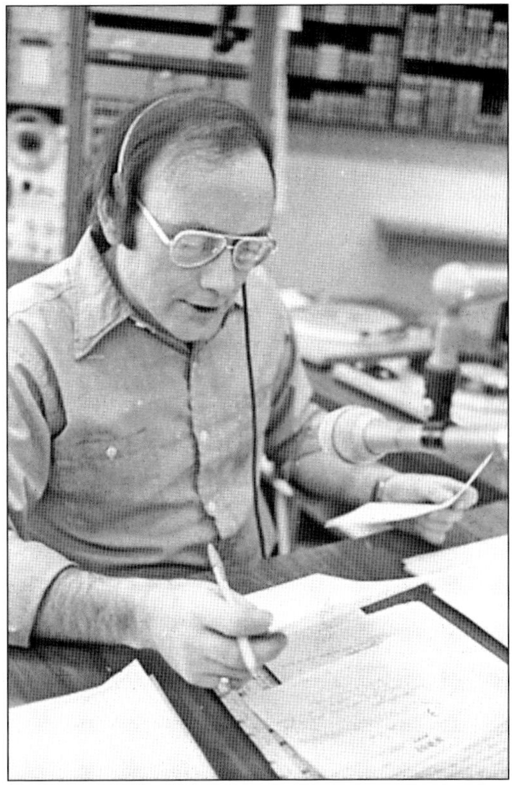

Snowmobilers working for the Red Cross checked parked vehicles for stranded motorists. Here, a flag tied to the antenna indicates that someone might be in the car. (NFPL.)

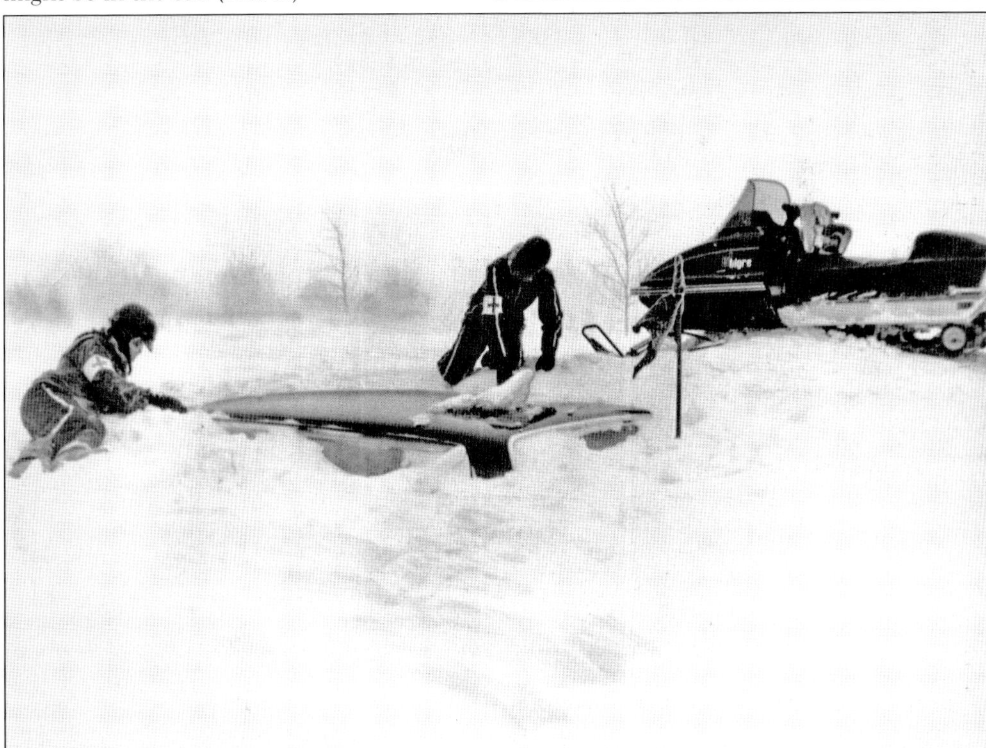

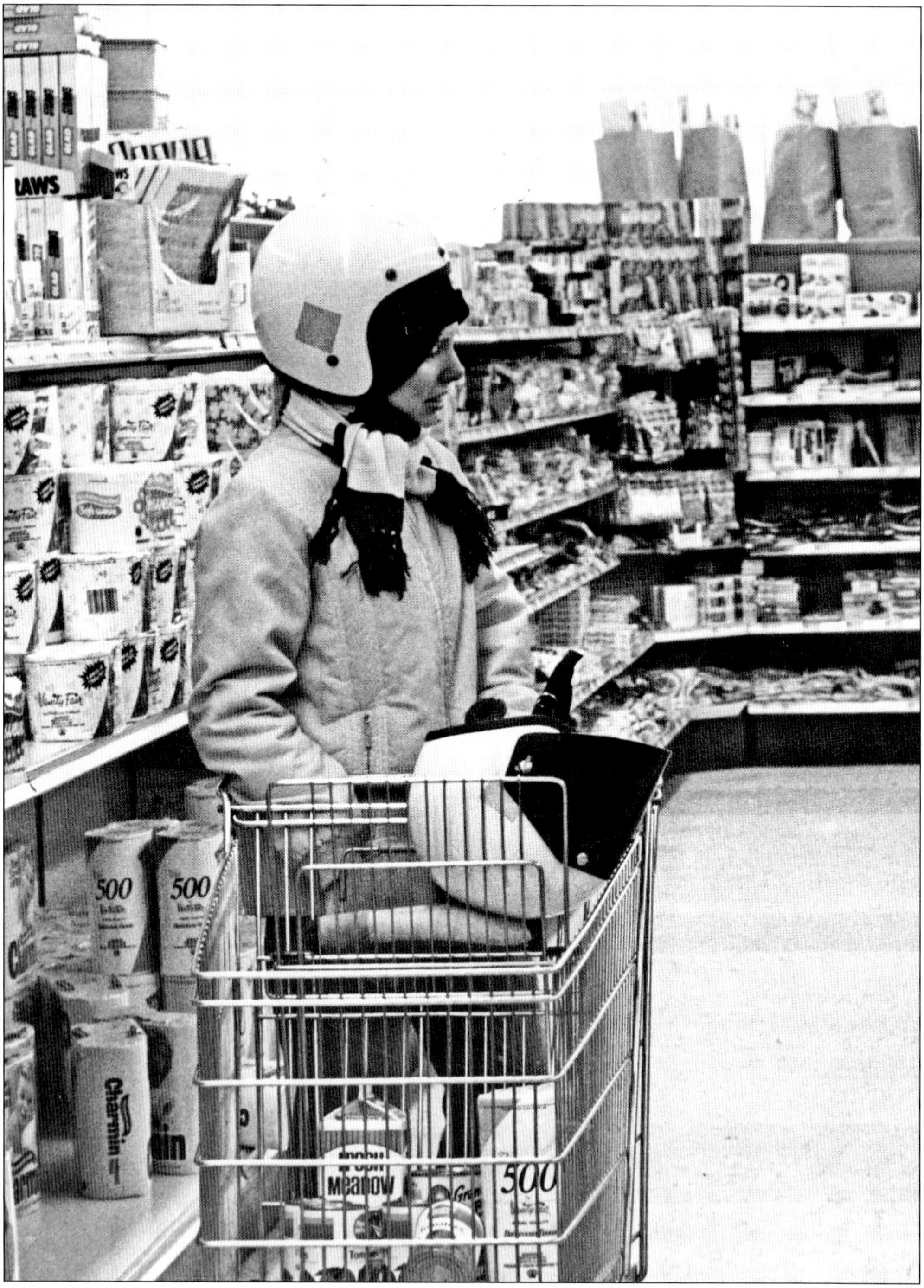

Snowmobilers assisted their communities by doing the shopping for those trapped in their homes. Everything from food to diapers to medicine needed to be delivered to hundreds of people stranded across the region. Volunteers working with different agencies either lent their snowmobiles or agreed to drive them to help their communities. (NFPL.)

Section 1 — Buffalo Evening News — Tuesday, February 1, 1977

THERE IS NO FOOD SHORTAGE AT BELLS!

We've got the staple items to meet the majority of your needs, and our employees are ready to do whatever it takes.

We're living through the worst winter in this century. Sub-zero temperatures. Record snowfalls. But we are pulling through it. There is no need to panic about food shortages.

Of course, there is some inconvenience. You may not be able to get a standing rib roast this week. Or your favorite imported cheese. But you will be able to get the staple items you need until this crisis is over.

Because Bells is going to do whatever it takes to get us through.

Every Bells Market listed below will stay open to meet the needs of the community it serves. Our employees are working long and hard. Our supplier, Peter J. Schmitt, is cooperating to the fullest. We're all in this together. So, don't start hoarding food.

Hoarding hurts everyone. It makes it hard to keep our stores stocked. It creates jams at checkout counters. And it's all unnecessary. Bells will make sure we have the food you have to have.

We can get through this crisis easily if everyone cooperates. So, do your part to help. Buy only what you need, when you need it. Remember, there is plenty of food to go around and we'll be making sure you get it.

Supermarkets worked hard to make sure they had necessary supplies. The now defunct Bells Markets put out a full-page ad to reassure customers its stores had what people needed. One grocery stored donated thousands of dollars' worth of bread to food pantries across the region. (Author's collection.)

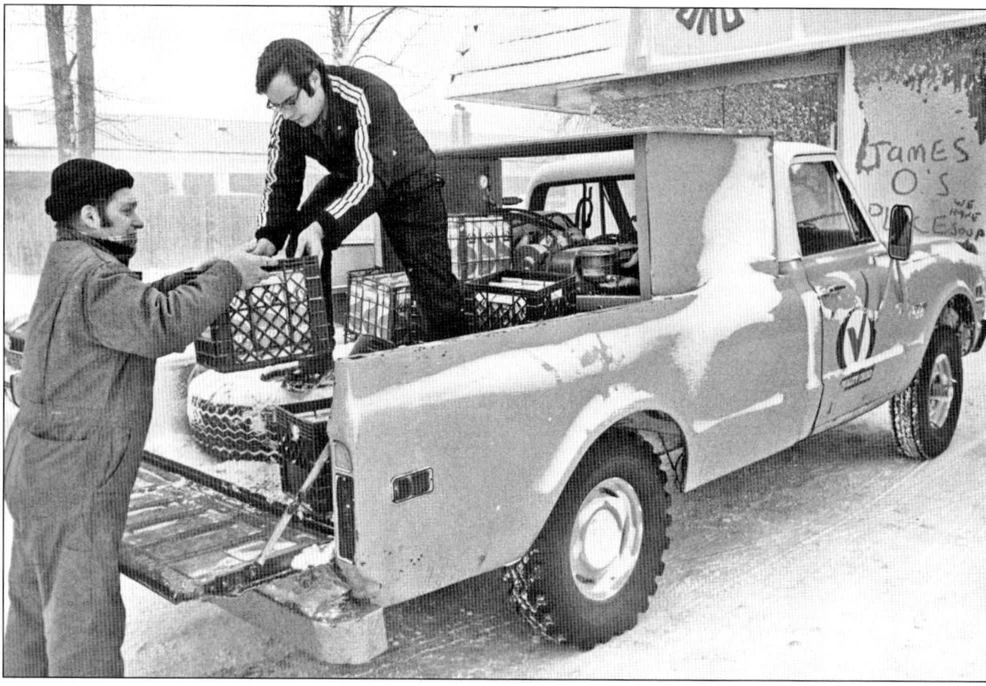

These Wendt employees in Niagara Falls picked up a milk supply for their customers. Wendt's Dairy operated in Niagara Falls from 1948 until it closed in 2008. (NFPL.)

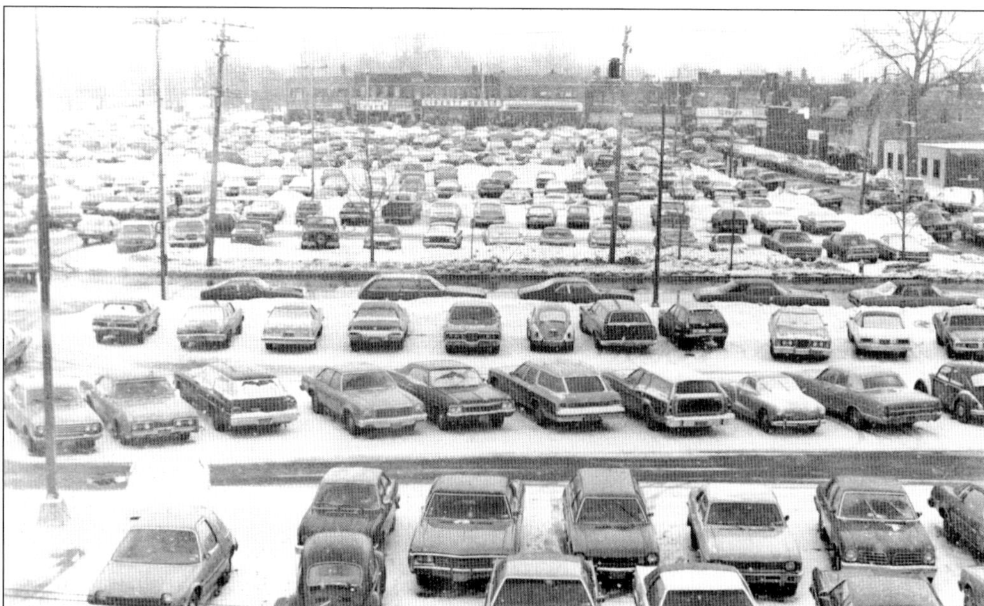

Food stamps were a big help to those who lost wages during the blizzard. Here, the city of Tonawanda looks like a giant parking lot. Individuals sought federal assistance in the aftermath of the storm. Food stamps were provided after President Carter declared nine counties in New York major disaster areas. (HST.)

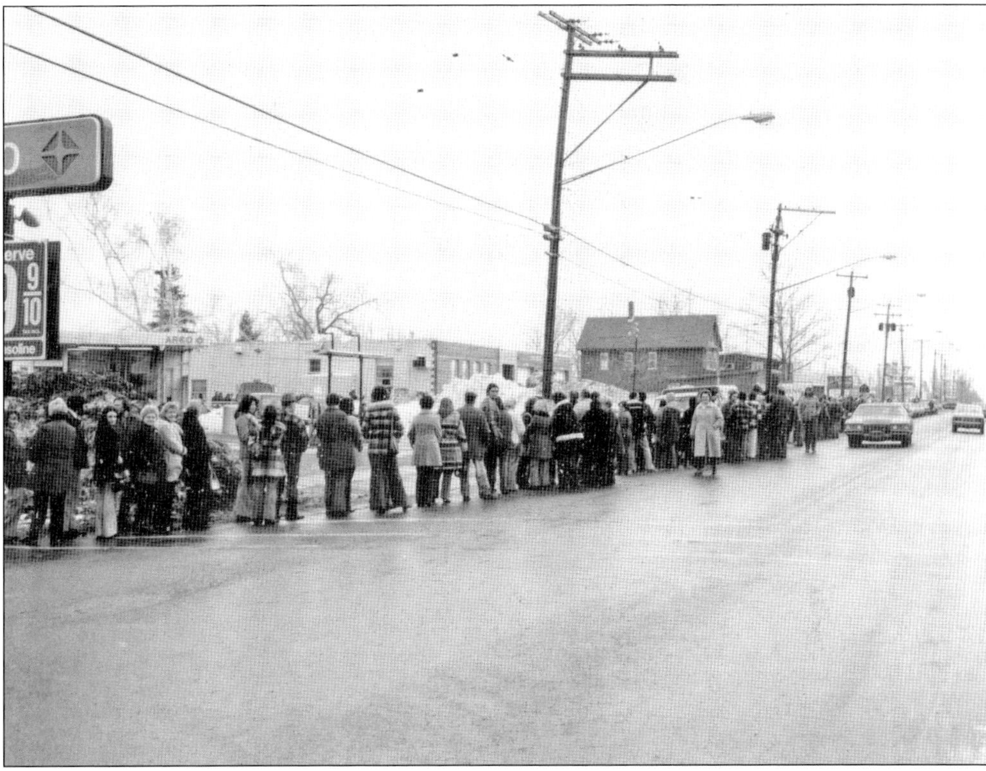

People waited in long lines in Alden for food stamps. The storm dislocated thousands of hourly workers in the area who lost wages during the blizzard and the subsequent ban on driving. Some people were eligible for unemployment compensation, but that did not fully replace their lost wages. (Leonard A. Weisbeck Sr.)

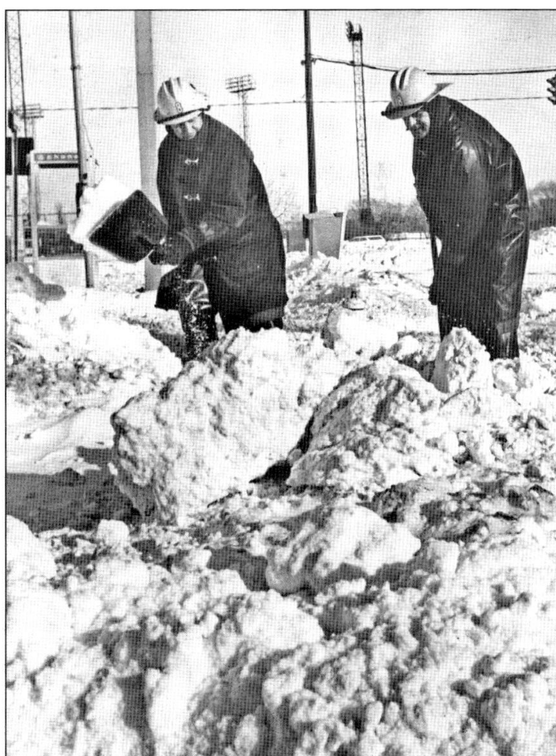

Utility workers had to dig in before they could get to work and restore vital services during the winter of 1976–1977. Fortunately, few people lost power during the blizzard. Some telephone lines went down. To repair these services, crews braved the cold. (NFPL.)

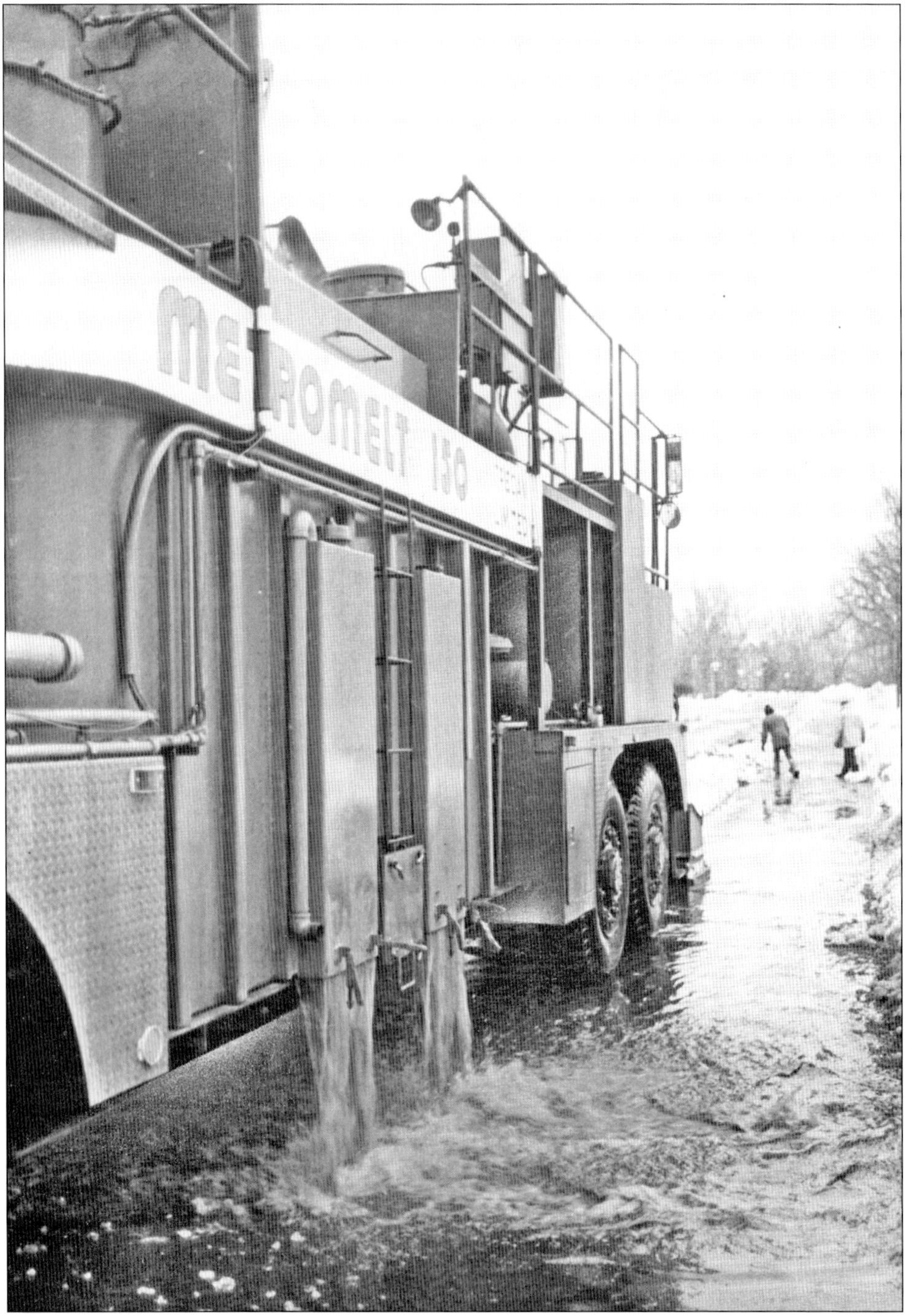

The people of Western New York received generous support from others across the United States and beyond. This snow melter was loaned to the City of Buffalo from Toronto, Canada. Snow melters were popular items in the 1960s and 1970s. They melted snow so it could be dumped into storm drains and sewers, thus saving crews from having to haul it away or attempting to find a location to put it. The winter of 1976–1977 was so snowy that there were few empty lots left to put the snow. (BLBS.)

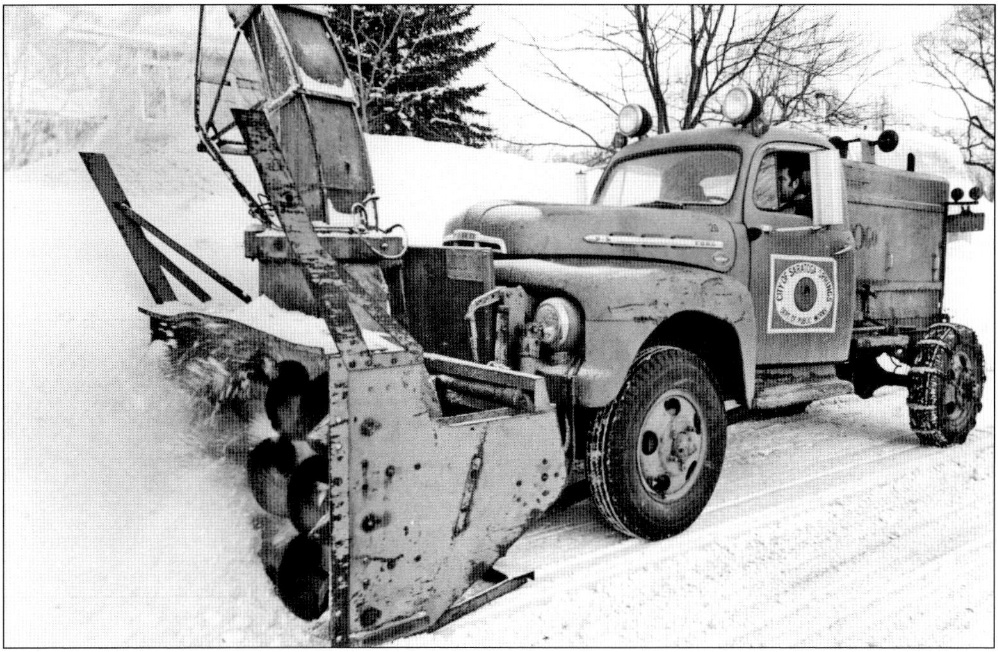

Saratoga Springs, New York, sent this plow to help the people of Batavia. Public works officials from across the state could empathize with the struggle of the crews in Western New York. Many offered men and matériel to assist in combatting the snow. (GCHD.)

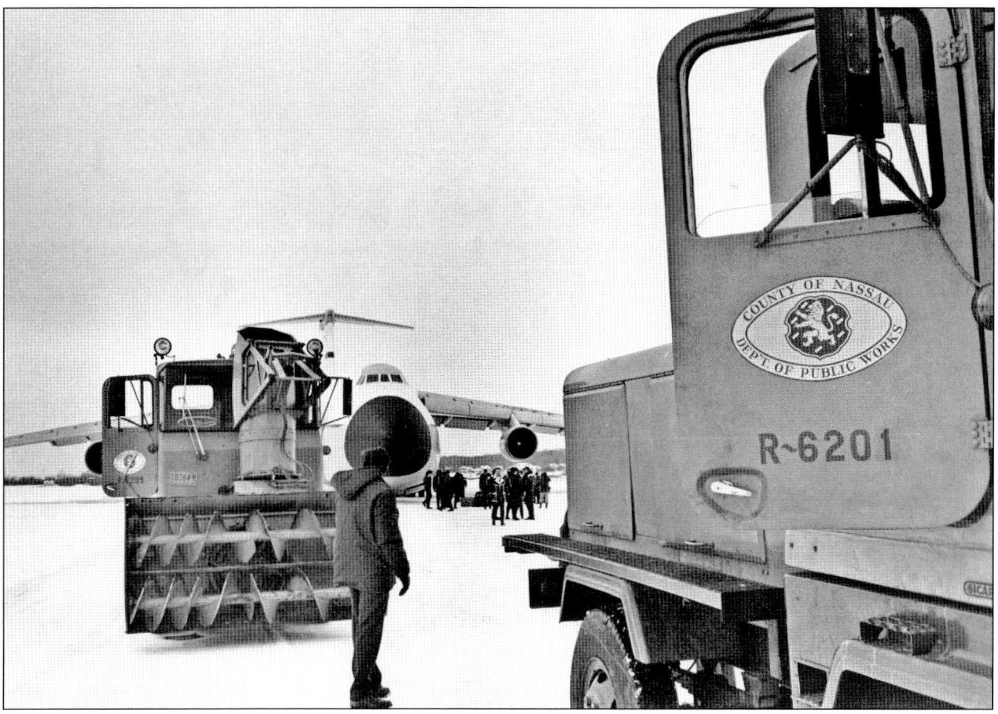

Nassau County lent giant snowblowers to move the snow. Like the snowblowers people use on their driveways, these industrial-sized versions blew the snow out of the roads rather than plowing it away. (BLBS.)

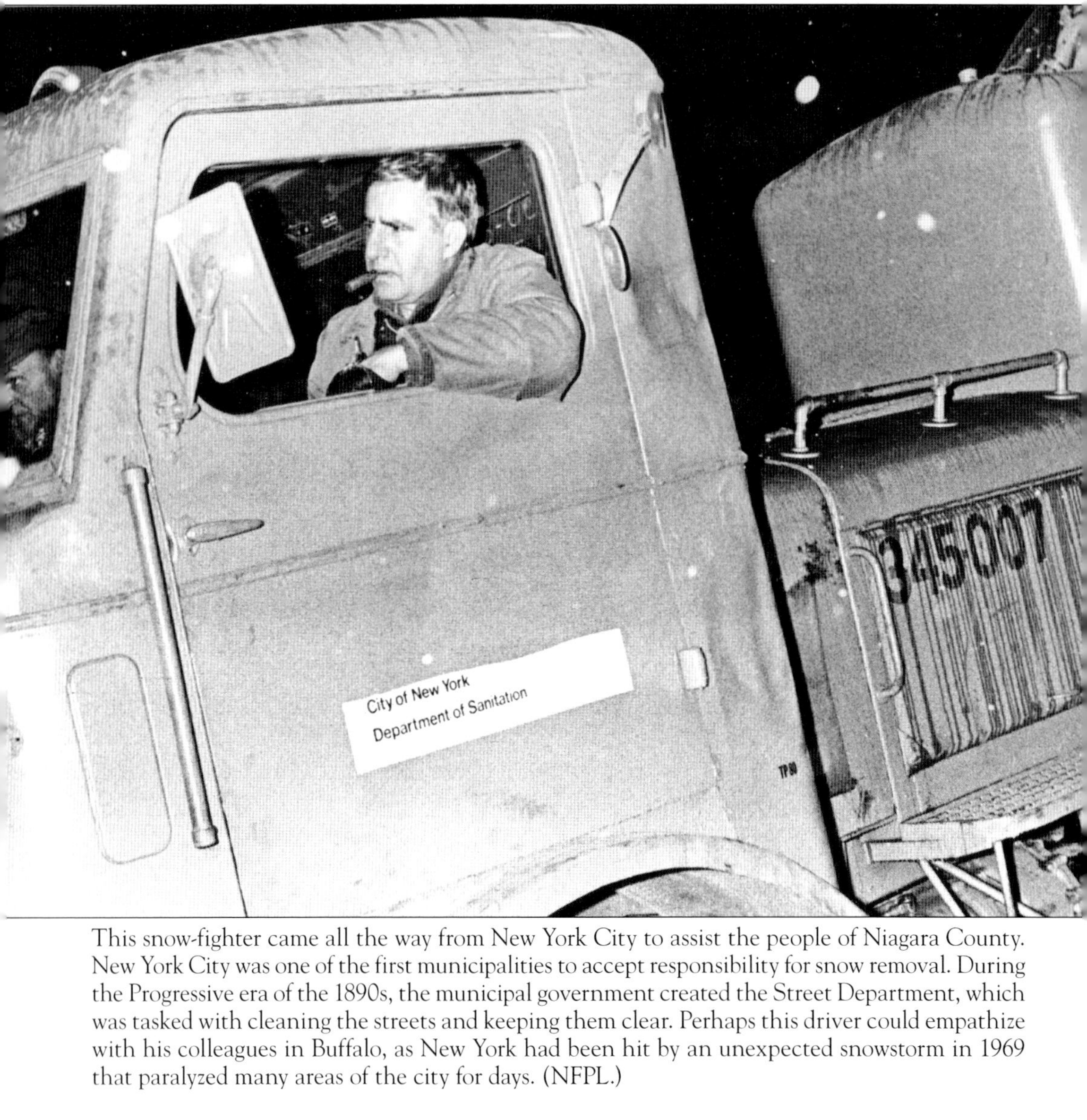

This snow-fighter came all the way from New York City to assist the people of Niagara County. New York City was one of the first municipalities to accept responsibility for snow removal. During the Progressive era of the 1890s, the municipal government created the Street Department, which was tasked with cleaning the streets and keeping them clear. Perhaps this driver could empathize with his colleagues in Buffalo, as New York had been hit by an unexpected snowstorm in 1969 that paralyzed many areas of the city for days. (NFPL.)

County Executive Ned Regan checks out the snowblower from Nassau County. Regan was a hands-on county executive and seemed to be everywhere at once during the crisis. (BLBS.)

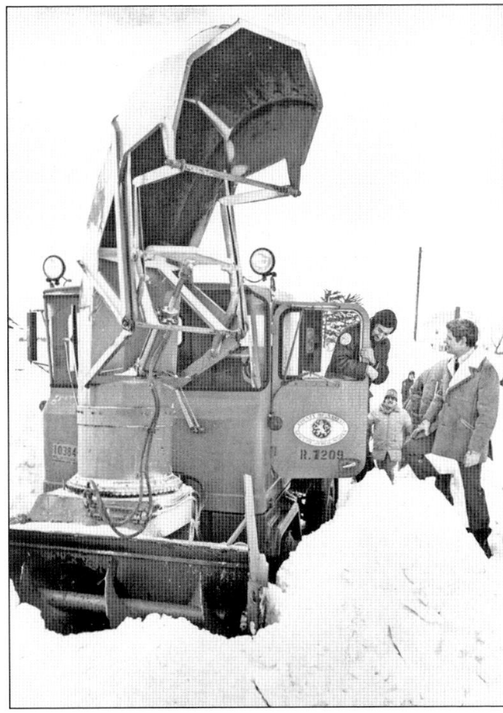

Crews from across the state helped clear snow and open roads. Between federal and state officials, the combined forces managed to clear the snow out of the major urban areas by mid-February. (NFPL.)

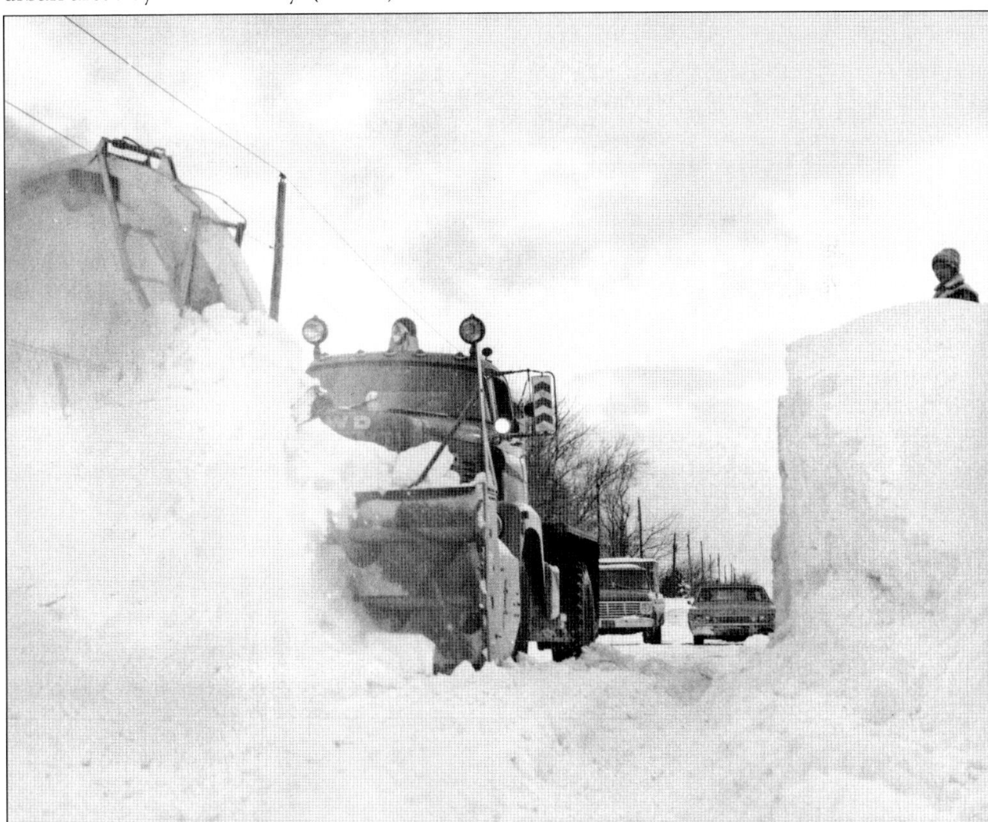

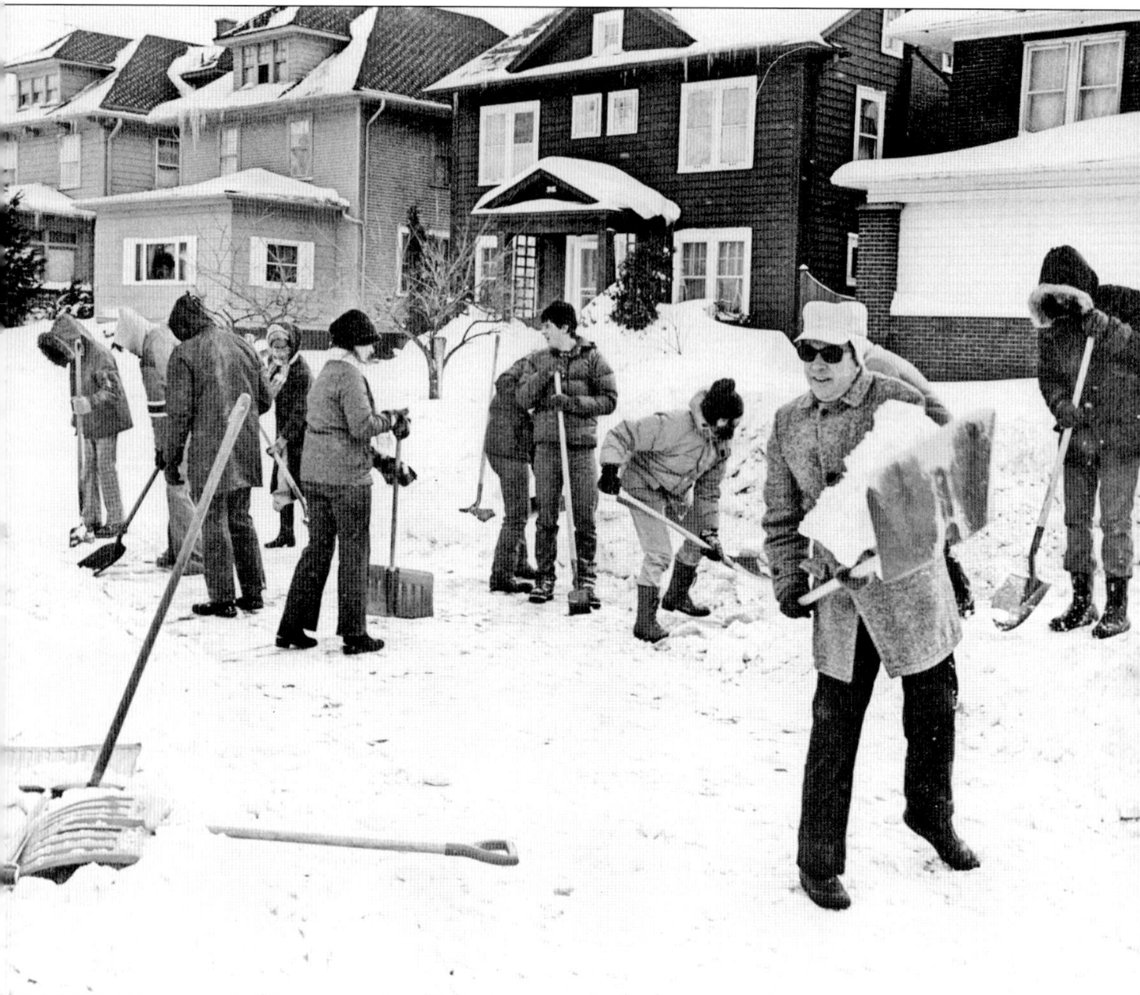

Neighborhoods banded together to open their roads and sidewalks. There are numerous stories of neighbors helping neighbors and of people combining their efforts to clear not just their driveways and sidewalks but also their streets. In some cases, people ended up feeding and housing complete strangers during the blizzard. (BLBS.)

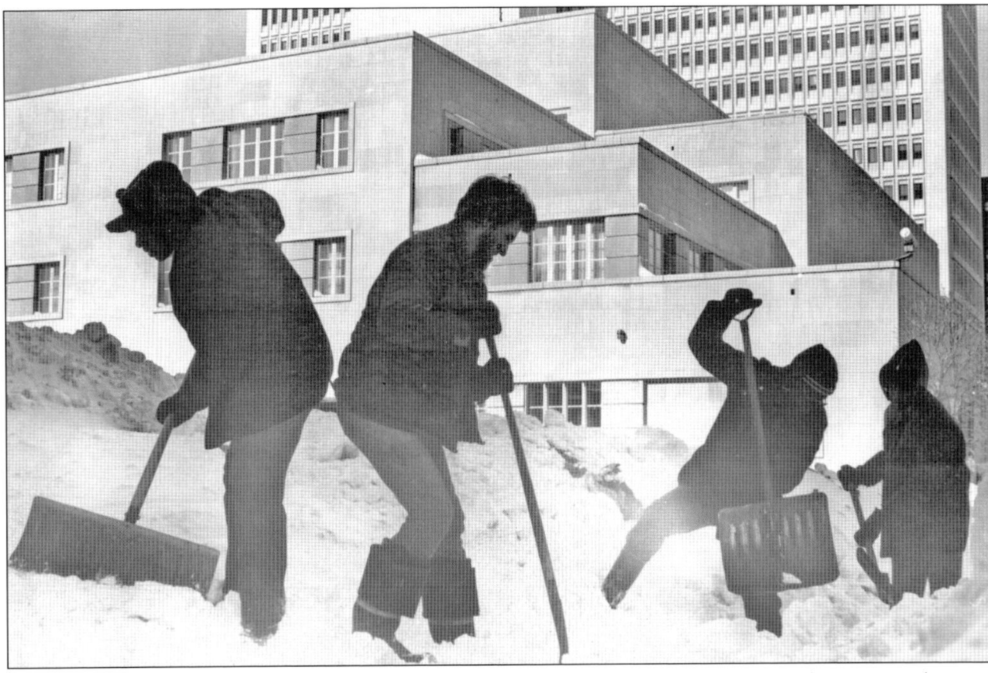

Helping one another out during the storm was essential to getting things back to normal. Here, students are shoveling the Buffalo State campus. (BLBS.)

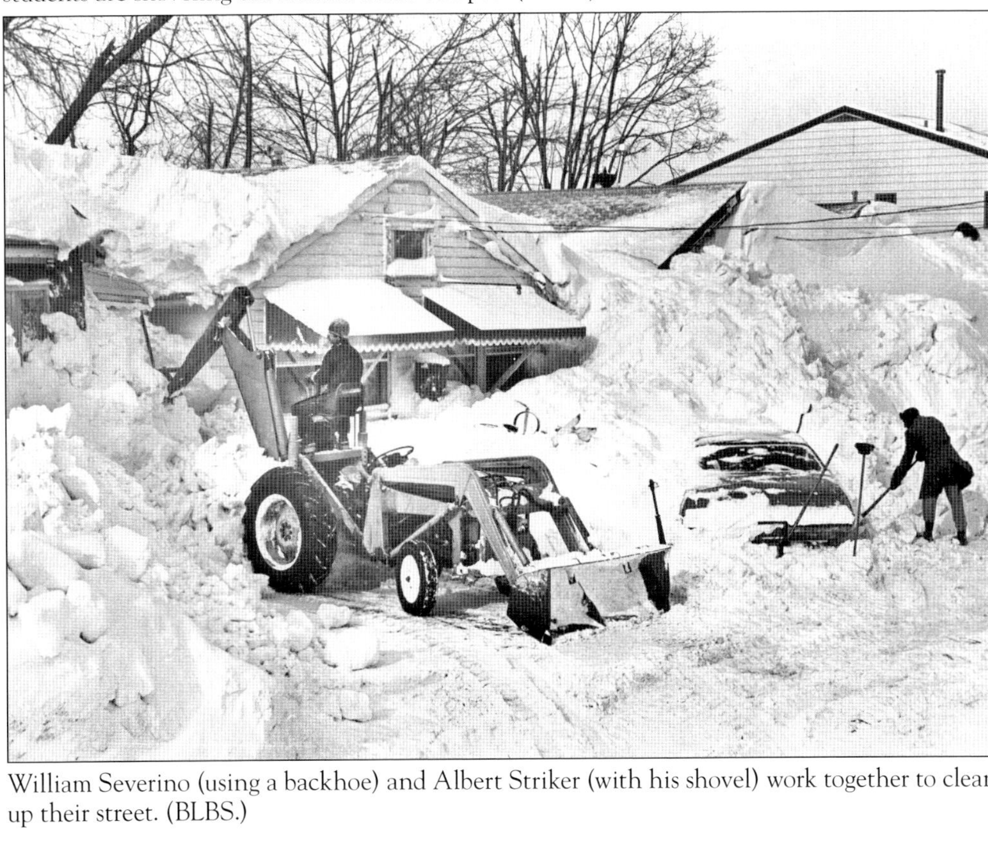

William Severino (using a backhoe) and Albert Striker (with his shovel) work together to clean up their street. (BLBS.)

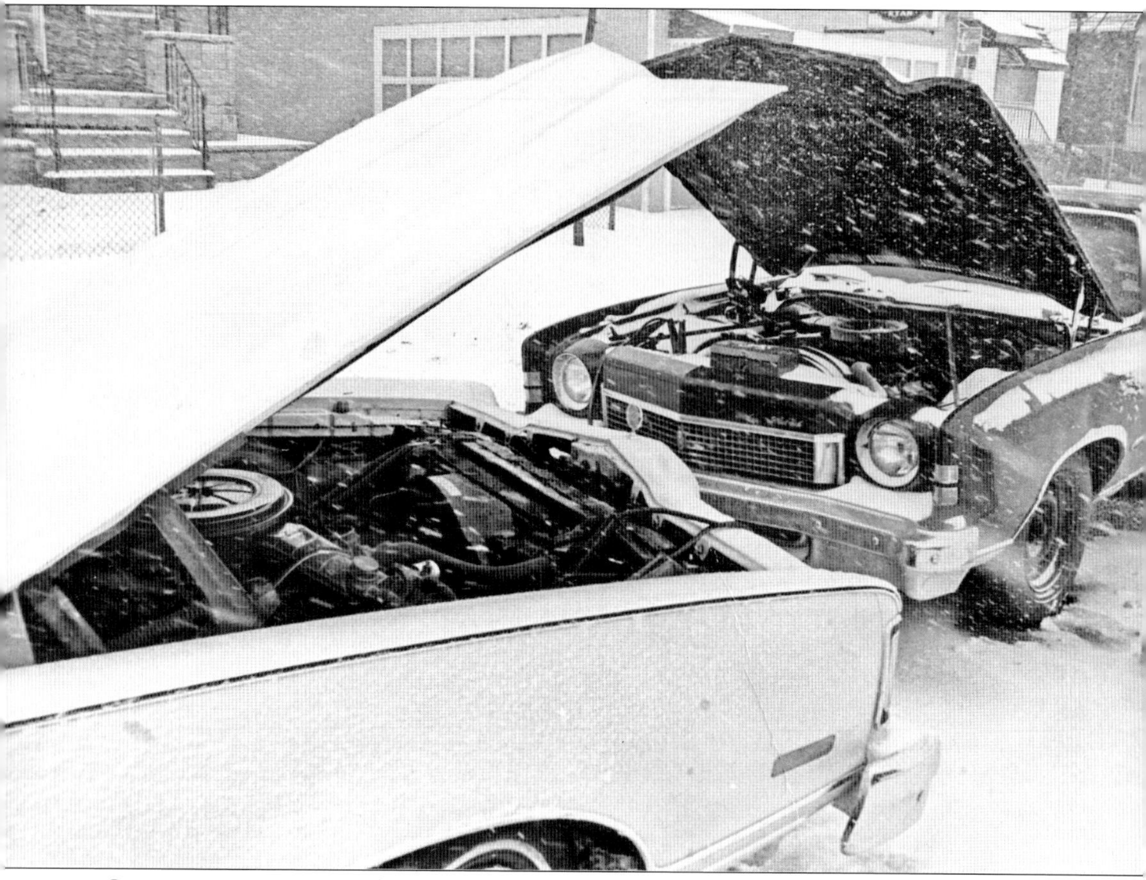

Starting one's car in the extreme cold often meant getting help from a friend or neighbor. (NFPL.)

Five

HAVING FUN

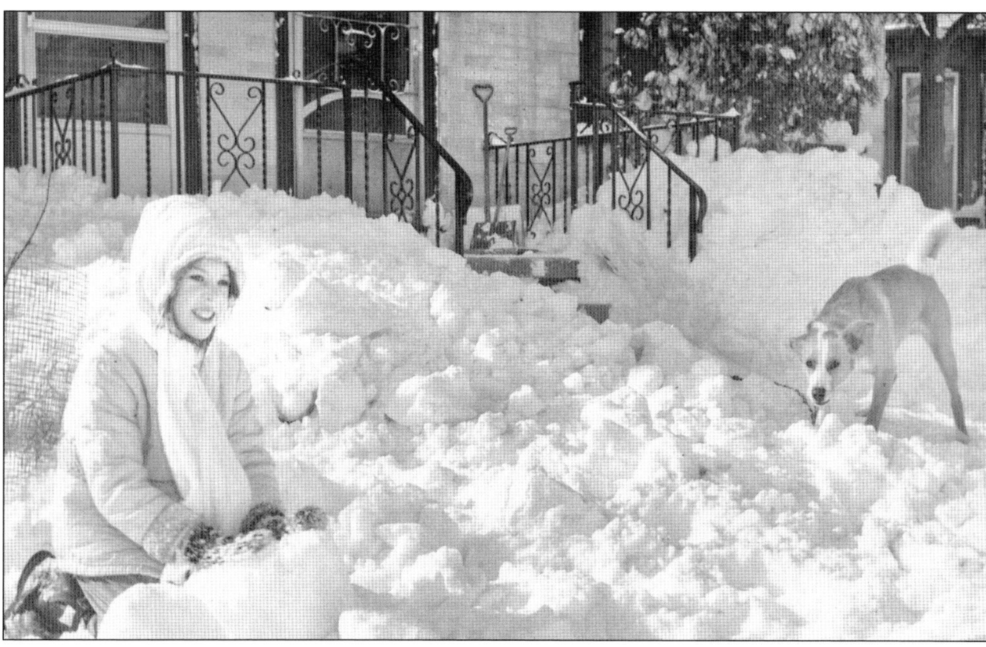

For many young people, the blizzard was an adventure. Many students in the Buffalo area had at least two weeks out of school due to snowstorms that occurred before the blizzard and the delay in getting streets and rural roads cleared. For children, the blizzard was one giant snow day and an opportunity to play in the snow or hang out with friends. What they remember about the blizzard is likely different from what their parents were thinking or feeling at the time. (HST.)

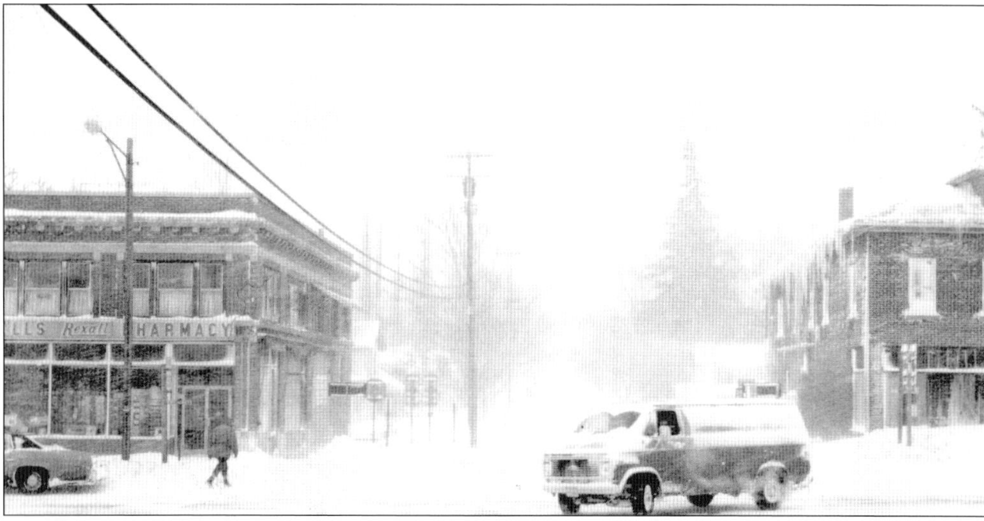

For adults, the blizzard may have meant a trip to the local pharmacy, like this Stowell's Pharmacy in Alden, at the corner of Broadway and Exchange Street. The pharmacy had prescription drugs, makeup, greeting cards, magazines, candy, and other novelties. Stowell's Pharmacy began in 1911 as Swain's Pharmacy. In 1920, Swain sold it Ralph Stowell, who started at Swain's as a stock boy. The Stowell family operated the pharmacy until 1985, when it was sold again and renamed the Alden Pharmacy. (Leonard A. Weisbeck Sr.)

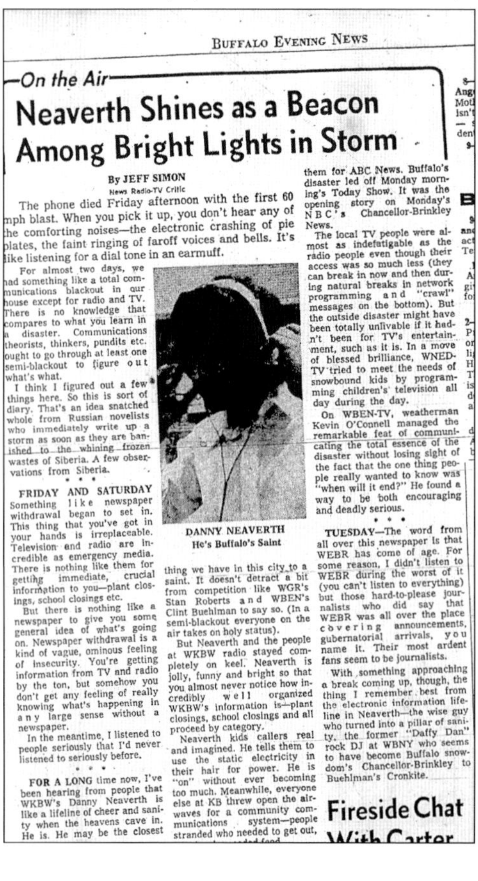

BUFFALO EVENING NEWS

—On the Air

Neaverth Shines as a Beacon Among Bright Lights in Storm

By JEFF SIMON
News Radio-TV Critic

The phone died Friday afternoon with the first 60 mph blast. When you pick it up, you don't hear any of the comforting noises—the electronic crashing of pie plates, the faint ringing of faroff voices and bells. It's like listening for a dial tone in an earmuff.

For almost two days, we had something like a total communications blackout in our house except for radio and TV. There is no knowledge that compares to what you learn in a disaster. Communications theorists, thinkers, pundits etc. ought to go through at least one semi-blackout to figure out what's what.

I think I figured out a few things here. So this is sort of diary. That's an idea snatched whole from Russian novelists who immediately write up a storm as soon as they are banished to the whining frozen wastes of Siberia. A few observations from Siberia.

• • •

FRIDAY AND SATURDAY Something like newspaper withdrawal began to set in. This thing that you've got in your hands is irreplaceable. Television and radio are incredible as emergency media. There is nothing like them for getting immediate, crucial information to you—plant closings, school closings etc.

But there is nothing like a newspaper to give you some general idea of what's going on. Newspaper withdrawal is a kind of vague, ominous feeling of insecurity. You're getting information from TV and radio by the ton, but somehow you don't get any feeling of really knowing what's happening in any large sense without a newspaper.

In the meantime, I listened to people seriously that I'd never listened to seriously before.

• • •

FOR A LONG time now, I've been hearing from people that WKBW's Danny Neaverth is like a lifeline of cheer and sanity when the heavens cave in. He is. He may be the closest thing we have in this city to a saint. It doesn't detract a bit from competition like WGR's Stan Roberts and WBEN's Clint Buehlman to say so. (In a semi-blackout everyone on the air takes on holy status).

DANNY NEAVERTH
He's Buffalo's Saint

But Neaverth and the people at WKBW radio stayed completely on keel. Neaverth is jolly, funny and bright so that you almost never notice how incredibly well organized WKBW's information is—plant closings, school closings and all proceed by category.

Neaverth kids callers real and imagined. He tells them to use the static electricity in their hair for power. He is "on" without ever becoming too much. Meanwhile, everyone else at KB threw open the airwaves for a community communications system—people stranded who needed to get out,

them for ABC News. Buffalo's disaster led off Monday morning's Today Show. It was the opening story on Monday's NBC's Chancellor-Brinkley News.

The local TV people were almost as indefatigable as the radio people even though their access was so much less (they can break in now and then during natural breaks in network programming and "crawl" messages on the bottom). But the outside disaster might have been totally unlivable if it hadn't been for TV's entertainment, such as it is. In a move of blessed brilliance, WNED-TV tried to meet the needs of snowbound kids by programming children's television all day during the day.

On WBEN-TV, weatherman Kevin O'Connell managed the remarkable feat of communicating the total essence of the disaster without losing sight of the fact that the one thing people really wanted to know was "when will it end?" He found a way to be both encouraging and deadly serious.

• • •

TUESDAY—The word from all over this newspaper is that WEBR has come of age. For some reason, I didn't listen to WEBR during the worst of it (you can't listen to everything) but those hard-to-please journalists who did say that WEBR was all over the place covering announcements, gubernatorial arrivals, you name it. Their most ardent fans seem to be journalists.

With something approaching a break coming up, though, the thing I remember best from the electronic information lifeline in Neaverth—the wise guy who turned into a pillar of sanity, the former "Daffy Dan" rock DJ at WBNY who seems to have become Buffalo snowdom's Chancellor-Brinkley to Buehlman's Cronkite.

Fireside Chat

Telephone lines went down, and television could be fuzzy in bad weather, but the radio was a constant companion to many people during the blizzard. It supplied information and entertainment. In the 1970s, WKBW radio was a Top 40 station and often No. 1 in the Buffalo market. Danny Neaverth is a legendary broadcaster. As the morning disc jockey for WKBW, he created a theater of the mind whose cast of voice characters included Artie, a foil for many of Neaverth's gags. During the storm, Neaverth balanced humor with good will and seriousness to keep people's spirits up and their sanity intact. (Author's collection.)

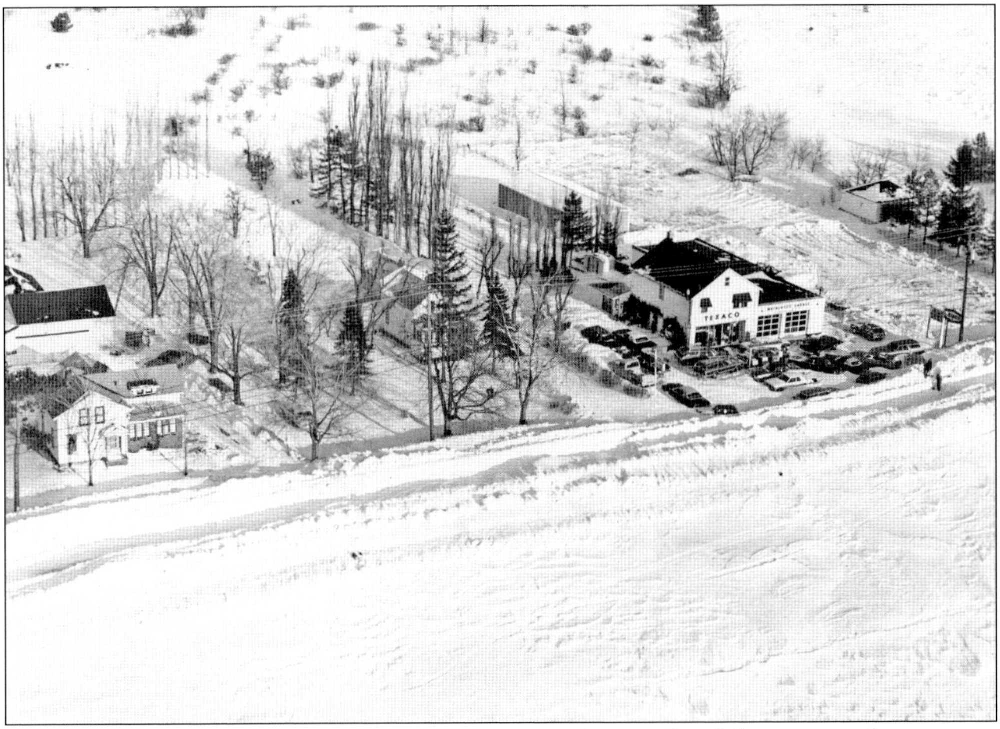

This image of Route 16, near East Aurora, New York, shows a closed down, snowed over scene. East Aurora, 16 miles south of Buffalo, is in the snowbelt and is ready and able to deal with indoor confinement in the winter. Stuck at home, many people amused themselves with typical indoor winter activities. People played board games, a popular family activity in the 1970s, while they ate toast and drank cocoa. Some knitted, put together jigsaw puzzles, or read. In the age before there was an Internet, people still found ways to bond during long stretches of winter. (BLBS.)

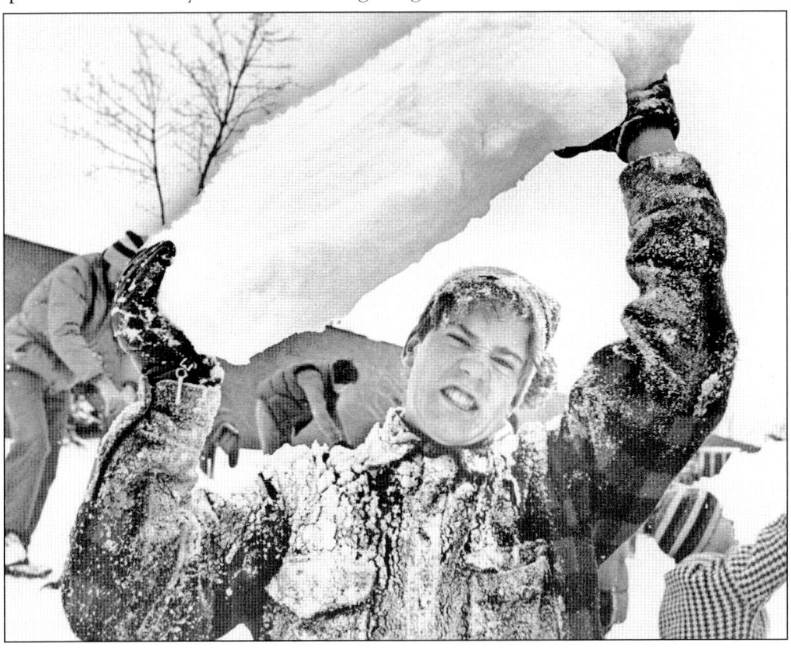

Feeling the effects of cabin fever, Kevin Carey of Buffalo found an easy way to work out his stress by hurling the snow out of his driveway. (BLBS.)

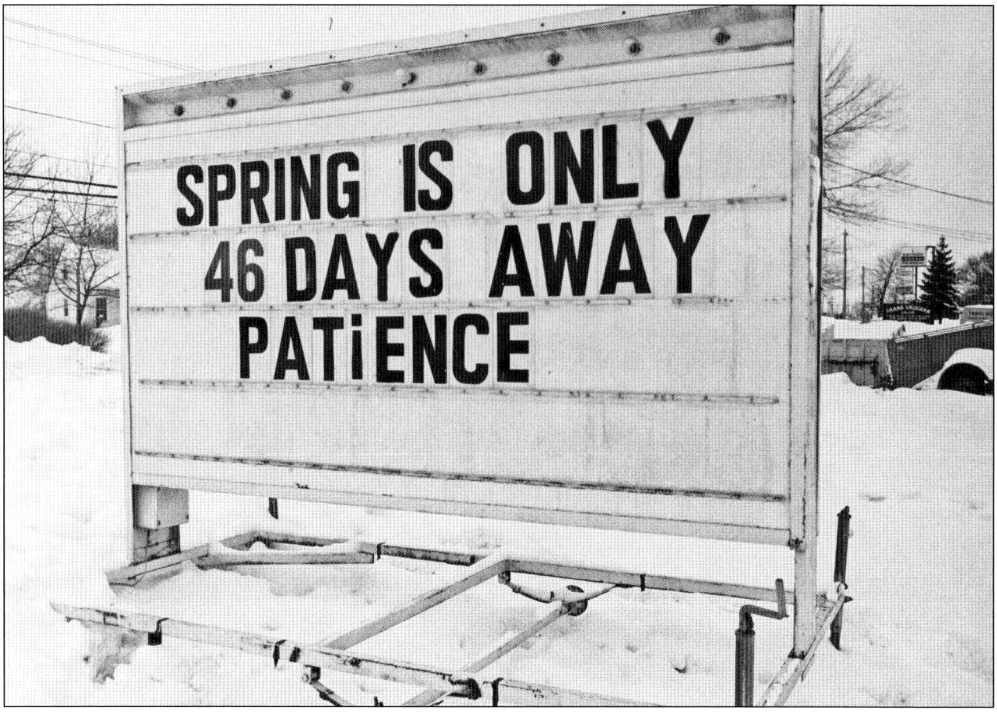

Some in Niagara County kept positive thoughts of spring as they struggled through the cold, wind, and snow. (NFPL.)

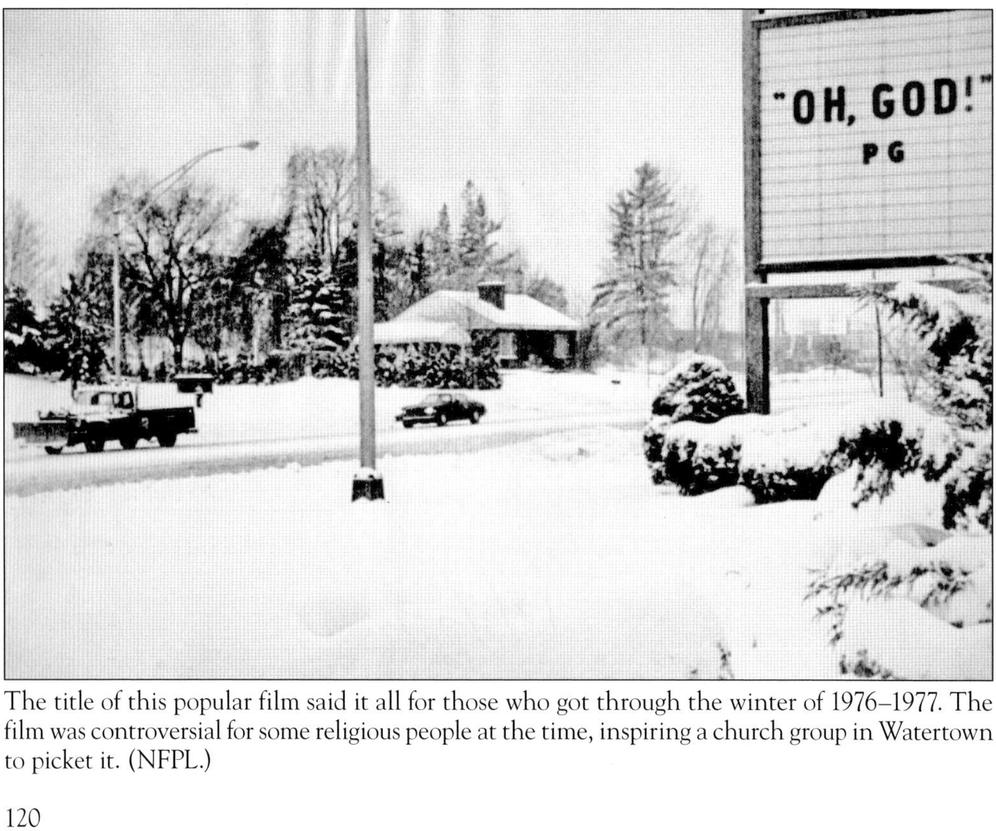

The title of this popular film said it all for those who got through the winter of 1976–1977. The film was controversial for some religious people at the time, inspiring a church group in Watertown to picket it. (NFPL.)

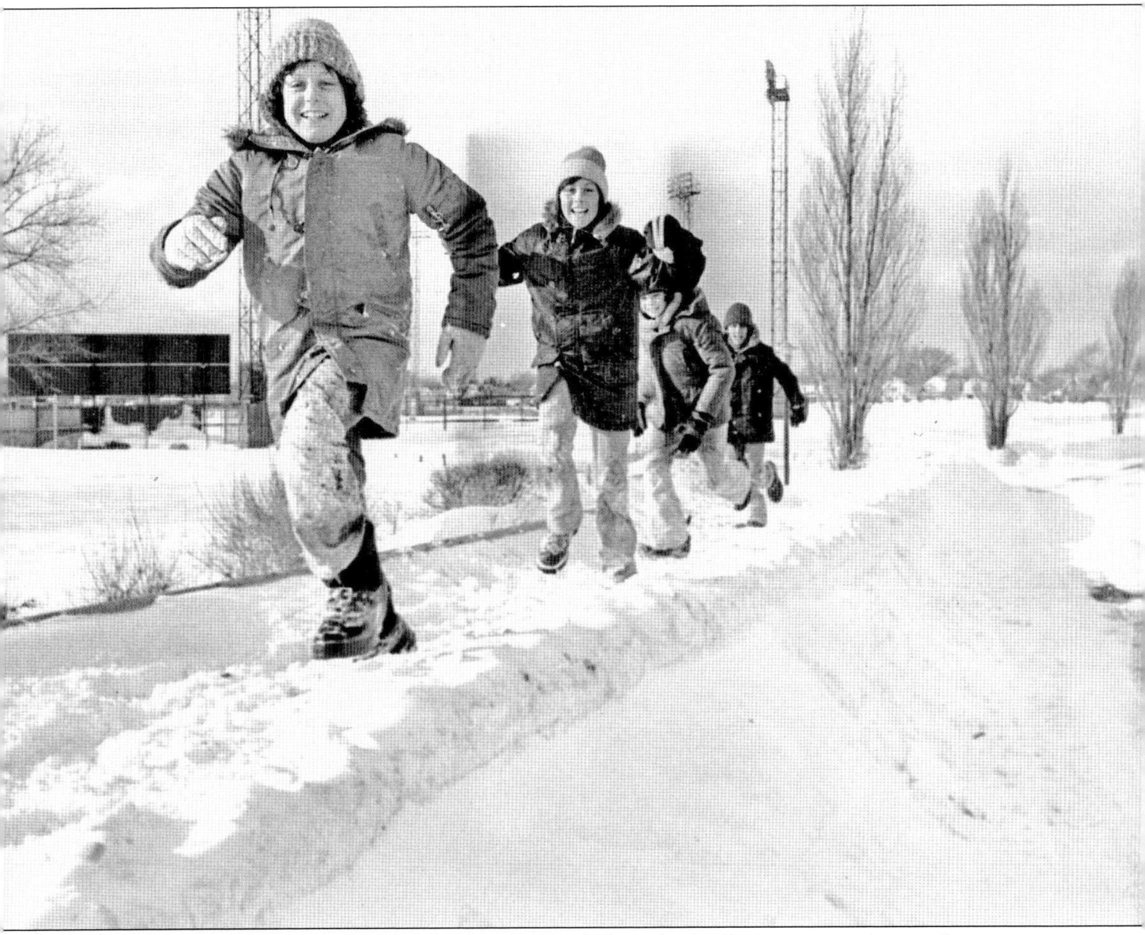

These children in Niagara Falls found that playing follow-the-leader was more fun in the snow. Trapped inside the house during the winter, children were happy to get outdoors after February 1. Many parents were probably also pleased that their children were outside getting fresh air and exercise and working off steam. These children are also exhibiting typical play behavior in the 1970s. This was a time when unsupervised, independently directed play was expected of children. Contemporary child-rearing practices are much different, with children today more likely to experience supervised and adult-directed play behavior. (NFPL.)

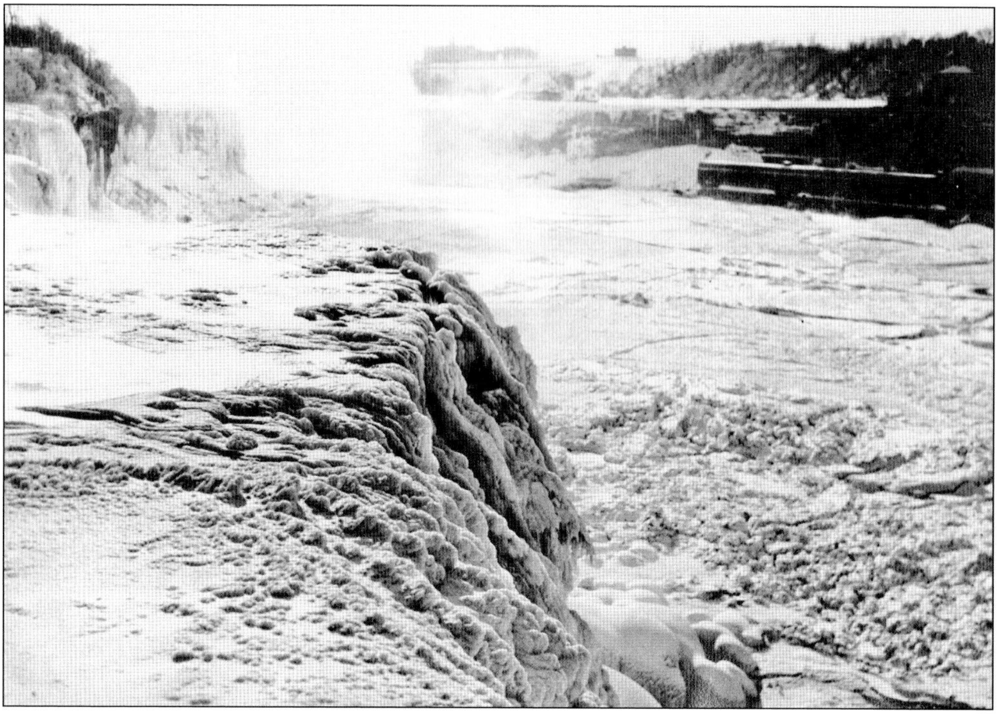

Once the weather broke, some people made their way to see Niagara Falls. Due to the historical cold weather, the falls froze. This is an image of the American Falls, with the Canadian Falls in the background. The American Falls and Canadian Falls are separated by Goat Island. (NFPL.)

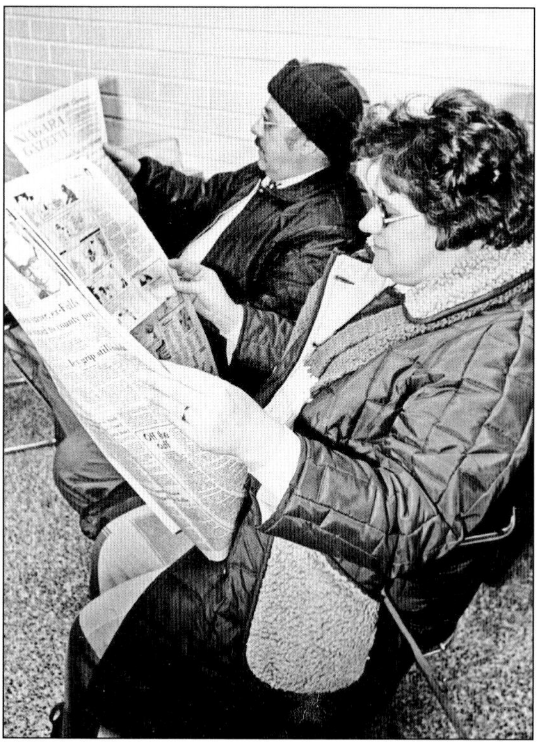

These adults, trapped by the blizzard, read the daily comics. These consisted of comic strips that may be familiar to readers today. Popular comics of the 1970s included *Blondie*, which began in 1930 and characterizes the adventures of Dagwood and his family; *Hagar the Horrible*, which began in 1973 and is a comic about the misadventures of a Viking and his family; and *Doonesbury*, launched in 1970 as a comic about politics and society. Less well known today were popular strips like *Love Is*, which began in 1960 and featured tastefully nude characters accompanied by a one-line sentence describing what love is, and *Momma*, begun in 1970 and featuring an overbearing, guilt-inducing mother who controlled her family through love and guilt. (NFPL.)

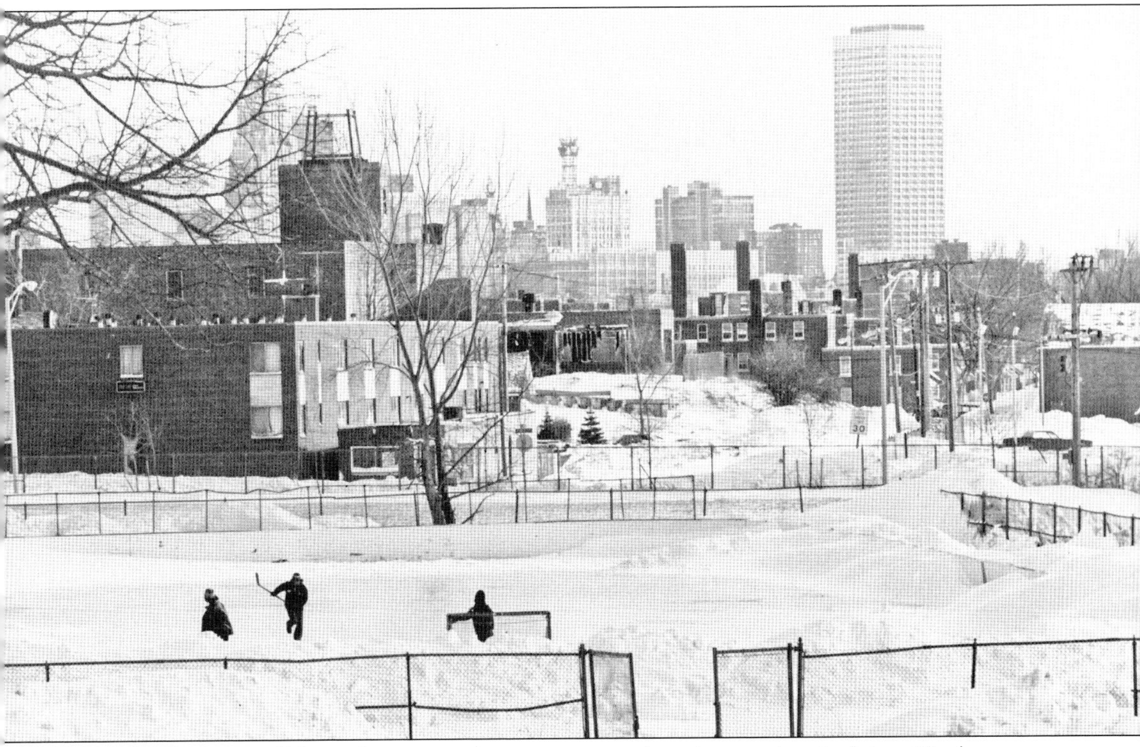

Playing hockey in Buffalo is always popular, no matter what the weather is doing. Hockey was often played in the Buffalo area on small ponds and community centers and town ice rinks. Games might be supervised but were spontaneous. Buffalo's professional hockey team, the Sabres, had been in the Stanley Cup finals against the Philadelphia Flyers in 1975 and inspired many young people to hockey fever. The city of Buffalo looms in the background. (BLBS.)

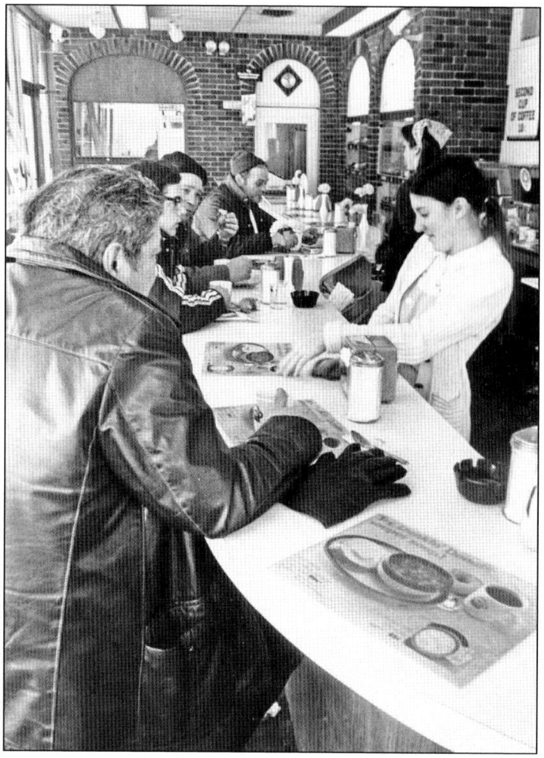

For adults, having fun meant getting out of house and grabbing a cup of hot coffee and a donut. These patrons swap stories about the blizzard at the Dunkin' Donuts on Pine Street in Niagara Falls. (NFPL.)

For these ducks, as for most other wildlife, once the storm ended, life returned to normal. This seems like a pleasant spot for this unidentified family to sit and feed the ducks. (NFPL.)

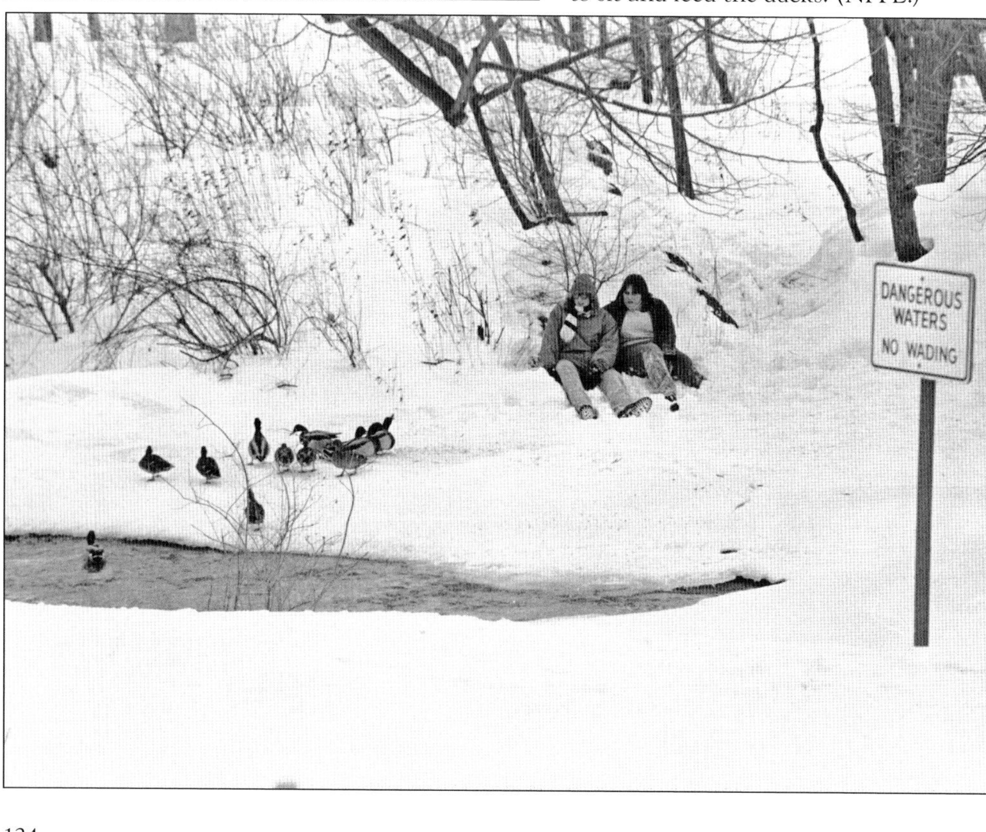

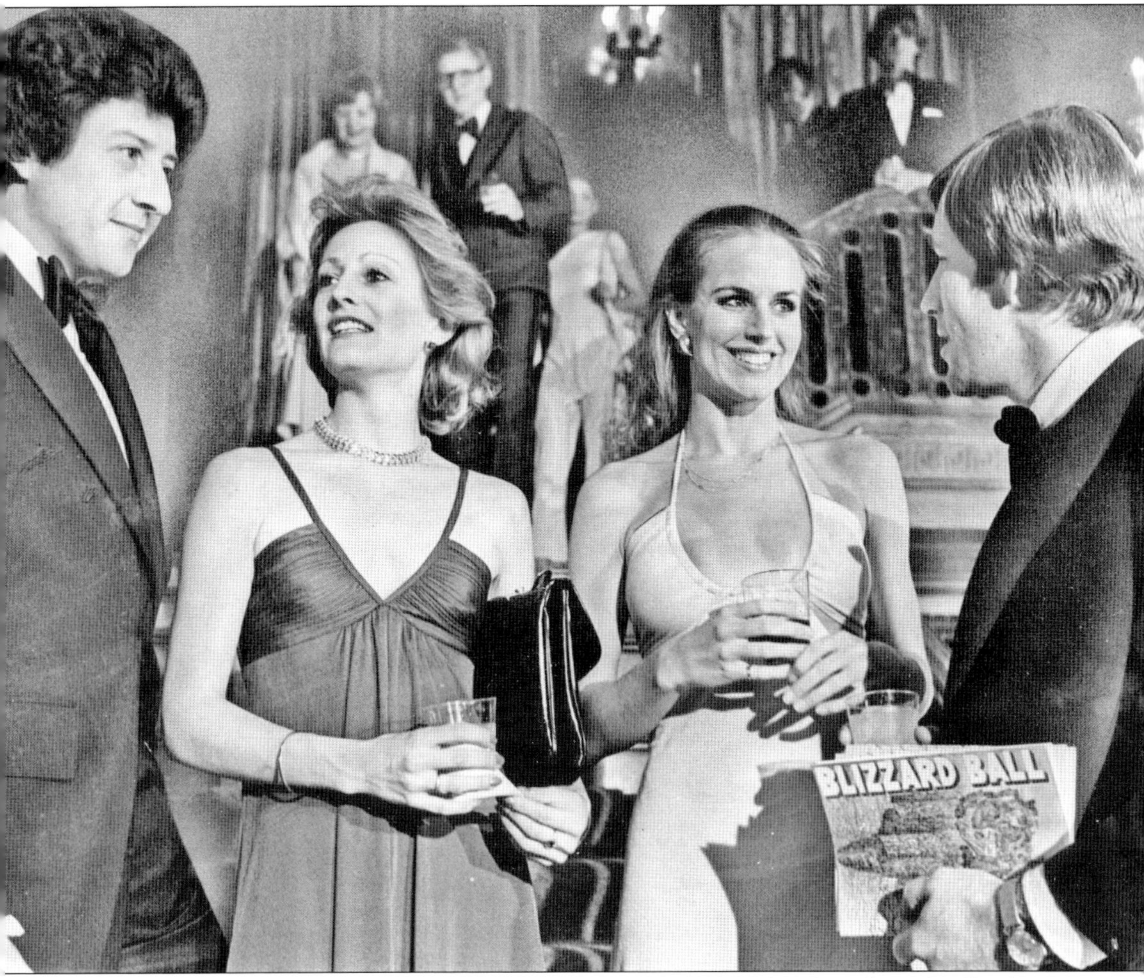

A year after the blizzard, the people of Buffalo celebrated their survival with a Blizzard Ball. The Blizzard Ball was an annual event for years after the blizzard of 1977. The first one was held at Butler Hall in Buffalo. (BLBS.)

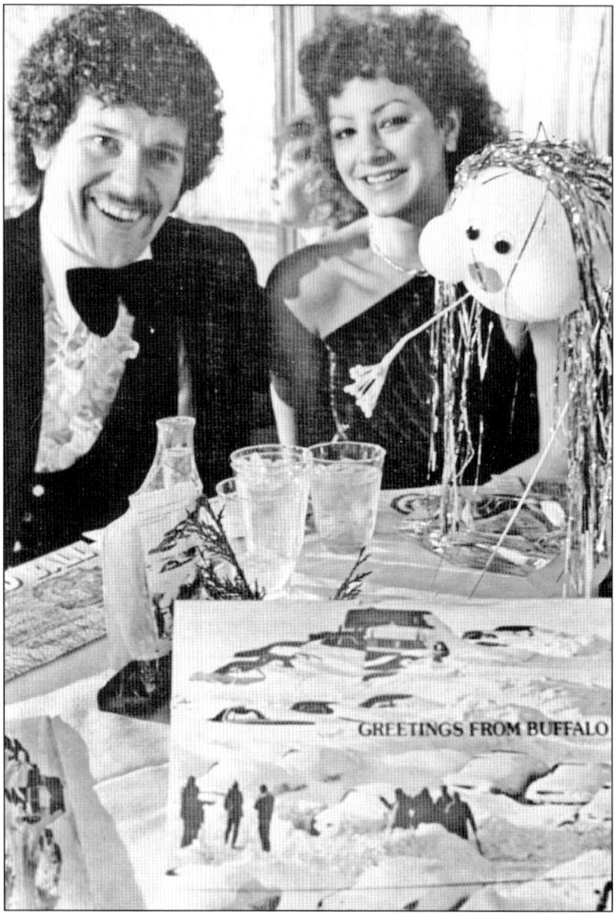

Although the blizzard of 1977 was a terrible event, the true grit and good spirits of the people of Buffalo and beyond returned as they commemorated the event at the Blizzard Ball. (BLBS.)

The Charr-Donn Company created a board game based on the events of the blizzard. Called the Blizzard of '77, the game featured a reversible board that required players to complete certain tasks to win. Players began on the sunny side of the board until one of them drew the "blizzard" card, which required the board be turned over to the blizzard side. On the blizzard side, players faced the kind of challenges common to those of the Buffalo area, such as travel cards that limited a player's movement and an increasing scarcity of food and other necessities. This game is one of the many items on display at the Strong National Museum of Play in Rochester, New York. (Author's collection.)

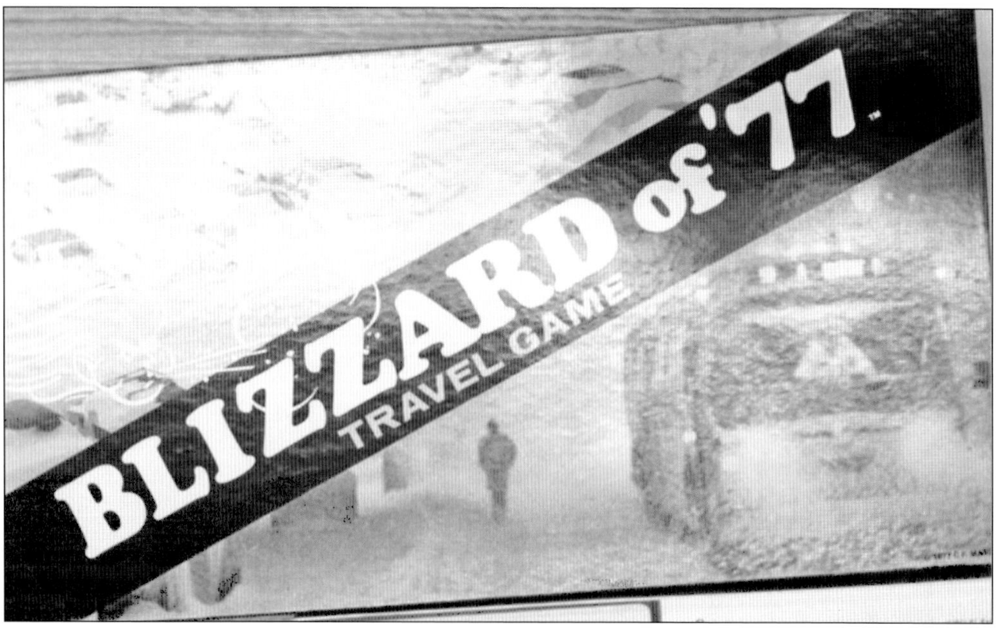

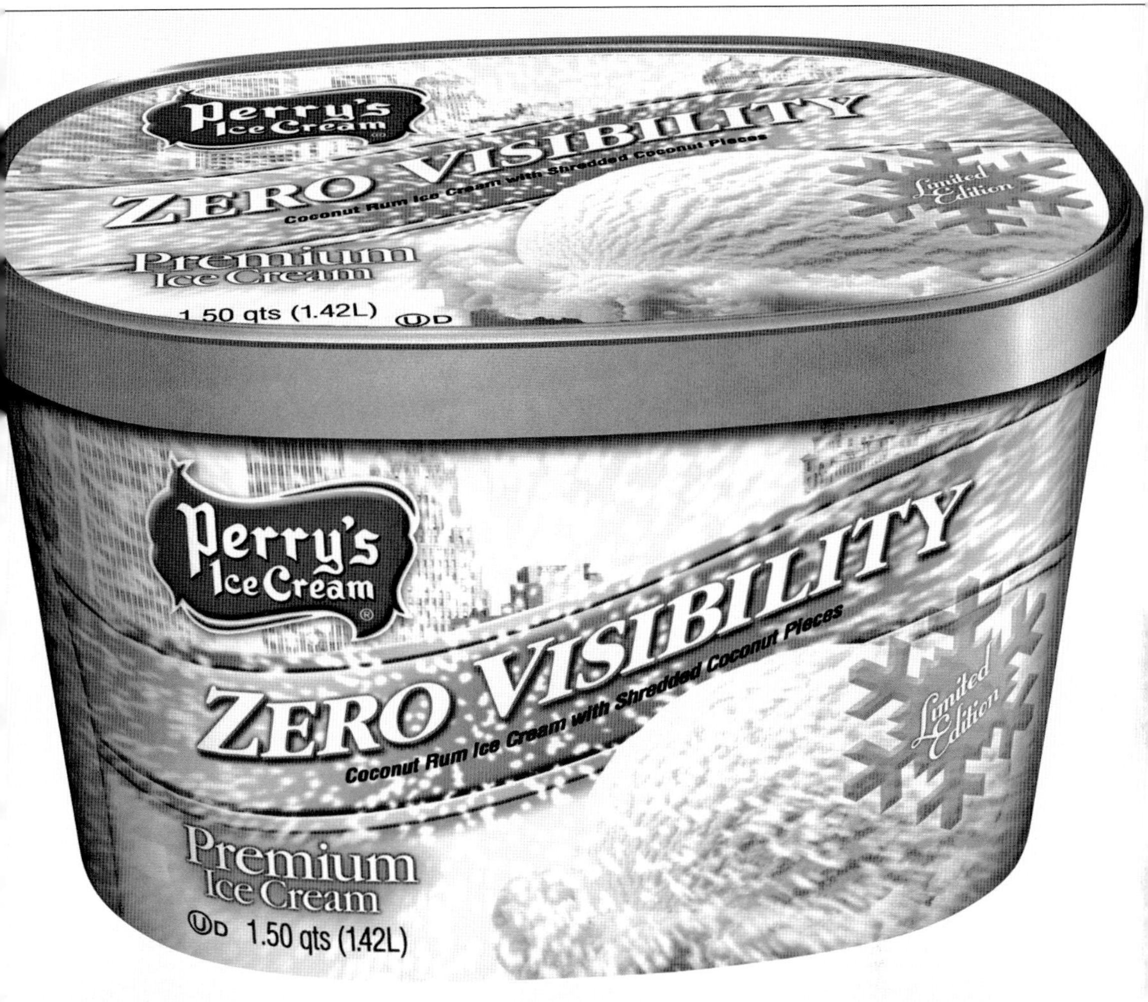

Perry's Ice Cream, which was founded in 1918 by H. Morton Perry, began making its Zero Visibility flavor in 1997 in honor of the 20th anniversary of the blizzard of 1977. Every five years, the company releases the flavor for a limited amount of time. The 40th anniversary of the blizzard falls in 2017. (Perry's Ice Cream.)